# Data Mining
# and
# Business Intelligence

*Data-driven strategy for business transformation*

Dr. Jyotiranjan Hota

**bpb**

www.bpbonline.com

First Edition 2025

Copyright © BPB Publications, India

ISBN: 978-93-65892-239

To View Complete
BPB Publications Catalogue
Scan the QR Code:

# Dedicated to

*My late parents*

*My wife **Mandakini***

*and*

*Daughters **Mugdha** and **Snigdha***

# About the Author

**Dr. Jyotiranjan Hota** is a distinguished academic with nearly 20 years of teaching, research and software consulting experience. He holds a B.E. in computer science and engineering from NIT Rourkela, a PGDBM from Xavier Institute of Management, Bhubaneswar, and a Ph.D. in Management Studies from Aligarh Muslim University, which was a joint program with AIMA, New Delhi. His areas of expertise includes business analytics, artificial intelligence, machine learning, data mining, text mining, visual analytics, and functional modules of SAP S4/HANA (SD, MM, PP, and FI-CO). He is also proficient in programming languages like R and Python and conversant with tools such as KNIME and Power BI. Dr. Hota's Ph.D. research delved into the adoption of Multivendor ATM technology in India. He analyzed challenges and opportunities from the perspectives of customers, suppliers, and bankers. Through this work, he developed and validated several qualitative and quantitative models addressing the drivers and barriers to technology adoption.

His broader interests focus on integrating information technology across various functional areas of management. An AIMA-accredited management teacher in the IT domain, Dr. Hota has an extensive record of publications in prominent top journals, including the International Journal of Bank Marketing, Asia Pacific Journal of Information Systems, International Journal of Management in Education, and The IUP Journal of Applied Economics, among others. He has also contributed to works by leading publishers such as Sage, Springer and Palgrave Macmillan. Dr. Hota has actively participated in international conferences in India and abroad, serving in key roles such as program committee member, advisory board member, technical committee member, track chair, and session chair. In recognition of his academic contributions, he was awarded with the ICBM-AMP Academic Excellence Award 2018 in the Best Professor in IT and Operations category in Hyderabad, India.

# About the Reviewers

❖ **Tong Zhi** is a seasoned data scientist and data engineer with expertise in the private equity sector. His professional experience encompasses the development and deployment of advanced analytical and predictive models, such as Markov Chain Monte Carlo simulations, sophisticated time series forecasting, and classification algorithms.

In addition to his role in private equity, he is also the founder of a startup venture, where he successfully architected and implemented a comprehensive business intelligence platform from scratch.

Tong holds a master of science degree in business analytics and a bachelor of science degree in finance. Recognized for his expertise, he has frequently been invited to speak at prestigious international data science conferences and events. Currently, he serves at RoundShield Partners, a firm specializing in private equity and private credit, while concurrently managing HireHarbour, an innovative executive assistant outsourcing agency.

❖ **Anup Sahoo** is a Cloud Technical Lead at Insight India with over 14+ years of rich experience in the field of Quality Engineering, Test Automation, and DevOps. As a seasoned professional and a lifelong learner, Anup is passionate about solving real-world problems by merging deep technical expertise with cutting-edge technologies.

He is a **Generative AI enthusiast and researcher**, exploring how large language models (LLMs) and AI-driven automation can transform the future of software testing and quality engineering. As a **Technical Author**, Anup has shared his insights through technical blogs, research-backed frameworks, and a growing portfolio of practical tools that aim to make QA smarter and more adaptive.

When he's not immersed in designing intelligent test frameworks or experimenting with AI-infused pipelines, Anup channels his energy into mentoring aspiring professionals, creating impactful DevOps and automation content, and exploring nature through trekking. His curiosity-driven approach and commitment to innovation make him a driving force in both the tech and learning communities.

# Acknowledgement

I would like to extend my heartfelt gratitude to everyone who has supported me on the challenging journey of writing this book as a sole author.

My wife, Mandakini, and my daughters, Mugdha and Snigdha, have been a constant source of love, motivation, and strength. Their encouragement and sentimental support have been a constant source of motivation.

At KSOM fraternity, I received consistent writing support from the early drafts to the final manuscript. The team's encouragement was instrumental in shaping this scholarly work into its final published version.

My sincere appreciation goes to BPB Publications for their invaluable guidance and expertise in bringing this book to life. I would also like to acknowledge the technical reviewers and editors who contributed their valuable feedback to this manuscript. Their insights and suggestions have greatly enhanced the quality of the book.

Last but not least, I want to express my gratitude to the readers who have shown interest in the book. Your support and encouragement have been deeply appreciated.

Thank you to everyone who has played a part in making this book a reality.

# Preface

In today's era of digital transformation, information has become the cornerstone of progress and innovation. The ability to uncover actionable insights from data and effectively use business intelligence tools is a skill that spans industries, domains, and geographies. This book is carefully crafted to provide readers with the knowledge, techniques, case studies, and practical applications required to thrive in this transformative era.

The book is divided into eight thoughtfully designed chapters which offers a balanced blend of theoretical understanding and practical exercises. It provides a gradual progression that takes readers from foundational concepts to advanced analytics to prepare them to navigate the complexities of real-world data challenges.

The journey begins with Chapter 1, which introduces the basics of data mining and business intelligence. This chapter highlights the significance of these fields, explains core principles and emphasizes the importance of leveraging data effectively. Readers are also introduced to key differences between **online analytical processing (OLAP)** and **online transactional processing (OLTP)** systems. Chapter 2 focuses on pre-processing techniques, regression, and classification methods. It equips readers with essential tools to improve data quality and build reliable predictive models, laying a strong foundation for tackling real-world challenges.

Chapter 3 presents association rule mining, which is key to discovering patterns and relationships in data. This chapter explains metrics such as support, confidence and lift while introducing algorithms like A priori for identifying valuable insights. Chapter 4 discusses clustering techniques and their applications across various domains. It provides practical examples to illustrate foundational methods like k-means clustering, as well as advanced algorithms for grouping and analyzing data effectively.

The middle chapters explore the domain of business intelligence. Chapter 5 introduces its fundamentals, examining the driving forces, market dynamics, and tactical applications that define this transformative field. Chapter 6 puts these ideas into practice by exploring business intelligence architecture, concepts such as slicing and dicing and utilizing Power BI to model data and create impactful dashboards.

As the book progresses, Chapter 7 introduces innovative methodologies such as text mining, cognitive analytics, and big data analytics. These approaches equip readers with techniques to handle structured, semi-structured, and unstructured data effectively. The final chapter, Chapter 8, discusses the ethical dimensions of data mining and business intelligence. It reflects on issues such as data governance, transparency, and responsible data practices, emphasizing the importance of trust and accountability in handling data in today's digital environment.

This book is thoughtfully written to be clear and useful for readers from various backgrounds, including students, professionals, and lifelong learners. With its clear explanations, practical examples, and comprehensive coverage, data mining and business intelligence provides a valuable resource for mastering the concepts and applications of these fields. It is hoped that this book inspires curiosity, fosters critical thinking, and empowers readers to unlock the potential of data to create meaningful and impactful solutions in their respective areas of study and work. Through practical examples, comprehensive explanations, sand a structured approach, this book aims to equip readers with a solid understanding of digital systems and technology. Whether you are a beginner or an experienced learner, I hope this book will serve as a valuable resource in your journey of exploring the foundations of data-driven insights.

**Chapter 1: Introduction to Data Mining and Business Intelligence -** This chapter briefly narrates the fundamental principles of data mining and business intelligence tools and techniques. Readers will gain an overall idea of how to use various techniques to extract meaningful information from large datasets. It also covers the scope, issues, and future trends.

**Chapter 2: Regression and Classification Techniques with Applications** - This chapter initially describes various pre-processing techniques with examples explained using R. Application of important supervised learning algorithms and applications of these algorithms on datasets from multiple functional areas are explained. Finally, ensemble algorithms are explained to improve the accuracy of prediction.

**Chapter 3: Concept and Application of Association Rule Mining Algorithm** - Association rule mining is an unsupervised learning algorithm that is used to decipher the best rules from frequent item sets to derive business insights. The most popular application of association rule mining is market basket analysis, which predicts the buying behaviors of customers in market place. Key metrics used to evaluate these algorithms are support, confidence and lift. These metrics evaluate the reliability, significance and strength of the generated rules to derive business decisions.

**Chapter 4: Clustering -** This chapter discusses clustering as an unsupervised learning algorithm which is used to group similar items based on their attributes. Here, different types of clustering algorithm like k-means clustering, hierarchical and density-based clustering are discussed with examples using R. Few advanced clustering algorithms are discussed to deal with very large datasets.

**Chapter 5: Introduction to Business Intelligence -** This chapter lays a solid foundation of elementary concepts of business intelligence. It covers basic defection, markets, various key vendors, scopes, benefits, and future trends to prepare the readers with groundworks to further delve into business intelligence applications.

**Chapter 6: Business Intelligence Architecture, Query and Reporting Practices** - This chapter discusses the architecture of business intelligence, data reconciliation process, concept of data marts, OLAP cubes, and various data modelling, dashboards, and visualization techniques. Various applications are discussed using Power BI exercises for the readers.

**Chapter 7: Advanced Data Mining and Business Intelligence Techniques -** This chapter narrates advanced data mining techniques to deal with large volume of data of various functional domains to extract meaningful insights. This chapter covers topics like text mining, big data, edge analytics, cognitive analytics and real-time analytics to integrate with data mining and business intelligence tools for making informed decisions in organizations. Organizations gain strategic intent by uncovering diamonds from large datasets.

**Chapter 8: Data Mining and Business Intelligence Ethical Framework -** The lifeblood of data mining and business intelligence is data. Primary responsibility and challenges of data governance revolve around data collection, access, preservation, security, privacy, and democratization. Fairness, transparency, and trust can be achieved through a proper ethical framework based on good data governance practices. This chapter discusses inhibiting and facilitating forces of ethical directions of data mining and business intelligence to ensure trust, transparency, lowering costs incurred in organizations, and social implications for society as a whole.

# Code Bundle and Coloured Images

Please follow the link to download the
*Code Bundle* and the *Coloured Images* of the book:

# https://rebrand.ly/30gtva2

The code bundle for the book is also hosted on GitHub at
**https://github.com/bpbpublications/Data-Mining-and-Business-Intelligence**.
In case there's an update to the code, it will be updated on the existing GitHub repository.

We have code bundles from our rich catalogue of books and videos available at **https://github.com/bpbpublications**. Check them out!

# Errata

We take immense pride in our work at BPB Publications and follow best practices to ensure the accuracy of our content to provide with an indulging reading experience to our subscribers. Our readers are our mirrors, and we use their inputs to reflect and improve upon human errors, if any, that may have occurred during the publishing processes involved. To let us maintain the quality and help us reach out to any readers who might be having difficulties due to any unforeseen errors, please write to us at :

**errata@bpbonline.com**

Your support, suggestions and feedbacks are highly appreciated by the BPB Publications' Family.

Did you know that BPB offers eBook versions of every book published, with PDF and ePub files available? You can upgrade to the eBook version at www.bpbonline.com and as a print book customer, you are entitled to a discount on the eBook copy. Get in touch with us at :

**business@bpbonline.com** for more details.

At **www.bpbonline.com**, you can also read a collection of free technical articles, sign up for a range of free newsletters, and receive exclusive discounts and offers on BPB books and eBooks.

# Piracy

If you come across any illegal copies of our works in any form on the internet, we would be grateful if you would provide us with the location address or website name. Please contact us at **business@bpbonline.com** with a link to the material.

# If you are interested in becoming an author

If there is a topic that you have expertise in, and you are interested in either writing or contributing to a book, please visit **www.bpbonline.com**. We have worked with thousands of developers and tech professionals, just like you, to help them share their insights with the global tech community. You can make a general application, apply for a specific hot topic that we are recruiting an author for, or submit your own idea.

# Reviews

Please leave a review. Once you have read and used this book, why not leave a review on the site that you purchased it from? Potential readers can then see and use your unbiased opinion to make purchase decisions. We at BPB can understand what you think about our products, and our authors can see your feedback on their book. Thank you!

For more information about BPB, please visit **www.bpbonline.com**.

# Join our book's Discord space

Join the book's Discord Workspace for Latest updates, Offers, Tech happenings around the world, New Release and Sessions with the Authors:

**https://discord.bpbonline.com**

# Table of Contents

# CHAPTER 1
# Introduction to Data Mining and Business Intelligence

## Introduction

In this chapter, we will discuss the fundamentals, techniques, applications, and challenges of data mining and business intelligence. We will initially focus on its importance and motivation to grasp the subject foundationally. The difference between **Online Analytical Processing (OLAP)** and **Online Transactional Processing systems (OLTP)** is explained through real-life examples. Emerging trends of data mining and business intelligence, top vendors, tools, and markets for data mining and business intelligence, are explained to build a foundation for subsequent chapters.

## Structure

This chapter covers the following topics:

- Reasons for studying data mining
- Evolution
- Introduction to OLTP, OLAP and data mining
- Associated fields of data mining
- Data mining techniques
- Business intelligence techniques

- Leading vendors of data mining

- Introduction to business intelligence

- Motivations

- Leading vendors of business intelligence

- Privacy issues

- Future trends

# Objectives

After going through this chapter, you will understand the fundamental principles of data mining and business intelligence tools, techniques, markets, and privacy concerns. Readers will also gain an overall idea of how to deal with various techniques to extract meaningful information from large datasets.

# Reasons for studying data mining

Although organizations today are sinking in data, they are starving for knowledge. Massive data is generated from social media, e-commerce transactions, online forums, **Internet of Things (IoT)** devices, and several streaming platforms. So, for competitive advantages, firms need to derive hidden patterns and insights from data. There is a curiosity to know the following:

- How to make use of data assets?

- How can organizations make the best use of generated data?

- How to decipher the gap from stored data to knowledge?

- What are the limitations of database queries in fetching the following results:

    o   Generate a list of customers likely to purchase products or services.

    o   Who are the prospects likely to respond to our advertising campaign?

In the correct context, data is abundant, and multiple data mining tools are readily available. It is not an uphill task to gather data in a warehouse. Similarly, computing power is cheap, and there is tremendous pressure on companies to build their strategic intent. Hence, it becomes indispensable to apply these tools and techniques to derive diamonds out of data for survival and excellence in the current business world.

**"Data is like a faint light when you are lost in a dark room. Follow it, try to make sense of it, and you might actually know where you are and what is around you."**

*- David Sides*

# Evolution

Data mining is a blend of statistics, mathematics, computer science, machine learning, and big data. Though there is no fixed timeline, its inception was in the late eighteenth century with the development of Bayes' theorem based on conditional probability. Currently, the Bayes theorem is applied extensively in data mining. Regression as a basic prediction technique in data mining was developed during the early nineteenth century. These rich applications strengthened the field of statistics, followed by the application of computing by the *Alan Turing* model and neural networks by the mid-twentieth century. *Charlee Babbage* surprised the entire human civilization with the power of computing by a machine. However, *Turing* took a step forward with the Turing machine model, which stated that a machine can also think like a human. Similarly, the introduction of neural networks laid the foundation for data mining by developing a model in 1943.

A drastic development in data mining happened after the mid-twentieth century due to databases, genetic algorithms, and further evolutionary computation in the era of computing. Real business applications gained momentum during the last decade of the twentieth century due to data warehousing and data mining as a prediction technique with the introduction of data science. Due to the rapid development of social media, big data, cloud usage, and IoT applications, there was an increased usage of data mining in all functional areas of business during the twenty-first century. The stages of evolution of data mining are specified in *Figure 1.1*:

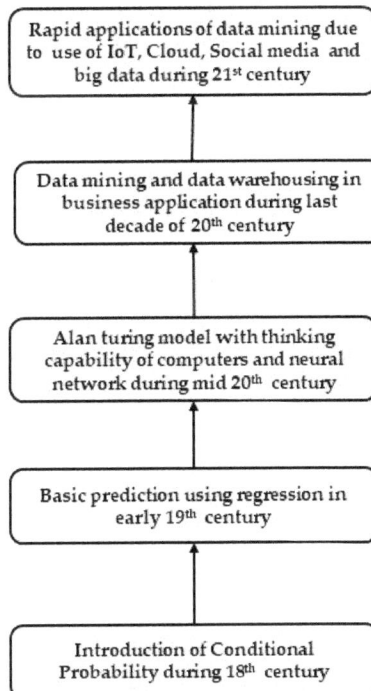

*Figure 1.1: Evolution of data mining*

# Introduction to OLTP, OLAP and data mining

Daily business transactions are captured in databases as online transaction processing in real-time. These OLTP transactions are captured online or offline. These transactions are common in all business activities like manufacturing, retail, sales, and finance. OLTP transactions are user-friendly and can be operated and managed by end users. Response time to these queries is quite fast. For example, withdrawal of money from ATMs, purchasing products online, and booking tickets are a few examples of OLTP systems. The volume of OLTP transactions is quite high, but transactions are small. Multiple users can access the OLTP system. So, a concurrency control mechanism is required to avoid data access by many users simultaneously. These transactions are basically database transactions. As past data is updated with new data, historical data cannot be retained for decisional analysis. However, OLAP systems are built offline, based on aggregate data from OLTP systems. These are offline systems that require huge resources, and the response time is high compared to OLTP systems.

The extracted data from OLTP systems is cleaned, transformed to a single format, and loaded into the data warehouse. Then OLAP queries are applied to these summary data. The queries touch a very large amount of data. Updates to OLAP systems are usually periodic and infrequent. As queries are complex, an individual query requires lots of resources. OLAP technology is based on a multidimensional data model. Ad-hoc queries can be applied linking functional areas like sales, marketing, operations, finance, and accounting for decisional analysis. OLAP uses cubes to store multiple categories of data. Usually, cubes have three dimensions. Say, for example, we take an example of a retail multidimensional model. The categories of dimensions can be product, customer and time dimensions. Actual transactions are stored as facts centrally. Further, analysis can be done using OLAP tools through multiple operations smoothly to derive insights from data. OLTP transactions are real-time transactions and OLAP transactions are offline transactions. So, OLTP and OLAP transactions are analyzed separately. There are three reasons for which we cannot mix both OLTP and OLAP queries. Firstly, performance requirements of OLTP and OLAP queries are not same. Since, OLTP queries require very less response time, and data should be always consistent. OLAP queries can saturate CPU time and consume lots of resources. Secondly, data modeling is different for both OLTP and OLAP. OLTP contains many tables with complex entity relationship models. However, OLAP contains very few dimension tables and a single fact table, which comprises transactions or facts. So fewer joins among tables are required as the architecture is different from OLTP. Thirdly, OLTP targets only a single source, whereas OLAP integrates data from multiple sources. So, OLTP and OLAP queries cannot be mixed. However, these queries are quite useful based on the requirements of different kinds.

Data mining techniques are applied to datasets to find hidden patterns and forecast future outcomes. The data mining technique uncovers hidden insights from data to facilitate decision-making. There are multiple applications of data mining in business. Telecommunication companies that use data mining techniques to predict when their customer will leave their company to join other competitors. In retail, the data mining technique helps decipher customers to whom we can go for product bundling promotional offers based on past transaction history and preferences. Data mining techniques also predict the life insurance policies the customers are likely to purchase in the future.

You may refer to *Figure 1.2* to go through the difference between OLTP, OLAP, and data mining:

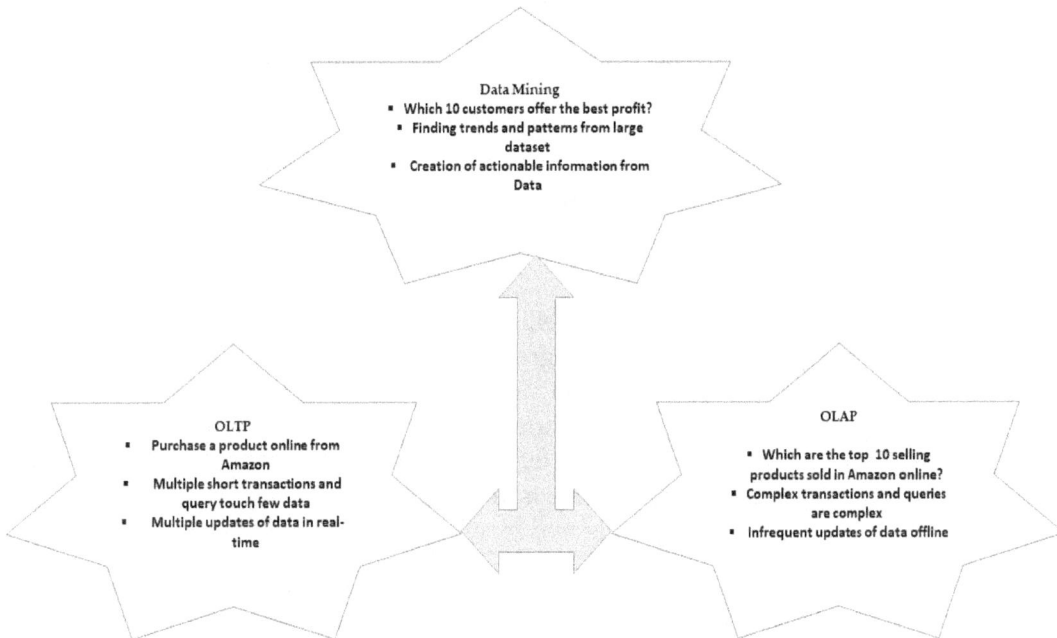

**Data Mining**
- Which 10 customers offer the best profit?
- Finding trends and patterns from large dataset
- Creation of actionable information from Data

**OLTP**
- Purchase a product online from Amazon
- Multiple short transactions and query touch few data
- Multiple updates of data in real-time

**OLAP**
- Which are the top 10 selling products sold in Amazon online?
- Complex transactions and queries are complex
- Infrequent updates of data offline

*Figure 1.2: Difference between OLTP, OLAP and data mining*

From the purchase history, data mining techniques can identify the pattern and association among purchased products. Subsequently, marketers can plan for techniques like cross-selling, upselling, and product bundling.

# Associated fields of data mining

Some associated fields of data mining are:

- **Statistics**: As a branch of applied mathematics, statistics deals with data collection, organization, interpretation, and presentation of data. As a related field of data mining, statistics is used to understand, described, and check the distribution pattern of data and also predicts using many statistical tools, like regression and clustering. Data visualization is an important contribution to statistics. Scatter plots, heat maps, histograms, and boxplots help to understand data pattern. To understand the performance of data mining, many metrics are used to access the quality of the model generated through statistical tools.

- **Database systems**: Database systems store, manage, and fetch structured data, based on relational database systems constraints. Data is stored as rows and columns. The number of columns is fixed in relational database systems. Real-time business transactions, like retail data and customer data related to banks, are stored in a database. Stored data can be accessed by data mining algorithms to identify trends. Similarly, data from the database are fetched using query language which can be used selectively to find out patterns.

- **Data warehousing**: Data from multiple operational systems are extracted, cleaned, transformed to a uniform format and loaded into a data warehouse for further processing to generate insights from data. These are basically historical data. Analysis of historical data is the primary objective of data mining. As data warehouse data are multidimensional summary data, analysis can be done in various ways based on a number of dimensions with operations like drill up and drill down for decisional analysis.

- **Artificial intelligence**: Artificial intelligence is a simulation of human intelligence that acts like a human as it is programmed to think and take action. **Artificial intelligence** (**AI**) is applied widely in education, retail, manufacturing, sales, customer services, healthcare, finance, and transportation. AI improves productivity, improves quality of life, and can address multiple problems where human cannot reach. Data mining is the foundation of AI. There are overlaps among statistics, AI, data mining and machine learning techniques.

- **Machine learning**: **Machine learning** (**ML**) learns from data using models to make a prediction or decision. However, data mining extracts meaningful information from a large dataset through human intervention. ML is a subset of AI that needs less data compared to data mining. ML algorithms have self-learning ability. ML can be classified as supervised, unsupervised, reinforcement, and evolutionary learning. In case of supervised learning, the algorithm is aware of both input and output features. Unsupervised learning algorithms do not have knowledge of output features. Similarly, reinforcement algorithms are uncertain about both input and output features. So, based on knowledge of features, appropriate algorithms are used to generate the model. There is another kind of evolutionary learning algorithm which follows natural evolution to solve an issue. Though, both data mining and machine learning apply algorithms to large datasets, there are differences. Data mining extracts rules from large datasets whereas machine learning learns from data to analyze the parameters.

- **Big data analytics**: Big data is a collection of very large datasets which are difficult to process using traditional data processing applications. Examples of big data can be social media data, stock exchange data, video data, sensor data, retail data and conversational data. These data can be structured, unstructured, and semi-structured in nature. Structured data have predefined formats like a table. RDBMS data are structured in nature. Unstructured data do not have any structure or the structure is unknown. Output obtained through Google search, image, audio and video data are examples of unstructured data. Semi-structured data contains both forms of data. CSV file, JSON file, and emails are examples of semi-structured data. Big data analytics is a process to extract meaningful insights from big data. Big data analytics is applied in marketing, finance, retail, manufacturing, and healthcare industries. There are various tools available in big data. Database tools are known as NoSQL. Databases of many vendors like Cassandra, MongoDB, and CouchDB. Similarly, Google BigQuery and Amazon Redshift are available in the market as common data warehousing tools. Open-source framework Hadoop supports the process of large datasets. Cloud framework, security tools, and distributed computing frameworks are available to manage large datasets of firms. These tools help derive business value from big data. So, big data analytics is built on the fundamental concepts of data mining.

*   **Bioinformatics**: The field of bioinformatics originated from biology and information technology. Bioinformatics uses statistical and datamining techniques to decipher patterns in protein structures, model complex biological systems and analyze biological data. The application of this field comprises areas like synthetic biology, identification of genetic diseases, cancer research, and agricultural biotechnology. Data mining plays a vital role in identifying patterns within large biological datasets. There are multiple bioinformatics tools available in the market, like *Cluster Omega* to compare RNA, DNA, and protein sequences, Genome browsers, Gene expression tools, and system biology modeling platforms like NetLogo.

Related data mining fields can be referred from the following figure:

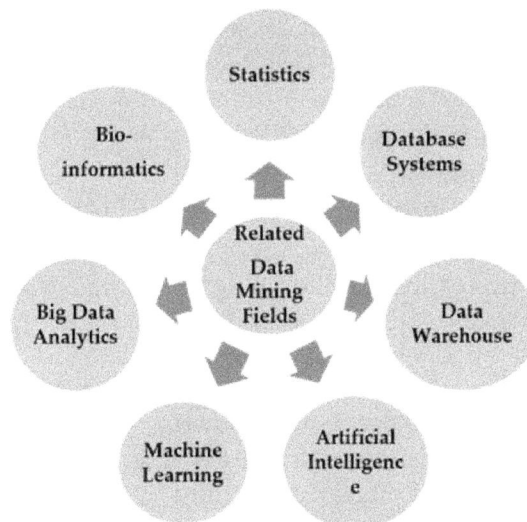

*Figure 1.3*: *Related datamining fields*

# Data mining techniques

The following list will describe important data mining techniques:

- **Regression**: *Sir Francis Galton* is known as the originator of regression analysis. Popularly known as the cousin of *Charles Darwin*, he first built the foundation of regression through two-dimensional plot sizes of daughter and mother peas. Regression is the simplest data mining technique available for prediction. Models are built using historical data to predict the dependent or outcome variable. This popular technique is widely applied in marketing, insurance, banking, the health sector, manufacturing, and related industries.

- **Classification**: This technique is used to group input variables into various categories based on specific features. Widely used algorithms include naïve bias classification method, logistic regression, decision tree, Support Vector Machines, neural networks, **k-nearest neighbor** (**KNN**), and random forest. Various metrics like the confusion matrix and the **receiver operating characteristics** (**ROC**) curve are used to measure the performance of the classification models. These predictive modeling techniques help in interpreting customer segmentation, fraud detection, predicting prices of stocks, medical diagnosis, categorizing news stories, and email spam, etc.

- **Association rule mining**: It is applied to generate the best rules out of many possible rules among transactions. A typical rule can be defined as *if a person purchases milk, then he/she is likely to purchase bread*. Once we know the important rules, we can design product bundling, cross-selling, and upselling marketing techniques. Popular algorithms of association rule mining are the priori algorithm, FP-Growth algorithm and the Eclat algorithms.

- **Clustering**: It is a technique to make homogeneous groups with similar data points. The technique is based on unsupervised learning algorithms and the classes are not known as priori like the classification techniques. To make multiple clusters, the technique uses many similarity or dissimilarity measures. Clustering is used in many real-life applications like fake news detection, customer segmentation, applications in medical imaging, genetic research, and transportation planning to avoid congestion.

- **Anomaly detection**: Anomaly detection is a technique applied to detect outliers in a dataset. Outliers are extreme values that are different from most the values in a dataset. There are many statistical techniques, data mining algorithmic methods, and data visualization techniques to detect outliers. Outlier treatment is one of the most challenging tasks of data mining experts. It is not always advisable to remove outliers during data analysis. Sometimes, outliers contain valuable information. So, treatment should be conducted carefully.

- **Text mining:** It is a technique to transform unstructured text data into a structured format to discover insights and decipher trends. An initial step in text analytics is to pre-process texts. Texts are made tokens. Stop words are removed and stemming and lemmatization tasks are performed before applying for modelling. Text analytics is widely used for sentiment analysis of customer reviews, topic modeling, text classification, and fraud detection in multiple functional areas of business. In the current context, there are several challenges in text analytics. Sometimes, unstructured data contains errors, noises, and multiple categories, which pose challenges. Similarly, there are issues in context-sensitive languages that contain ambiguities. Sarcasm, polarity, bias of employee feedback and audio-visual data pose challenges for text analytics professionals in reducing issues.

- **Graph mining**: The graph mining technique is used to find patterns in real-life collections of graphs. This technique is used in social network analysis, analysis of web data, cybersecurity, understanding barriers and optimization of inventory and logistics in the supply chain, understanding the pattern of congestion in traffic, and bioinformatics. Graph mining is also not free from issues. Comparison of the model results or metrics with results of past studies is not possible due to a lack of standardization. During analysis, we find governance issues with protecting the privacy of sensitive data. While dealing with large graphs, there is complexity in storage and processing time to maintain scalability.

The following table describes techniques with real-life application:

| Data mining technique | Input dataset | Real-life application |
|---|---|---|
| Regression | The input dataset for regression comprises both independent variables and respective dependent variable. Input variables can be continuous and be categorical. Categorical features are encoded to numeric before applying to the model. | There are multiple applications of regression in real-life. Linear regression technique can be used to measure the effect of supply of water and fertilizer on yield of crops. Different amount of water and fertilizers can be applied on different fields to know how it affects the yield of crops. Yield of crop can be dependent feature. Amount of water and fertilizers are independent features. For example, students are studying how water and fertilizer influence crop yield. By collecting data, they establish a regression equation: *Crop Yield (tons)=0.9 × Water (liters) + 2 × Fertilizer (kg) + 11* This equation predicts that for each additional liter of water, the yield increases by 0.9 tons and for each additional kilogram of fertilizer, the yield increases by 2 tons. |

| Data mining technique | Input dataset | Real-life application |
|---|---|---|
| Classification | The input dataset for classification techniques can be combination of different types or diverse. The output data is categorical which represent a class. Input data are levelled. That means, data set contains input and corresponding output data. | There are many real-life applications of classification technique. Say, we want to know whether a borrower of a loan will default or pay loan in time. We take a dataset with available personal information like income, age, marital status, number of dependents etc. and apply this dataset to a classification model to classify. |
| Association rule mining | The input dataset for association rule mining can include transactional data of customers purchased from stores, social media data, medical diagnostics data and patient data etc. Output data are mostly generated rules which help to provide insights in business to make decisions. | Real life example of association mining is helpful in recommendation to customers. For example, a customer who previously purchased bread may be advised to purchase butter or related complementary products. |
| Clustering | Input data for clustering can be diverse like categorical, continuous, text data and web-based data etc. Output data is quite important to analyse the result of clustering and to derive insights. | Clustering algorithm is applied to decipher various groups based on customer preferences, behaviour and purchasing patterns. Based on the result of clustering, firms can make their strategy to target the customer segments. For example, clustering technique is applied to analyze customer purchasing dataset with algorithms like k-means to group shoppers based on variables like purchase frequency, average spending and product preferences. This process reveals different customer segments such as frequent small spenders and occasional big spenders to enable organizations to customize marketing strategies like personalized promotions or loyalty programs for each group. By analysing these clusters, one can visualize how data-driven insights can transform raw data into effective business decisions. |

| Data mining technique | Input dataset | Real-life application |
|---|---|---|
| Anomaly detection | Through detection of anomalies or unusual patterns, firms can address the issues and improve operational efficiency. | Application of anomaly detection in medical cases relating to patient is quite useful. Real time monitoring of heart rate, temperature, blood pressure is analysed by medical professionals to detect any unusual pattern which may require any medical emergency. So, there can be intervention by doctors early to take proper care of the patients. This effort also reduces the cost of medical treatment. |
| Text mining | From unstructured text data, insight can be derived using techniques like natural language processing, ML and text mining. | Sentiment analysis is a good example of product review using text analytics. Positive, negative and neutral are categorised to understand the scope for improvement of the products. |
| Graph mining | Graph mining extracts meaningful insights from graph structured data. | Spotify uses graph mining to interpret linkage between singers, users and songs to maintain personalized playlist and recommendation. Platform engagement and user experience can be improved on the platform. |

*Table 1.1: Data mining techniques*

# Business intelligence techniques

The following list will describe important business intelligence techniques:

- **OLAP**: Using OLAP techniques, it is possible to conduct high performance analysis and easy reporting on large volume of data with multiple dimensions. Multidimensional analysis supports fast and flexible summarization of data with reporting capability. There are multiple vendors of OLAP are present to conduct slicing, dicing and pivoting operations on multidimensional data relating to many functional areas.

- **Query and reporting technique**: Business intelligence reporting techniques enable self-service reporting, easy use of wizard-driven interface and integrating analytics results and processes. These techniques support in fetching information in a timely manner in order to make informed business decision. It is also possible to make reports of varying complexity to meet a wide set of information needs. Naive and specialized users can access and use these techniques based on their needs due to process standardization.

- **Data visualization**: Data visualization is one of the primary business intelligence techniques. This technique presents complex data in simple visual formats like graphs, charts and dashboards. To support story telling of data, data visualization tools can present the key performance indicators and metrics of firms in interactive way to provide deeper meaning. With self-service business intelligence capability, these tools enable firms to share and show quantitative data for employees, end users and customers in user friendly manner.

- **Statistical analysis**: Statistical analysis is a technique of collecting and analyzing large volume of data to decipher trends and insights from data. Two major categories of statistical analysis are descriptive and inferential statistics. Descriptive statistics techniques are used for data summarization. Inferential statistics uses sample data to estimate characteristics of large population and to test hypothesis of a population.

- **Extract, transform and load (ETL)**: This is a crucial technique of extracting data from multiple sources. Further, the data is cleaned and transformed into a single format to load in a warehouse for further analysis using business intelligence tools. However, ETL is a time consuming and complex process. This technique is useful in situation where data is changing very slowly.

The following table describe business intelligence techniques with applications:

| Business intelligence technique | Description | Applications |
|---|---|---|
| OLAP | OLAP technology facilitates the analysis of multidimensional data extracted from data warehouse. These data are stored in data cubes. | Here, queries are complex and updates are infrequent on offline data. The following OLAP queries can be addressed. <br><br> • Who are the top ten profitable customers? <br><br> • Which are the top ten profitable products? <br><br> • Which customers defaulted on their loan payment in last three years? |

| Business intelligence technique | Description | Applications |
|---|---|---|
| Query and reporting techniques | Valuable insights can be derived from data for strategic planning in organisations. The process of data analysis is structured though automation of manual operations. Real time access possible with collaboration with multiple users. Sharing of reports and dashboards is possible through BI query and reporting. | Here, the role of business user is vital. Regardless of the skill levels, it is possible to generate report as per requirements. |
| Data visualization | Data visualization is used to quickly translate complex data to visual formats for easy understanding through charts, graphs, dashboards and maps. | Food delivery industry utilizes data visualization for interpretation of customer orders, popular dishes, peak time for ordering and order frequency etc. The most preferred delivery route for driver is suggested based on duration of delivery time, traffic pattern and distance. The analysis improves operational efficiency, customer satisfaction and profit. |
| Statistical analysis | Statistical analysis helps firms to understand and identify the **key performance indicators (KPI)**. It is possible to know the factors affecting the KPIs in a firm. Based on historical data, statistical analysis can derive valuable insights. | Manufacturing companies can use statistical analysis in supply chain to optimise operations, improve satisfaction of customers and facilitates to standardise processes for competitive advantages. Issues of supply chain efficiency and process improvements are possible through statistical analysis. |
| ETL | ETL process is used to extract data from multiple operational systems, cleaned, transformed to single format and to load to data warehouse for analysis. | ETL process facilitates call detail record analysis in telecommunication companies. Data like phone call data, type of call, duration of call and details of subscribers are pulled using ETL process. The data is cleaned and loaded through ETL process to warehouses for analysing pattern of phone calls and improvement of quality of services. |

*Table 1.2: Business intelligence techniques*

# Processes of data mining

Data mining processes generally comprises the following steps:

- **Understanding business objectives**: Clearly understanding the objective of the data mining project is quite crucial. This initial phase includes defining the goals, objectives, and factors affecting firms' key performance indicators. Once the business problem is clearly understood, it becomes easy to drive the project smoothly.

- **Understanding data and data collection**: Data is collected from multiple sources like internal sources, online or external sources. Hence, basic exploratory techniques are required to produce graphs and charts of data to understand the pattern and nature of data. This is due to various types of data such as web log data, survey data and specific data, like demographic data. Data may be collected in multiple ways. Various ways of data collections can be manual, web scrapping, automatic data extraction and import of data. There are multiple tools available for data collection based on the method selected to collect data.

- **Data preparation**: In this stage of data preprocessing, raw data is converted into a meaningful standard format. Data is cleaned initially, removing missing values, duplicates, errors, and outlier treatments. Sometimes, it is necessary to reduce the volume of data by merging it. Based on requirements, we may scale the data to a smaller range through normalization as a data transformation method. In some cases, we group the continuous data to reduce the size of the data. Many different tools are available to prepare data. The selection of these tools depend on the type of data and needs of data preparation.

- **Model building**: Once the data is prepared, the correct algorithm, as per the nature of the data, is selected to be applied to train the model on a dataset for evaluation. In some cases, the input and output features or variables are known to the algorithm. These kinds of datasets are known as leveled datasets, and supervised learning algorithms are applied here. Some examples are linear regression and classification algorithms like logistic regression, decision tree, and KNN, etc. In some situations, only the input variables or features are known to the algorithms. Due to unleveled data, unsupervised learning algorithms, such as clustering algorithms, are applied to these datasets. In some situations, there is uncertainty of both input and output features. Here, reinforcement learning algorithms are applied. There is a situation where we deal with natural evolution with evolutionary learning. We apply genetic algorithms here.

- **Evaluation of result**: As we discussed, there are various kinds of models in data mining. There are also numerous metrics for evaluating a data mining model based on its type. Mostly, the dataset is divided into training and test datasets. The model is built using training dataset and the same is tested using test dataset to know the accuracy of the model. We find various metrics to evaluate based on the type of the model.

- **Model deployment**: Based on the business objective, we have to decide the deployment of the model for decision making. For example, if we try to judge the purchasing behavior of consumers, we may examine the evaluation metrics to know how accurately the number of consumers are found out. So, a final decision may be taken to apply the model into production environment.

- **Model monitoring after deployment**: Once the model is deployed into practice, continuous monitoring is accomplished to understand its performance. Feedback from users, accuracy, and resource utilization of the model are measured for analysis. Professionals use dashboards, and scorecards and conduct data storytelling to communicate this information to the right kind of organization strategists for future course of action.

The following figure describes the processes in sequence:

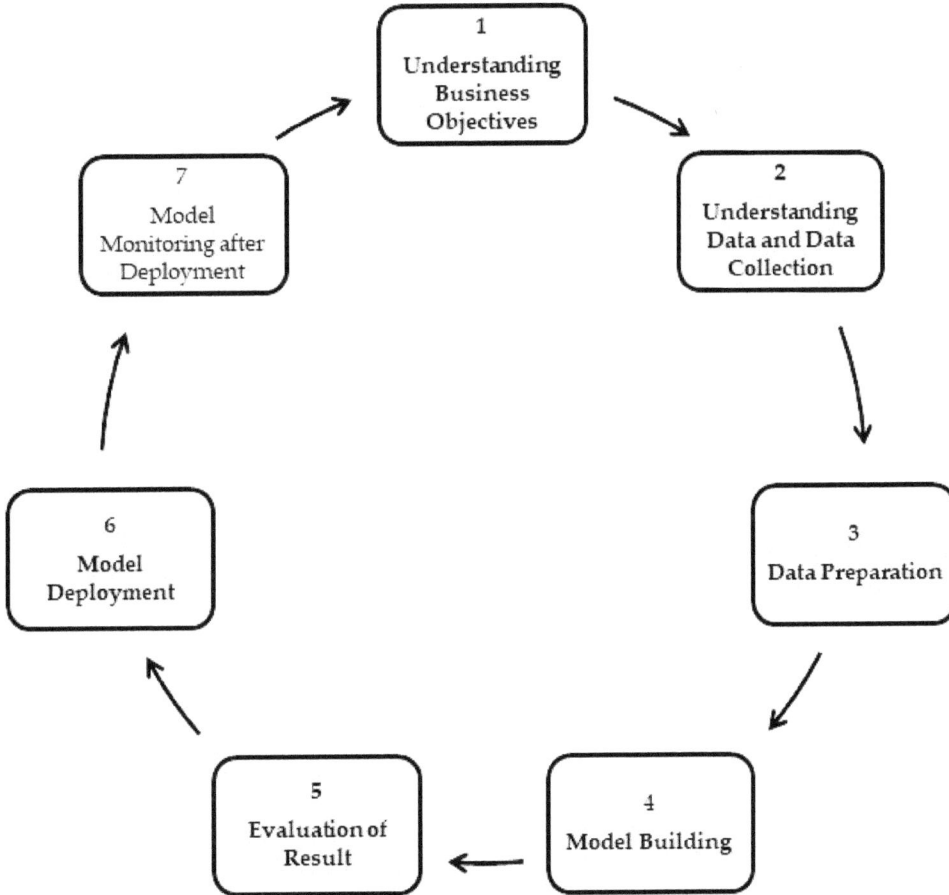

*Figure 1.4*: Processes of data mining

# Leading vendors of data mining

The emergence of various data mining vendors creates a competitive advantage for organizations. There is a paradigm shift in data analysis orientation in the current era with the following leading vendors of data mining:

- **RapidMiner**: RapidMiner was developed in 2001 at the *Technical University of Dortmund*. The tool is supported by both public and private clouds. It can extract data from multiple sources, perform preprocessing, predictive modeling, and visualize data. RapidMiner was developed using the Java programming language. Python and R scripting can be extended with RapidMiner. RapidMiner is easy to use, scalable, flexible and support collaboration and version control. It has a strong community support and can quickly build models. This tool is quite comfortable for experts and beginners.

- **KNIME**: KNIME stands for Konstanz Information Miner. KNIME was developed in 2004 at the *University of Konstanz* as an open-source platform. The initial purpose of this development is to make KNIME a generic data analysis platform for multiple functional areas. This open-source tool is popularly termed a no-code tool. Apart from the ETL process, data modeling, and visualization, this tool is widely used for sentiment analysis, text analytics, and is extended for R and Python-based applications. Users can comfortably create workflows through drag and drop operations of nodes. It is an open architecture that supports to integrate with other platforms easily. It can be deployed on cloud infrastructure.

- **Orange**: Orange is an open-source tool developed in 1996 at the *University of Ljubljana* and the *Jozef Stefan Institute*. It is platform-independent and has programming support. Experienced, and beginners can use this tool comfortably for visualization and modelling through workflows with interactive visualization capability. There is an add-on scope for bioinformatics and text mining. This tool is quite suitable for elementary data mining tasks and good for medium to small-sized datasets. Of course, orange is not recommended for large complex projects due to scalability issues.

- **SAS Enterprise Miner**: SAS Enterprise Miner was developed in 1998. This tool is suitable for advanced data visualization and predictive modelling. Huge datasets can be handled comfortably to derive insights. The integration of this tool is possible with other SAS tools. The automation of model construction, scoring, and deployment is also quite easy with the presentation of results. Due to high license cost, it is not popular among small and medium enterprises. This tool is highly dependent on SAS for all supports, training and updates. It is adoption is limited to large organizations due to high cost and limited flexibility.

- **Python**: Python was initially developed in 1989 by a Dutch programmer during the Christmas holidays. This is an open-source object-oriented language, and can easily do data visualization. The language is supported by multiple user groups and libraries like *NumPy, pandas, Matpotlib, Seaborn,* and *Plotly* to apply ML algorithms and statistical modeling for data mining. Many user-friendly **integrated development environment (IDEs)** like *Google Colab, PyCharm,* and *Spyder* are useful for executing data mining tasks.

- **R**: R was initially developed in 1992 at the *University of Auckland*. As an open-source language, it is popularly used through a tool, Posit. Further extension and customization scopes are available for users. Package installations, pre-procession and application of data mining techniques can be comfortably applied using Posit. Further, evaluation, interpretation and deployments are also hassle-free with the help of this tool. Integration with multiple databases and other tools is less cumbersome here, although using big data and data set handling is quite challenging.

- **IBS SPSS Modeler**: This tool was initially known as Clementine and developed during the early 1990s in Unix platform. It is used for data preparation, data visualization, predictive modelling and related analytics tasks. It supports wide range of data mining algorithms, and integration with other systems is easy. Due to high cost and limited flexibility, it is adoption is limited to large organizations.

- **Weka**: Weka was initially developed by a student during his coursework in the *University of Waikato* in New Zealand during the late 1990s. Though Weka was initially applied to the agricultural domain, this tool was later used extensively in academics and research. In the current context, integration of Weka is easy with other data mining tools through Java-based APIs. Weka is quite user-friendly for professionals without any coding knowledge and supports a variety of data mining algorithms.

# Introduction to business intelligence

Business intelligence is an essential part of all progressive enterprises. Organizations build their competitive strength through **business intelligence (BI)** tools designed for multiple categories of users based on their job roles. BI tools explore and visualize various processes or enterprises with the help of associated technologies and concepts like data warehousing, data mining, knowledge management, statistics, mathematics, and business analytics. There is a paradigm shift in organizations to use historical data for predicting future courses of action. BI references various business applications, technologies, and practices for elucidation, data modeling, and visualization of business information. Data warehouses pull data from multiple operational systems or sources. With the help of the ETL process, the data is loaded into data warehouses. Data mining and further BI techniques are applied to explore the hidden pattern in the data. Some BI tools are MS Excel, OLAP tools, business performance management tools, and reporting tools. Access to data, analysis, decision, and implementation time, till the action is applied, is reduced in BI systems. Due to this, the value is saved, which is the difference of values between the action implementation time of operational and BI systems. Metrics like return on investment, contribution margin, churn rates, customer acquisition cost, etc., are essential to developing firms' strategic intent. The overall performance of firms is improved through the analysis of metrics and key performance indicators with the help of BI tools. The status of these metrics in real time can be analyzed using BI dashboards. Here, real-time data is extracted from various operational systems. On a single screen, a BI dashboard can consolidate and make the data visible for interpretation. MS Excel is also a popular external tool from which datasets can be uploaded into any dashboard environment.

# Motivations

BI can provide competitive advantages, improve a firm's performance and produce data-driven decision-making. Organizations can have better control over their business processes based on inputs from the business dashboard, which shows the entire state of the organization. Data is the new oil of the twenty-first century, and BI can be considered a lamp that provides value. In the current context, knowledge of BI is required for career enhancement. Once the reporting of organizations is automated, strategists can get more time to concentrate on many important nonroutine activities.

> **"If you can't measure it, you can't manage it."**
>
> *– Peter Drucker*

# Evolution of business intelligence

BI was first introduced in 1865 by author *Richard Millar Devens*. He informed the collection and application of relevant information by a banker before his competitors could. The application of technology to gather BI was first explored in 1958 by a scientist of *IBM*. Evolution of BI stages is specified in the following figure:

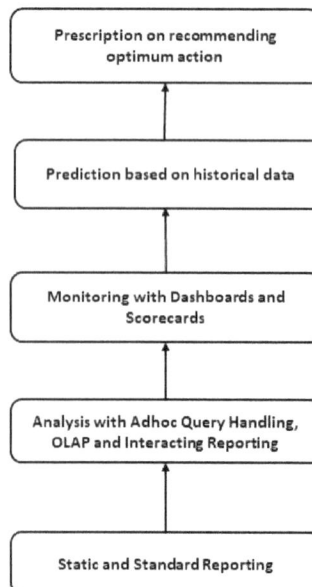

*Figure 1.5: Evolution of BI*

During the post-World War II period, the generation of data was stupendous. There was a need to derive meaningful information from the data. Database applications started during the 1970s, termed as the golden era. So, commercial organizations started entering data into database. During the 1980s, computers were quite popular in advanced countries like the US. Static reporting practices started where queries were determined before.

Concepts of **decision support system (DSS)** and **executive information system (EIS)** evolved due to the introduction of data warehouses at the beginning of the last decade of the twentieth century. Here, the concept of user-defined or ad-hoc queries could be handled. Interactive reporting and the use of multidimensional modeling or OLAP were initiated. Data warehouses were built by extracting data from multiple operational or OLTP systems. These OLTP systems are fundamentally for the storage of data in database systems. After extracting operational data from OLTP systems, the data is transformed and loaded into data warehouses periodically. These data warehouses are maintained offline. BI queries in ad hoc format can be posted to extract the relevant information through OLAP software.

Interactive reports were also possible to generate based on requirements. Subsequent progress was made in BI through business performance management. It is a framework for organizing and analyzing business metrics, dashboards, scorecards, and scenario modeling. The tracking of organizational goals with the key performance indicators can be monitored using BI tools for scorecards. However, visual reflection of real-time KPIs of the firm can be presented through dashboards. Once objectives and metrics are clearly understood, there will be success for BI practices. Similarly, many applications benefit from using historical data to predict future trends or possible outcomes using predictive modeling. Predictive modeling use statistics, and machine learning to forecast future trends. During the twenty-first century, prescribing an action optimally is possible through prescriptive analytics. The main idea of prescriptive analytics is: What action should we take to achieve our goal? This tool recommends the best course of action for a firm.

# Leading vendors of business intelligence

The BI market is fiercely competitive now. Multiple vendors are emerging to provide actionable insights from data. The following vendors are dominating the marketplace with multiple tools and technologies that facilitate firms to build their strategic intent:

- **Power BI**: Power BI is a data visualization and data modeling platform used by varied levels of professional competencies, from end-users to BI professionals. This tool was developed initially by *Ron George* in 2010. It is user-friendly in deriving insights from datasets through what-if analysis, data visualization, and data modeling, and it has the capability to understand natural language queries with interpretation and real-time report generation. To meet the needs of organizations, Power BI can improve data governance features. Three different platforms, Power BI Desktop, Power BI services and Power BI Mobile are available.

- **Tableau**: Tableau was developed in 2003. This tool is primarily used for interactive data visualization and BI for the usage and sharing of information. Programming knowledge is not a prerequisite to learning and using Tableau. This tool is extensively used in finance, marketing, healthcare, and retail to gain insights and derive trends. It is quite easy for users to connect multiple data sources to pull data and perform storytelling with data visualization without extensive technical knowledge. Even large datasets can be handled easily, which usually require complex tabulation and forecasting. Challenges of scalability and cost prevent many small enterprises from using Tableau. Optimum utilization of this tool may not be possible in all circumstances. Particularly, the use of various advanced features requires specialized training programs.

- **QlikView**: The first version of QlikView was released in 1994. It is one of the leading tools for **enterprise resource planning (ERP)** data visualization. Complex data analysis is possible through linking QlikView to multiple data sources. Data analysis of huge and complex dataset is accomplished quickly due to in-memory computing capability. Here, data analysis is done in memory which saves the time of data transfer between CPU and system RAM. However, implementation and license costs are a bit high.

- **SAS**: SAS was founded in 1976 by *Jim Goodnight*. It has been used across the industry for a long time as a BI tool. SAS is used for advanced BI and machine learning applications for big organizations with the capability to handle large datasets. However, this tool is not very popular now due to its high license cost and complexity of using the package.

- **Micro strategy**: The tool was developed in 1989. It supports advanced BI capability and makes it easy to pull data from a variety of sources with scalability as an enterprise BI tool. Interactive dashboards, reports, charts, and graphs can be presented with this tool, and they are quite easy to understand. Privacy and security can be maintained through the the encryption of ,data maintaining confidentiality.

- **IBM Cognos**: BM Cognos was developed in 1969 by *Alan Rushforth* and *Peter Glenister*. This tool is equipped with self-service features that assist users in analyzing data as a BI tool. However, a novice user will struggle to use all its advance features. The package is also a bit costly for small business users.

- **SAP BusinessObjects**: The SAP BusinessObjects was developed in 1990 by *Bernard Liautaud* and *Denis Payre*. This tool supports small enterprises and individual business users through Crystal Report and dynamic reports can be generated from anywhere, either online or offline, using it. Apart from Crystal Report, SAP BusinessObjects supports SAP Lumira, Query as a Web Service, Web Intelligence and SAP BusinessObjects Dashboards. Web intelligence applications can be accessed through the web browser to conduct data analysis, generate reports, and send these results to Microsoft Excel or PDF. SAP Lumira supports users to find business related data themselves and build customized interactive dashboards. QaaWS is used to construct and publish web services.

- **Zoho Analytic**: As a self-service BI tool, Zoho Analytics is an interactive data visualization tool with cloud support. Zoho Analytics was initially developed in 2009. As it is completely hosted in cloud, no such technical assistance is mandatory to set up this tool. It facilitates firms to simplify operations and optimize resources. It is scalable and flexible for business of all sizes. However, it is more suitable for small and medium enterprises and startup firms.

# Privacy issues

Currently, huge amounts of data are generated in social media, the internet, and interactions due to IoT devices. Much of this data is real data due to individuals' transactions. There are many third-party providers of data who can easily access sensitive demographic data, financial data, and purchase transaction data of customers. Multiple issues arise during the collection, fetching, storing, and presenting of data, and data governance becomes essential. Once data governance is achieved optimally, there is a drastic reduction of cost, and transparency and trust can be built among the stakeholders. As advanced data mining techniques are increasingly applied in recently, there are also concerns of multiple breaches. We are now collecting data from multiple sources. The sources can be online questionnaires, surveys, generated data from IoT devices, internet, social media, and third-party vendors. So, proper consent must be taken from the right respondents in an ethical and transparent manner. In case we collect data from social media or the internet, care should be taken to check for biased and fake data. Sometimes, personal data is collected without proper understanding.

As a consequence, apart from required personal data, other personal data is collected, which is prone to privacy. Once, data is encrypted, the issues of privacy invasion can be checked. At the same time, employees must be aware of the regulations of practices of data collection.

Preservation of data should be enforced with data integrity and confidentiality without any unauthorized access. Correct methods to back up data are also essential. Proper data access strategy and data encryption techniques can be applied. Similarly, the presentation of data is one of the most crucial phases of the data mining process to communicate findings through data storytelling or data visualization. To build trust with stakeholders, sensitive information along with the confidentiality of the individuals should be taken care of. Similarly, leakage of data and incorrect interpretation of the data create confusion. Proper security measures for multiple employees with different job roles should be taken for accessing data before presentation. So, a proper data governance policy should be implemented so that the right employees can access the data intended for their presentation using data mining tools.

# Future trends

In the current context, data is generated from multiple sources. The complexity and dynamics of data is creating bright scope for future of data mining and business intelligence. The following emerging areas signify the future areas of focus in data mining and BI landscape:

- **Sustainable data mining**: The main purpose of sustainable data mining is to maintain data democratization, remove bias in data, address the concerns of all stakeholders, maintain societal values, and fulfill environmental sustainability. Proper ethical standards should be followed while sharing and dealing with the entire data's lifecycle with a third-party. Data mining and BI applications require computing power and resources. So, many organizations follow green computing practices. For example, a firm can follow energy-efficient computing resources, reduce carbon emissions in data centers, and dispose off electronic wastes.

- **DataOps**: DataOps practices synchronize and automate the collection, processing, and analysis of data to ensure data integrity as a holistic approach. With data Ops, data quality is not compromised. Here, the barriers are eliminated to improve agility. It improves the data management processes of the firms through deriving insights from data. Sometimes, resistance to change from silo to process based culture create issues in implementing DataOps practices.

- **Responsible data mining**: Responsible data mining ensures ethical standards while collecting, processing, and analyzing data. Transparency, fairness, accountability, privacy of individuals, and compliance are the key traits here. The model's proper explanation ability, the right way to mitigate bias, and the explainability of the model should be mentioned clearly. So, adoption of responsible data mining builds trust and helps to care for individuals, organizations and society as a whole.

- **Cloud-based BI**: Cloud-based BI is scalable for data usage and user requirements, and it delivers BI services using the cloud instead of procuring physical infrastructure on-premise. Here, the incurred IT cost is covered through revenue expenses instead of capital expenditure. The service can be availed rapidly from anywhere using the internet. Implementation time and complexities can be avoided.

- **Natural language processing**: **Natural language processing** (**NLP**) helps computers understand human language both in text and voice format and interpret its meanings accurately. NLP is a subset of artificial intelligence that conducts applications like sentiment analysis, speech recognition, language translation, and summarization of texts and chatbots. For example, customer review of an *Apple* iPhone in *Flipkart* can be analyzed to know the positive, negative and neutral sentiments. Here, the customer reviews are extracted through web scrapping. Further, these data are cleaned and applied to a model for sentiment analysis.

- **Edge analytics**: Huge data is now generated at an alarming rate from cloud systems, social media feeds, IoT devices, smart phones, and video streaming. This process of data generation is the cause of edge analytics adoption. Here, data is processed and analyzed close to the originating source. So, analysis can be done in real-time without sending the generated data to a data center or any central location. Data transmission and storage costs are reduced due to edge analytics. Edge Analytics is now quite popular due to a wide adoption of Internet of Things.

- **Augmented analytics**: With the help of AI and ML, augmented analytics automates the data preparations and analyzes and improves insights presentation. This technology facilitates end users in analyzing and data storytelling accurately. Due to advancement in natural language processing and edge computing, the future of augmented analytics is quite bright in the coming years.

The future of data mining in long run will be focusing on integrating artificial intelligence, machine learning and big data analytics. This integration effort has the potential to revolutionize the way the data is analyzed to utilize decision making across industries. It is likely that the effort will be more for ethical practices to eliminate or curb bias and privacy issues.

# Conclusion

In this chapter we covered the fundamentals of data mining and BI. The foundational understanding of data mining and BI techniques, applications and trends are illustrated. In the next chapter, we will learn about regression and classification techniques and their applications.

# Multiple choice questions

1. **Queries touch large amounts of data and consume a lot of resources in case of what?**
   a. Decisional queries
   b. Transactional queries
   c. Void queries
   d. None of these

2. **Which one among the following is a popular and basic data mining technique?**
   a. Decision tree
   b. Artificial neural network
   c. Random forest
   d. Linear regression

3. **Who are our top 100 profitable customers? This ad-hoc query can be answered using what?**

    a. A data mining technique

    b. OLAP query

    c. OLTP query

    d. None of the above

4. **If a customer buys a potato, then they are most likely to purchase an onion. This can be found out using which technique?**

    a. Regression technique

    b. Association rule mining

    c. Cluster analysis

    d. Logistic regression

5. **Power BI is a product of?**

    a. Oracle Corporation

    b. SAP

    c. Microsoft

    d. None of these

6. **What do we need to do to achieve our goal? This can be answered which tools?**

    a. Descriptive analytics

    b. Predictive analytics

    a. Prescriptive analytics

    b. None of these

# Answers

1. a

2. d

3. b

4. b

5. c

6. c

# Practice exercises

In this chapter, readers learnt the fundamentals of data mining and business intelligence. They are expected to understand different techniques, their applications and the challenges involved. There is an attempt to explore the differences between OLTP and OLAP systems. Let us go through the following interesting scenarios.

1. You are a data analyst at a large supermarket called Miku_FreshMart. Miku_FreshMart collects massive data every day, just like what items customers buy, how much they spend, and how often they shop. However, they have not used this data to improve their business yet. Answer the following questions:

   a. List the types of data Miku_FreshMart collects that could be useful for understanding customer behavior. Explain how this data can reveal shopping patterns.

   b. Choos between OLTP and OLAP. Describe in simple terms what OLTP and OLAP systems are. Decide which system Miku_FreshMart should use to analyze customer data and explain why.

   c. Suggest a data mining technique that could help Miku_FreshMart discover which products are often bought together. Explain how this information can help Miku_FreshMart increase sales.

   d. Propose one way Miku_FreshMart can use data insights to make shopping better for customers. Identify any challenges they might face and suggest how to overcome them.

2. You are part of the team at Jinu_MovieFlix, an online streaming service. Jinu_MovieFlix wants to give better movie and show recommendations to keep users happy. They have information on what users watch, when they watch it, and how they rate what they have seen. Answer the following questions:

   a. Identify the kinds of data that can help Jinu_MovieFlix understand what users like to watch. Explain how this data shows user preferences.

   b. Briefly describe OLTP and OLAP systems. Decide which system Jinu_MovieFlix should use to analyze viewing habits and explain your reasoning.

   c. Suggest a data mining technique to personalize recommendations. Explain how this technique would help users find shows they will enjoy.

   d. Propose a feature or idea that uses data insights to keep users subscribed. Consider any challenges and suggest how to address them.

3. You are helping Speedy Deliver, a package delivery company, to make their deliveries faster and more efficient. They have data on delivery addresses, package sizes, delivery times, and traffic conditions. Answer the following questions:

a. List the pieces of data that could help Speedy Deliver plan better routes. Explain why each piece of data is helpful.

b. Explain in simple terms what OLTP and OLAP systems are. Decide which system would help Speedy Deliver analyze their delivery data and explain why.

c. Recommend a data mining technique that could help optimize delivery routes. Describe how this technique can lead to quicker deliveries.

d. Suggest one change Speedy Deliver could make based on the data. Identify any possible obstacles and propose solutions.

# Join our book's Discord space

Join the book's Discord Workspace for Latest updates, Offers, Tech happenings around the world, New Release and Sessions with the Authors:

**https://discord.bpbonline.com**

# CHAPTER 2
# Regression and Classification Techniques with Applications

## Introduction

In this chapter, we will discuss various pre-processing techniques with examples explained using R programming language, like missing data analysis, bias-variance trade-off, regression, classification techniques, and combining classifiers for better model performance. Missing data analysis under various situations is also explained using R. The concept of bias-variance trade-off is presented using a particular case with few features. The application of important supervised learning algorithms and applications of these algorithms on datasets from multiple functional areas are explained. Finally, ensemble algorithms are explained to improve the accuracy of prediction.

## Structure

This chapter covers the following topics:

- Data cleaning, transformation and normalization
- Bias and variance
- Regression
- Decision tree
- Logistic regression
- Other classification techniques

# Objectives

After going through this chapter, you will understand the data cleaning procedures, transformation, and normalization of data. Readers will acquire knowledge on various classification techniques, and regression and understand the combination of classifiers for improvement of model performance. Practical examples are specified using the R programming language to explain classification techniques.

**Without clean data, or clean enough data, your data science is worthless.**

*— Michael Stonebraker, Adjunct Professor, MIT*

# Data cleaning, transformation and normalization

Significant effort and time are spent during the pre-processing of data. Data cleaning deciphers errors, inconsistencies, and missing data and ensures the quality of data through validation to prepare data for modelling. A systematic procedure to clean data is done through the following methods:

- **Removal of duplicate rows**: In many cases, the same values are present in all columns of multiple rows in dataset. Sometimes, similar or few columns may have same values in few rows of dataset. So, various techniques are applied to remove these redundancies. For improving quality of dataset, removal of duplicates is essential. However, care should be taken to avoid any important data loss and context sensitive data protection.

  Let us take an example with R Codes.

  Duplicates can skew analysis and lead to incorrect conclusions. Removing them improves data quality.

  Example with R codes.

  The following R Codes remove the duplicate records:

```
# Create a data frame
df <- data.frame(
ID = c(1, 2, 1, 2),
Name = c("Gopal Sharma", "Ram Pandey", "Gopal Sharma", "Ram
Pandey"),
Product = c("Laptop", "Tablet", "Laptop", "Tablet"),
Quantity = c(1, 2, 1, 2),
Price = c(900, 300, 900, 300))
```

```
# Remove duplicate rows
df_cleaned <- df[!duplicated(df), ]
# Display the cleaned data frame
print(df_cleaned)
```

- **Standardization of formats**: To ensure data quality, standardization of formats is quite essential. The same information may be represented differently in collected data. Standardization is required to convert all these differently represented data into a consistent format. Various techniques like normalization, encoding of categorical data, time and date standardization are applied based on situational requirements. In data normalization, data are scaled up to a range from -1 to +1, which avoids issues with values spread in wide ranges. Similarly, encoding methods are used to convert categorical data to numeric or continuous data. Date and time features should be properly formatted during data cleaning to get accuracy during analysis. There are various ways to treat date and time fixing. The data types should be converted to the exact data and time-type using tools. In case a string contains data and time, extraction may be done, and the proper time zone must be applied. Automated Python libraries and other tools are available to locate and correct issues in data and time datatypes. Similarly, Invalid data can be of different categories like missing data, data in incorrect format, and outliers. The quality of the dataset can be improved by removing inconsistencies of these invalid data through various methods.

Standardization converts data into a uniform format.

Example with R codes:

```
# Create initial dataframe
df <- data.frame(
TransactionID = c("T001", "T002", "T003"),
Date = c("01/08/2023", "2023-08-01", "August 1, 2023"),
PaymentMethod = c("Credit Card", "credit card", "CC"),
stringsAsFactors = FALSE)
# Standardize the Date column
df$Date <- as.Date(df$Date, tryFormats = c("%d/%m/%Y", "%Y-%m-%d",
"%B %d, %Y"))
# Standardize the PaymentMethod column
df$PaymentMethod <- tolower(df$PaymentMethod)
df$PaymentMethod[df$PaymentMethod %in% c("credit card", "cc")] <-
"credit card"
# View the standardized data frame
print(df)
```

- **Missing values treatments**: Sometimes data is missing a few features and does not get recorded in a few cases. The treatment of these missing values is quite vital to get an accurate result from the model. There are various techniques used to treat missing values. Methods can be opted to delete the missing value, treat the missing value with proper imputation method and a model-centric method. Based on various data types, data distribution and type of missing data, the treatment method is chosen.

  Example with R codes: The R Codes impute missing age with the mean age and impute missing score with the mean score:

```
# Create initial data frame which comprises missing values
df <- data.frame(StudentID = c("S001", "S002", "S003"),
Name = c("Deepti Gupta ", " Arati Tripathy ", " Badri Sehgal "),
Age = c(17, NA, 18),
Score = c(88, 92, NA),
stringsAsFactors = FALSE)
# Impute missing Age with mean age
mean_age <- mean(df$Age, na.rm = TRUE)
df$Age[is.na(df$Age)] <- mean_age
# Impute missing Score with mean score
mean_score <- mean(df$Score, na.rm = TRUE)
df$Score[is.na(df$Score)] <- mean_score
# View the data frame after imputing missing values
print(df)
```

- **Treatment of outliers**: In datasets, it may so happen that few observations are quite different from all other observations. These observations are known as outliers. In some cases, outliers are context-based. For example, there may be an observation of a younger age group present near a group of elderly age-group observations. It may so happen that a subgroup with collective different data distribution is present in a group. So, these outliers should be treated differently so as to get accurate result.

  Outliers can distort analysis. Identifying and addressing them ensures more accurate results.

  R codes:

```
# Create the sales data frame
sales_data <- data.frame(Day    = c("Monday", "Tuesday", "Wednesday",
"Thursday", "Friday"),Sales = c(1200, 1150, 1180, 10000, 1220))
Identifying the Outlier:
```

```
# Calculate basic statistics
mean_sales <- mean(sales_data$Sales)
sd_sales   <- sd(sales_data$Sales)
# Identify outlier (values beyond mean ± 2*SD)
sales_data$Outlier <- abs(sales_data$Sales - mean_sales) > 2 * sd_
sales
# View the data with outlier flagged
print(sales_data)
```

- **Merging and splitting columns**: Merging columns during data cleaning can be done in various ways. If there are multiple datasets, merging can be accomplished through a common column using a **Structured Query Language** (**SQL**) query. Similarly, R and Python functions can be written to merge. Similarly, if multiple columns contain similar information, they may be merged into a single column. Similarly, one can split columns in case a column contains both numeric and text data types based on a condition. Sometimes, string functions can be used to extract substrings based on requirements. We plot box plot, use **Inter Quartile Range** (**IQR**) method, and calculate z score to detect outliers.

  o **Merging columns using R codes**: You can merge datasets using the merge() function.

  **R code for merging:**

  ```
  # Employee Details Data Frame
  employee_details <- data.frame(EmployeeID = c("E001",
  "E002"),FirstName  = c("Rajesh", "Anjali"),
    LastName   = c("Kumar", "Singh"))
  # Department Info Data Frame
  department_info <- data.frame(EmployeeID = c("E001",
  "E002"),Department = c("Engineering", "Marketing"))
  # Merging the Data Frames on 'EmployeeID'
  merged_data <- merge(employee_details, department_info, by =
  "EmployeeID")
  # Displaying the Merged Data
  print(merged_data)
  ```

  **Output:**

| EmployeeID | FirstName | LastName | Department |
|---|---|---|---|
| 1 E001 | Rajesh | Kumar | Engineering |
| 2 E002 | Anjali | Singh | Marketing |

o **Splitting columns**: For splitting, the **tidyr** package streamlines the process.

**R code for splitting**:

```
# Install 'tidyr' if not already installed
# install.packages("tidyr")
library(tidyr)
# Full Address Data Frame
addresses <- data.frame(FullAddress = c("123 MG Road,
Bengaluru, Karnataka 560001","456 Park Street, Kolkata, West
Bengal 700016"))
# Splitting the 'FullAddress' Column into Separate Columns
addresses_split <- addresses %>% separate(FullAddress, into
= c("Street", "City", "State", "PIN_Code"), sep = ",\\s|\\
s(?=\\d)")
# Displaying the Split Data
print(addresses_split)
```

**Output**:

| Street | City | State | PIN_Code |
|---|---|---|---|
| 1 123 MG Road | Bengaluru | Karnataka | 560001 |
| 2 456 Park Street | Kolkata | West Bengal | 700016 |

# Bias and variance

Once preprocessing is accomplished, it is essential to check that the dataset is not affected due to bias and variance. Bias is the difference between the average prediction of the model and the right value that we are attempting to predict. Bias is high due to over-simplified assumption. For example, in simple linear regression, we assume the relationship among two variables is linear. In real cases, it may not be linear. In case of high bias, the model cannot capture the true relationship among data and variables. High bias is also termed as under-fitting of data. Algorithms like linear regression, logistic regression and discriminant algorithms are high-bias algorithms.

In case of high variance, for different datasets, the model fit is also significantly different. Here, the dataset overfits. So, in case of a particular dataset, the model fits very well. However, on a different dataset, the model does not fit well in case of high variance. Error rates in these cases are very high on test data, though the model fits very well with training data. Algorithms like decision trees, Support Vector Machines, and k-nearest neighbors are examples of high-variance algorithms. The following figure shows the trade-off of bias variance:

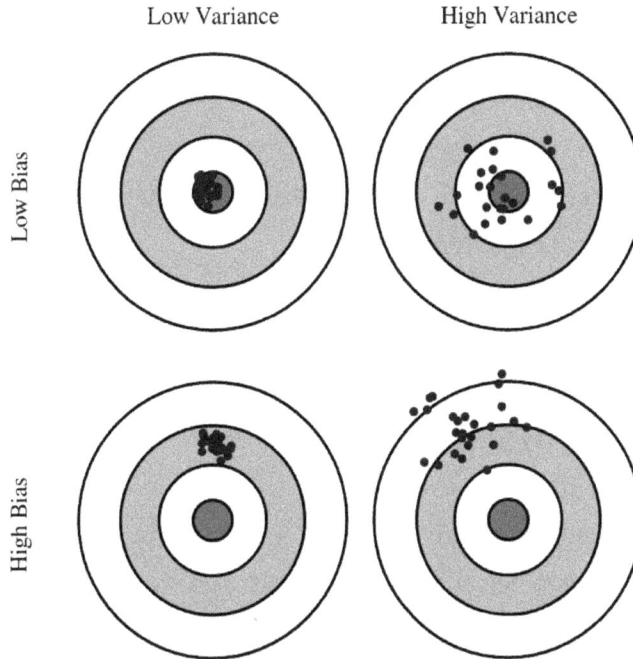

**Figure 2.1**: *Bias variance trade-off*
**Source:** *https://scott.fortmann-roe.com/docs/BiasVariance.html*

We have to make a balance of bias and variance. To fix bias, we may increase the number of features or increase the complexity of the algorithms by adding polynomial features.

Let us take an example to understand the concept and take a decision to choose the optimal degree of an example. The following R code shows how to choose the optimal polynomial degree for regression using the **mtcars** dataset. It forecasts miles per gallon based on car weight by fitting polynomial models of degrees one to five. For each model, it calculates the Root Mean Squared Error on the test data to measure performance. By plotting the test RMSE against the polynomial degrees, the code identifies the degree with the lowest RMSE. This shows which model best balances bias and variance, helping to illustrate the bias-variance tradeoff in a practical way.

R codes:

```
# Load the mtcars dataset
data(mtcars)
# Set seed for reproducibility
set.seed(123)
# Split data into training and testing sets (70% train, 30% test)
train_indices <- sample(1:nrow(mtcars), size = 0.7 * nrow(mtcars))
```

```
train_data <- mtcars[train_indices, ]
test_data <- mtcars[-train_indices, ]
# Define degrees of polynomial to test
degrees <- 1:5  # Testing degrees from 1 to 5
# Initialize a vector to store testing RMSE for each degree
test_rmse <- numeric(length(degrees))
# Loop over polynomial degrees
for (i in degrees) {
  # Fit polynomial regression model
  model <- lm(mpg ~ poly(wt, i), data = train_data)
  # Predict on test data
  predictions <- predict(model, newdata = test_data)
  # Calculate Root Mean Squared Error (RMSE) on test data
  rmse <- sqrt(mean((test_data$mpg - predictions)^2))
  test_rmse[i] <- rmse
}
# Identify the degree with the minimum test RMSE
optimal_degree <- which.min(test_rmse)
cat("Optimal polynomial degree:", optimal_degree, "\n")
# Plot Test RMSE vs. Polynomial Degree
plot(degrees, test_rmse, type = "b", pch = 19, col = "blue",
     xlab = "Polynomial Degree", ylab = "Test RMSE",
     main = "Test RMSE vs. Polynomial Degree")
points(optimal_degree, test_rmse[optimal_degree], col = "red", pch = 19)
```

The plot generated is as follows:

**Test RMSE vs. Polynomial Degree**

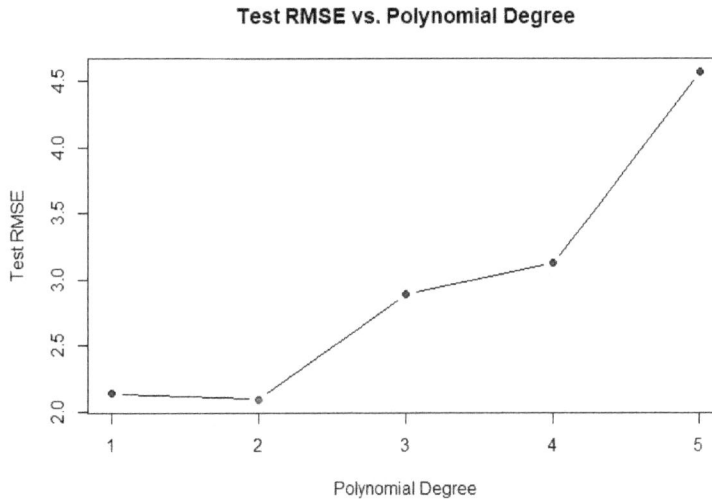

*Figure 2.2*: *Bias variance trade-off*
*Source: Author's R Studio*

The optimal polynomial degree from the preceding plot can be concluded as 2 which minimizes the test RMSE. This means that a quadratic model best balances bias and variance when predicting miles per gallon from car weight in the **mtcars** dataset. A degree 2 polynomial effectively captures the underlying relationship without overfitting to provide the most accurate predictions on new data.

Sometimes, we can decrease regularization term also. The regularization concept will be discussed in the *Regression* section. Similarly, to fix variance, we may add more data, go for cross validation technique, reduce no of features to retain the important features just required for the model and increase the regularization term. So, an optimal balance of bias and variance will never underfit or overfit the model.

# Regression

Linear regression predicts the output or dependent variable with a linear function of predictors $y = k0 + k1x1 + k2x2 + \cdots + kjxj$,

Here, $x1, x2, \cdots, xj$ are predictors, y is the response to predict, and $k0, k1, \cdots, kj$ are coefficients to learn. The dependent variable or response variable is a continuous variable. However, the independent or predictor variables can be a combination of categorical or continuous variables. The primary task of regression is to minimize the prediction errors of all data points available in a dataset. In order to interpret the regression model, we have to understand the metrics of regression.

# Metrics and coefficients of regression

Some important metrics of regression are as follows:

- **$R^2$**: This value represents the proportion of variance in the dependent variable that is collectively explained by all the independent variables. The value of $R^2$ lies between 0 and 1. The higher value signifies that the regression line will pass through a higher percentage of data points. Similarly, the lower value states that the regression line will pass through a smaller number of data points. The higher the value of R2, the better the model explains variation. However, in case of multiple independent variables, we have to check the adjusted R2 also, which is as follows:

  o **Adjusted R2**: R2 square value always increases when we go on adding more variables to the model. Once we add more useless or redundant independent variables to the regression model, the adjusted R2 will decrease. So, adjusted R2 is a determinant to stop once the exact number of independent variables which are just sufficient for the regression model.

- **Mean Absolute Error (MAE)**: The MEA is the average of the absolute difference between observed and predicted values of data in the dataset. It calculates the absolute difference between each prediction and actual value and then averages these differences. These metrics can be used to measure the performance of regression models:

$$MAE = (1/k) \ \Sigma(i{=}1 \ to \ k) \ |y\_i - \hat{y}\_i|$$

Where:

  o k is the number of observations in the dataset

  o y_i is the observed value

  o $\hat{y}$_i is the predicted value

MAE is easy to interpret, and the calculation is also simple. These metrics is relatively less sensitive to outliers and can be applied to non-normal data.

- **Mean Square Error (MSE)**: MSE is the average of the squared difference between the observed and predicted data of the dataset. It is nothing but the variance of the residuals. This is a popularly used metrics to evaluate the performance of regression models. Mean absolute error penalizes all errors equally. However, the Mean Square Error penalizes large errors more severely. MSE is also sensitive to outliers due to squaring. Refer to the following:

$$MSE = (1/k) \ \Sigma \ (i{=}1 \ to \ k) \ (y\_i - \hat{y}\_i)^2$$

Where:

  o k is the number of observations in the dataset

  o y_i is the observed value

- o ŷ_i is the predicted value

- o MSE is easy to calculate and sensitive to outliers

- **Root Means Square Error (RMSE)**: RMSE is computed by taking the square root of the mean of squared differences between the predicted and observed values. This measures the standard deviation of the differences between predicted and actual observations. This metric is widely used to measure the accuracy of regression models:

$$RMSE = SQRT[(1/k) \; \Sigma \; (i{=}1 \; to \; k) \; (y\_i - \hat{y}\_i)^2 ]$$

RMSE is a metrics balances bias and variance trade off but sensitive to outliers. It is easy to interpret and a popular metrics of regression.

- **Standard Error of Coefficient**: This is an estimate of the standard deviation of the coefficient. It signifies how much uncertainty there is with the coefficients. The smaller the standard error, the more accurate the estimate. We can also say, how much the coefficient may change if the change the sample is different:

*p value: \*\*\*(<.001), \*\*(<.01), \*(<.05) and so on*

- **Residual Standard Error**: The average amount that the actual values differ from the predictions. We can also say, it measures the variability of errors or residuals in a regression model.

- **F Statistics**: It is a good indicator of whether there is a relationship between independent and dependent features or variables. The farther the F Statistics from 1, the better it is.

# Assumption of linear regression

To make a meaningful prediction from data and storytelling on hidden relationships between variables, assumptions should be satisfied.

Assumption of linear regression:

- The total number of observations must be greater than number of independent variables.

- Residuals of the linear regression model are normally distributed.

- Residuals of the model have a mean of zero.

- Residuals of the model have the same variance, that is, homoscedasticity is maintained.

- Residuals of the model should be statistically independent of each other.

- There should not be autocorrelations, especially for time series data.

The following four plots explain the issues of regression model, like non normal residuals, nonlinear relations, non-constant variance and influential data:

- **Residual vs. fitted plot**: This plot shows the predicted value on the x-axis and residuals or errors on the y-axis. Here, it is possible to locate relationship among the errors. This plot should not show any pattern in data. Residuals should be randomly scattered. In that case, it can be comprehended that the model quality is good.

- **Normal QQ plot**: This plot checks the normality of the residuals. This is a scatter plot which compares quartile of dataset with quartile of a normal distribution. QQ plot analyses how closely the data follows a normal distribution. If the data fall approximately a straight line, then normal distribution is followed. If data points deviate from straight line or there is pattern in data, then the data distribution is not normal. For linear regression, normality is essential.

- **Scale-location plot**: This plot examines homoscedasticity or constant variance across all levels of the predictor variables. This plot examines the relationship between square root of the absolute residual and the fitted value of the model. There should be a horizontal line in plot in case variance of the errors are constant to obey homoscedasticity assumption.

- **Residual versus leverage plot**: This plot calibrates the influence or leverage of observations on x-axis and residual on y-axis. This plot deciphers influential observations that may affect the output of the model. This plot is also known as cook's distance plot. Proper treatment of outliers and influential observation improves the accuracy of the model.

The following R codes generate diagnostics plot:

```
data("mtcars")
names(mtcars)
[1] "mpg"  "cyl"  "disp"
[4] "hp"   "drat" "wt"
[7] "qsec" "vs"   "am"
[10] "gear" "carb"
model <-  lm(mpg ~ cyl + wt,data=mtcars)
#Diagonostic Plot
plot(model,pch=18,cex=2)
```

The following four diagnostics plots shown in the following figure, collectively examine the regression model's fit, assumption, and reliability:

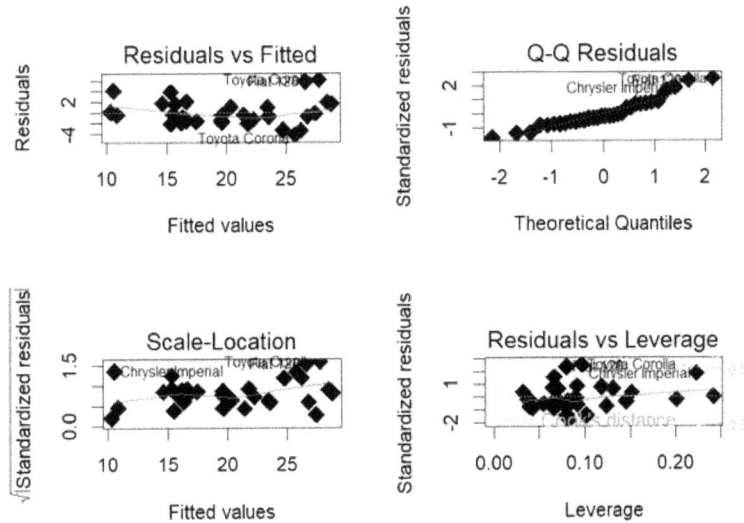

**Figure 2.3**: *Diagnostic plots*
*Source: Author's R Studio*

# Case study

A firm is conducting an analysis on its current and past employees. The dataset is adopted from Kaggle.

All the features of the dataset are:

- Satisfaction level (ranges from 0 to 1)
- Number of projects
- Average monthly hours
- Time spent at the company (in years)
- Work accident (0: No or 1: Yes)
- Promotion in last 5 years (0: No or 1: Yes)
- Sales (departments of employees)
- Salary (low, medium, high)
- Left (0: No or 1: Yes)

Here, we will apply linear regression and apply multiple regression with the dependent variable as **"No of projects"** and independent variables as **"average_montly_hours"**, **"satisfaction_level"**,**"Work_accident"**,**"promotion_last_5years"**,**"sales"**    and **"salary"** using R and interpret the result. The following R codes generated in the writer's RStudio solves the purpose:

```
library(psych)
setwd('D:/BPB_Publication_BOOK')
Reg_DM<- read.csv (paste ("HR_comma_sep.csv", sep=""))
describe(Reg_DM)
#linear regression on number of projects done
mlm <- lm (number_project ~ satisfaction_level+average_montly_hours+Work_
accident+promotion_last_5years+sales+salary, data = Reg_DM)
summary(mlm)
#
# Call:
#lm (formula = number_project ~ satisfaction_level + average_montly_hours +
#     Work_accident + promotion_last_5years + sales + salary, data = Reg_DM)
#
# Residuals:
#     Min      1Q  Median      3Q     Max
# -2.9320 -0.9334 -0.0846  0.8333  3.7053
#
# Coefficients:
#                          Estimate   Std. Error   t value    Pr(>|t|)
#(Intercept)              2.0636094    0.0594599    34.706     <2e-16 ***
# satisfaction_level     -0.6711281    0.0364662   -18.404     <2e-16 ***
# average_montly_hours    0.0102268    0.0001812    56.449     <2e-16 ***
# Work_accident           0.0254529    0.0257838     0.987     0.3236
# promotion_last_5years  -0.0065286    0.0628034    -0.104     0.9172
#sales                    0.0077595    0.0032958     2.354     0.0186 *
#salary                   0.0158775    0.0144571     1.098     0.2721
# ---
# Signif. codes:  0 '***' 0.001 '**' 0.01 '*' 0.05 '.' 0.1 ' ' 1
#
# Residual standard error: 1.108 on 14992 degrees of freedom
# Multiple R-squared:  0.1926, Adjusted R-squared:  0.1923
# F-statistic: 596.1 on 6 and 14992 DF,  p-value: < 2.2e-16
```

The linear regression on **number of projects done** presented that **satisfaction level** and **the average monthly hours** are the most significant.

Let us start a similar simple analysis with a regression graph using another important variable from the same dataset. This time, we will explore how employee satisfaction relates to the number of projects they have been assigned. Understanding this relationship can offer valuable insights into workload management and its impact on employee morale. We will look at plot regression equation also:

```
# Load the dataset
Reg_DM <- read.csv("HR_comma_sep.csv")
# Fit the regression model
simple_lm <- lm(satisfaction_level ~ number_project, data = Reg_DM)
# Plot the data points
plot(Reg_DM$number_project, Reg_DM$satisfaction_level,
     xlab = "Number of Projects",
     ylab = "Satisfaction Level",
     main = "Satisfaction Level vs. Number of Projects")
# Add the regression line
abline(simple_lm)
```

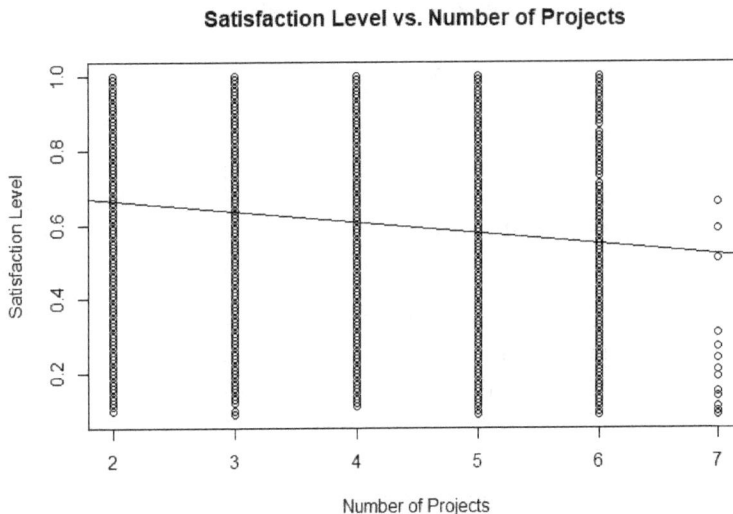

*Figure 2.4*: Diagnostic Plots

Source: Author's RStudio

# Holdout and cross-validation in classification tasks

We do not use all the observations in the dataset to build a model. There are various ways to construct the models. Let us discuss two important methods. The basic way is popularly known as hold-out method. Here, the entire dataset is split into a training and a test dataset. The training dataset is used to build the classification model, and the test dataset is used to test the accuracy of the model. This is done by comparing the observed dataset with the predicted dataset. The accuracy will be good if the distribution of training and test dataset are approximately same.

Cross validation or k fold validation is a method where the dataset is spilt into k folds. One of the folds is taken as a test dataset and the other folds as training dataset. The holdout method is repeated until each fold is used as test set. Here, more possible data are subjected in both training and test datasets compared to holdout method. The holdout method is useful when the dataset is large, and time pressure is there.

There are many performance matrices to judge the model performance.

# Performance metrices of classification techniques

There are various ways to measure the performance of classifiers. Some popular methods are Confusion Matrix, Lift Chart, **Kolmogorov-Smirnov Chart (KS Chart)**, **Receiver Operating Charecteristic (ROC)** and **Area Under the Curven (AUC)**. Let us understand a popular matrix of classification, that is, the confusion matrix among the five metrices specified:

- **Confusion matrix**: The confusion matrix is a popular tool to measure the performance of the classification model. The following table specifies accuracy, precision, recall or sensitivity and specificity. These ratios facilitate to interpret the classifiers.

    o **Accuracy** is the proportion of correctly classified prediction in total number of predictions. However, in case of imbalanced dataset, the interpretation is not correctly present the result. A dataset is imbalanced where once class contains significantly higher number of samples. The formula to calculate accuracy is as follows:

    $$Accuracy = (TP+TN)/(TP+FP+FN+TN)$$

    o **Recall**: It computes the proportion of true positives among all actual positives points of the dataset. It is easy to interpret and can be used in imbalanced datasets. However, this ratio is suitable for binary classification and ignores false positives. The formula to calculate recall is as follows:

    $$Recall/True\ positive\ rate/Sensitivity = TP/TP+FN$$

o **Precision**: Precision computes the proportion of true positives among all predicted positive points in the dataset. It is easy to interpret and can be used in imbalanced dataset also. However, it is suitable for binary classification and ignores false negatives. The formula to compute precision is as follows:

$$Precision = TP/TP+FP$$

o **Specificity**: Specificity computes the proportion of true negatives among all actual negative instances of the dataset. It is easy to interpret and suitable for binary classification problems. It is suitable for imbalanced dataset analysis also. It may be misleading in case dataset comprises large number of true positive cases. The formula to compute specificity is as follows:

$$Specificity \ or \ true \ negative \ rate = TN/FP+TN$$

o **F1 score**: F1 score is used as a balanced measure which combines both precision and recall. However, this score is sensitive to threshold of classification model. Though 0.5 threshold is a default choice, in real world applications, tuning of threshold is required. Threshold tuning is also beneficial to optimize F1 score as per requirement. F1 score is useful for binary classification problems. F1 score is calculated as follows:

$$F1 \ score = 2 * (precision * recall) / (precision + recall)$$

You can check *Table 2.1* to go through the ratios explained previously:

| | | Actual outcome | | | |
|---|---|---|---|---|---|
| | | **Positive** | **Negative** | | |
| Predicted outcome | Positive | **True positive (TP)** | **False positive (FP)** | Positive predictive value or precision | *TP/TP+FP* |
| | Negative | **False negative (FN)** | **True negative (TN)** | Negative predictive value | *FN/FN+TN* |
| | | Sensitivity or recall or true positive rate | Specificity or true negative rate | *Accuracy = (TP+TN)/(TP+FP+FN+TN)* | |
| | | *TP/TP+FN* | *TN/FP+TN* | | |

*Table 2.1: Confusion matrix*

Let us discuss the following small situation:

Out of the 200 emails, 80 emails are actually spam in which the model correctly classifies 60 of them as spam. Out of the 200 emails, 120 emails are not spam, in which the model correctly classifies 100 of them as not spam. Out of the 200 emails, the model incorrectly classifies 20 non-spam emails as spam. Out of the 200 emails, the model misses 20 spam emails and identifies them as non-spam. The next step is to classify the outcomes into the following four categories:

- True positive: 60
- True negative: 100
- False positive: 20
- False negative: 20

$$Accuracy = (TP+TN)/(TP+FP+FN+TN) = (60+100) / (60+100+20+20) = 160/200 = 0.8$$

$$Precision = TP/(TP+FP) = 60 / (60+20) = 0.75$$

$$Recall\ or\ sensitivity = P/TP+FN = 60/ (60+20) = .75$$

$$F1\ score = 2 * (precision * recall) / (precision + recall) = 2 *(.75*.75)/ (.75+.75) = .75$$

$$Specificity = TN/FP+TN = 100 / (100+20) = 0.84$$

Sometimes, we come across an imbalanced dataset. In those situations, the F1 Score is crucial, which balances recall and precision because, when precision increases, recall decreases. When recall increases, the precision decreases. Decision makers should balance and go for a tradeoff. Precision can have serious consequences in financial fraud cases due to false positive cases. Similarly, in medical situations, recall use is crucial once the model fails to dragonize detrimental.

# Decision tree

A decision tree is a supervised learning tool where we continuously split data based on certain parameters. This tool is extensively used in the field of statistics, ML, and data mining. Nonlinear datasets can be handled quite effectively using a decision tree. We can use the decision tree in various real-life cases relating to business applications, engineering, law, and civil planning. It is easy to prepare and clean data for decision tree. Reading and interpretation of this tool also require less effort.

## Terminologies of decision tree structure

For understanding and interpreting decision trees, it is essential to understand the following terms associated with a decision tree:

- **Nodes**: Node is a fundamental item of a tree which is a variable or feature. The node from which the tree starts is known as a root node.

- **Branches/Edges**: Edge or branch connects two nodes to display that there is relationship between two nodes based on a decision to any particular circumstances.

- **Leaf nodes**: The node where the tree ends is known as a leaf node, which also signifies a class of the dataset as final decision or outcome.

- **Decision criteria**: Decision criteria is a rule used to determine how the dataset should be divided at a decision node. The criterion is based on comparison of the value of features against a threshold value.

- **Pruning**: Pruning is a process to remove a branch of a decision tree which do not provide predictive power to classify the instances. To understand the concept of a decision tree, let us take an example. Suppose we wish to know the fitness of an individual based on his age, physical activities, and eating habits. The decision nodes are *What is his age?, Does he exercise?, Does he frequently eat red meats?* The outcome as leaves of the tree as is either fit, or not fit:

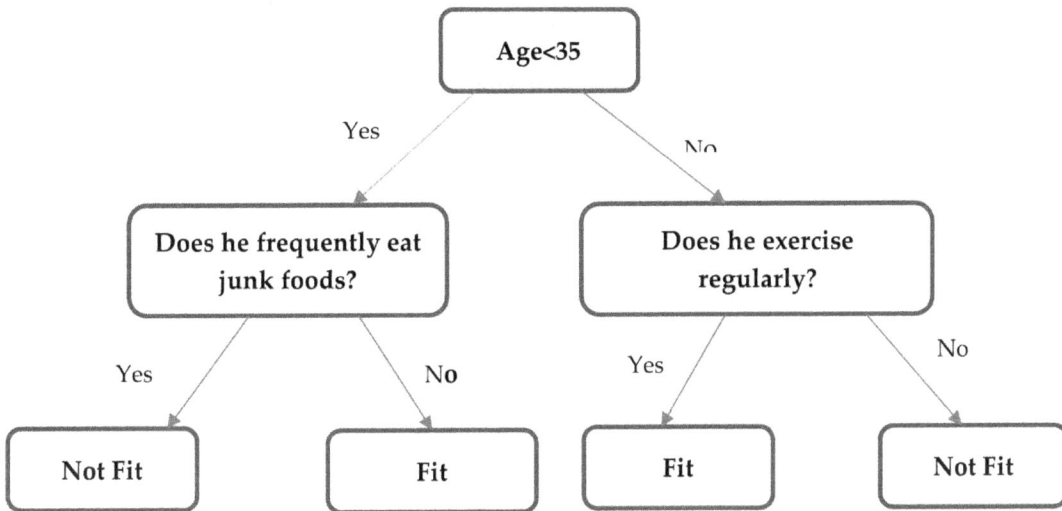

*Figure 2.5: Example of a decision tree*

# Tree construction and metrics of decision tree

Decision trees are usually classified into regression and classification trees. Regression trees deal with continuous variables, and classification trees deal with categorical target variables. The final output is generated as class levels in the classification tree, whereas the output of regression trees are continuous values. The criteria to split the classification tree are based on information gain. In the case of regression trees, MSE or variance reduction techniques are used. Algorithms like ID5 and **Classification and Regression Tree (CART)** can be used in both classification and regression cases. Let us try to understand one of the simplest classification algorithms, that is, **Iterative Dichotomizer 3 (ID3)**.

A decision to make a split to determine the root node of a decision tree for a given dataset with multiple features affects the accuracy of decision tree. To determine the root node, the information gain must be calculated. The node or feature with the highest information gain is chosen as the root of the decision tree. Entropy should be calculated to compute information gain. Entropy is the measure of impurity of a specified dataset. For each node, entropy is calculated before splitting and after splitting the tree. The difference in entropy before and after splitting is the information gain of that node.

If a dataset has x number of classes and the probability of randomly choosing data from a class, $k$ is $P_k$, then entropy is expressed as:

$$Entropy(E)= (P_k log_2 P_k)$$

Say we have a dataset with eight students on a tutorial belonging to two different classes with results as pass and fail. If five students passed and three students failed, then the entropy will be calculated as follows:

$$Entropy(E)= -(P_{pass} log_2 P_{pass} + P_{fail} log_2 P_{fail})$$

Here, the probability of pass is 5/8 and the probability of fail is 3/8.

$$So,\ Entropy(E)= -(5/8* log_2 5/8 + 3/8* log_2 3/8) \approx .9542$$

If all eight observations belong to one class, then entropy will be zero as the node is pure:

$$Entropy(E)= -(1 log_2 1) = 0$$

If four observations belong to pass and another four observations belong to fail class:

$$Entropy(E)= - (4/8 * log_2 4/8 + 4/8 * log_2 4/8) = 1$$

So, impurity is the maximum here.

# Gini value

Gini value or impurity is also a metric like entropy in decision tree. The most appropriate feature is selected here as root by using Gini values. A high Gini value of a feature signifies high impurity, and a low value signifies low impurity.

If a dataset has x number of classes and the probability of randomly choosing data from class, and k is $P_k$, then the Gini value is expressed as the following:

$$Gini\ Index\ Gini(G) = 1\ \sum_{k=1}(Pk)^2$$

Here, $P_k$ is the probability of the kth class in G. Once G is split into $G_1$, $G_2$, ......, $G_n$, then goodness of the spilt is computed, as follows:

$$Gini_{split}(G)= \sum_{i=1}P(Gi)\ Gini(Gi)$$

Let us calculate the Gini value of the preceding example:

$$Gini(G)= 1- \sum k=1(Pk)^2 = 1- [(5/8)^2 + (3/8)2] = .468$$

Gini calculation is much faster than entropy calculation. However, entropy calculation is more accurate compared to Gini calculation. The application of logarithm makes entropy calculation complex.

**Example**: Let us take a dataset to demine the root of the decision tree:

| Cases | Height | Hair | Eye | Attractiveness |
|-------|--------|------|-----|----------------|
| C1 | Tall | Dark | Blue | Not beautiful |
| C2 | Short | Dark | Blue | Not beautiful |
| C3 | Tall | Blond | Blue | Beautiful |
| C4 | Tall | Red | Blue | Beautiful |
| C5 | Tall | Blond | Brown | Not beautiful |
| C6 | Short | Blond | Blue | Beautiful |
| C7 | Short | Blond | Brown | Not beautiful |
| C8 | Tall | Dark | Brown | Not beautiful |

*Table 2.2: A dataset*

The preceding dataset comprises eight number of cases belonging to two different classes with result as not beautiful and beautiful. Here, five cases are not beautiful and three cases are beautiful.

So, $Entropy(E) = -(5/8* log2\ 5/8 + 3/8* log2\ 3/8) \approx .954$

Let us calculate the information gain of hair:

$$Entropy\ (E, hair) = 3/8* [-3/3 * log23/3-0/3 * log20/3- 0/3*log20/3] + 1/8*[-0/1 * log20/1-1/1 * log21/1] + 4/8*[-2/4 * log22/4-2/4 * log22/4] = 0.5$$

$$Information\ gain(hair) = 0.954- 0.5 = 0.454$$

Now, let us calculate the information gain of height:

$$Entropy(E, Height) = +3/8 (-1/3\ log\ 1/3 - 2/3\ log\ 2/3) + 5/8 (-2/5\ log\ 2/5 - 3/5\ log\ 3/5) = 0.951$$

$$Information\ gain(Height)=0.955 - 0.951 = 0.004$$

Now, let us calculate the information gain of eyes:

$$Entropy(E, Eyes)= +5/8 (-3/5\ log\ 3/5 - 2/5\ log\ 2/5) + 3/8 * 0 = 0.607$$

$$Information\ gain(Eyes)= 0.955 - 0.607 = 0.348$$

So, the feature with highest information gain is hair, so hair will be chosen as the root of the ID3 decision tree. Let us construct the tree using hair as the root:

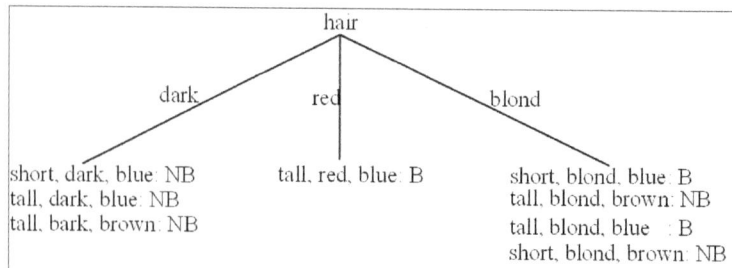

*Figure 2.6: Decision tree with Hair as Root (NB: Not beautiful, B- Beautiful)*

As classes are already determined for dark and red hair, let us select the best attribute among eyes and height:

So, *entropy before splitting the subtree = -2/4log22/4 – 2/4log22/4 = -log21/2=1*

*Height: short (1 B, 1 NB)*

$\qquad$ *tall (1 B, 1 NB)*

*Eyes:* $\qquad$ *blue (2 B, 0 NB)*

$\qquad$ *brown (0 B, 2 NB)*

Now,

$\qquad$ *Information gain(height) = 1 – 2/4\*E(1 B,1 NB) – 2/4\*E(1 B,1 NB) = 1-1 = 0*

$\qquad$ *Information gain(eyes) = 1 – 2/4\*E (2 B,0 NB) – 2/4\*E(0 B,2 NB) = 1 – 0 – 0 = 1*

Information gain of eyes is maximum and will be chosen as sub root of the branch. Let us build the decision tree as shown in the following figure:

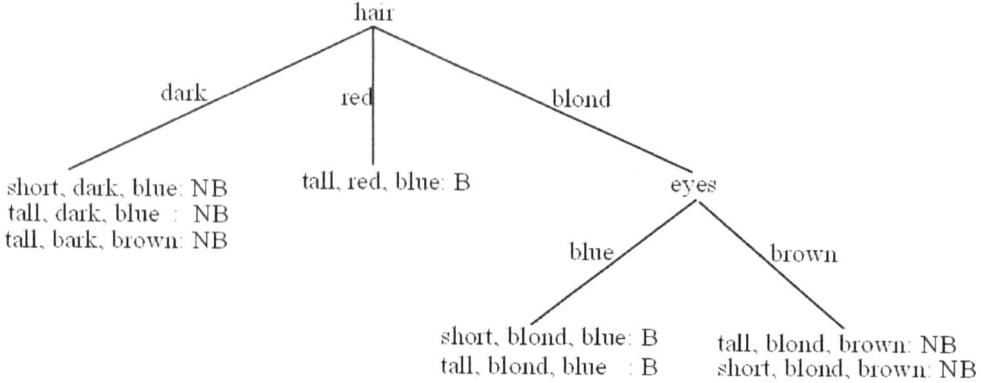

*Figure 2.7: Complete tree*

Let us build a decision tree to understand the practical usefulness in R.

The following decision tree is built using IRIS dataset in R. Party package is a popular library in R for constructing and visualizing a decision tree:

```
install.packages("party")
library(party)
names(iris)
[1] "Sepal.Length"
[2] "Sepal.Width"
[3] "Petal.Length"
[4] "Petal.Width"
[5] "Species"
str(iris)
'data.frame':150 obs. of  5 variables:
 $ Sepal.Length: num  5.1 4.9 4.7 4.6 5 5.4 4.6 5 4.4 4.9 ...
 $ Sepal.Width : num  3.5 3 3.2 3.1 3.6 3.9 3.4 3.4 2.9 3.1 ...
 $ Petal.Length: num  1.4 1.4 1.3 1.5 1.4 1.7 1.4 1.5 1.4 1.5 ...
 $ Petal.Width : num  0.2 0.2 0.2 0.2 0.2 0.4 0.3 0.2 0.2 0.1 ...
 $ Species     : Factor w/ 3 levels "setosa","versicolor",..: 1 1 1 1 1 1 1
1 1 1 ...
# devide dataset into two subsets: training (70%) and test (30%);
#setting of  a fixed random seed to make output reproducible
set.seed(12345)
outr <- sample(2, nrow(iris), replace = TRUE, prob = c(0.7, 0.3))
train.data <- iris[outr == 1, ]
test.data <- iris[outr == 2, ]
```

Now, let us build the tree with target feature as Species and independent features which are:

"Sepal.Length","Sepal.Width" , "Petal.Length" and  "Petal.Width".

```
tree_build <- Species ~ Sepal.Length + Sepal.Width + Petal.Length +
Petal.Width
ctree <- ctree(tree_build, data = train.data)
# checking of   the prediction
table(predict(ctree), train.data$Species)
```

| # | setosa | versicolor | virginica |
|---|--------|-----------|-----------|
| # setosa | 40 | 0 | 0 |

```
# versicolor              0                    37                    3
# virginica               0                    1                     31
 Accuracy is  96.42% . Misclassification rate is 3.58%
#
## Conditional inference tree with four terminal nodes
#
#Response: Species
# Input features : Sepal.Length, Sepal.Width, Petal.Length, Petal.Width
# Total  number of observations: 112
# 1) Petal.Length <= 1.9; criterion = 1, statistic = 104.643
# 2)* weights = 40
# 1) Petal.Length > 1.9
# 3) Petal.Width <= 1.7; criterion = 1, statistic = 48.939
# 4) Petal.Length <= 4.4; criterion = 0.974, statistic = ...
# 5)* weights = 21
# 4) Petal.Length > 4.4
# 6)* weights = 19
# 3) Petal.Width > 1.7
# 7)* weights = 32
```

The following plot is a detailed one with node number, probability estimates, splitting conditions. These plots are suitable for small trees when visualization of specific details is required.

**plot(ctree):**

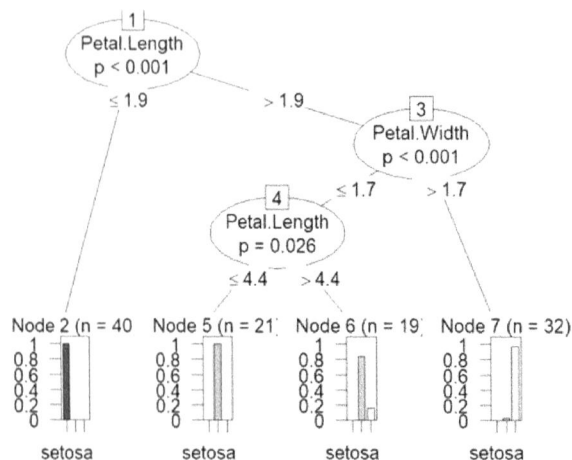

*Figure 2.8: Complete tree plot ctree*

The following plot is simplified visualization with class levels. These types of plots are suitable when we want high level overview. The readability of complex trees is improved with types such as **"simple"**.

**plot (ctree, type = "simple"):**

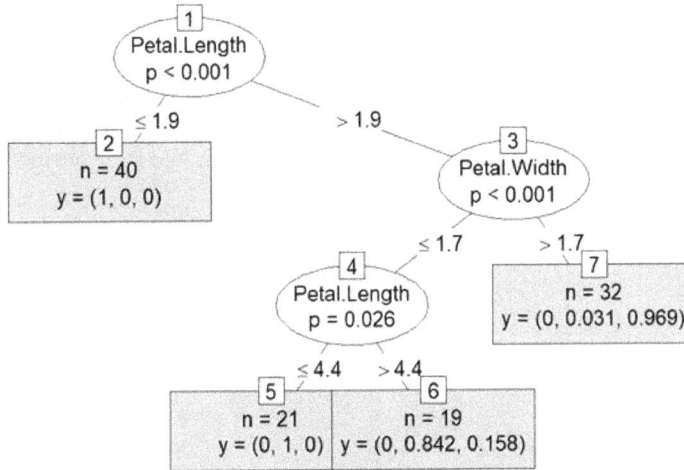

*Figure 2.9: Complete tree plot ctree, type is simple*

Prediction using test data:

```
#prediction using test data
# predict on test data
testPred <- predict(ctree, newdata = test.data)
table(testPred, test.data$Species)
#
# testPred        setosa      versicolor       virginica
# setosa            10             0               0
# versicolor         0            12               2
# virginica          0             0              14
```

Accuracy is 94.4% and misclassification or error percentage is 5.6%.

# Logistics regression

Logistics regression is a popular predictive modeling and classification technique applied across industry applications. Classification may be binary, multinomial, or ordinal. The independent or response variable is categorical. The input features or variables are either continuous or categorical. In binary logistics regression, the response variable can take two values. The values can be yes or no (0 or 1), that is, the probability of an event occurring based on a threshold probability value. If the probability value is above the threshold value, then it is 1 or a positive class. If the value is less than the threshold, the value is 0 or a negative class. The logistic function is used to model the probability of an event. The function is as follows:

$$P(Y=1) = eZ \,/\, 1+ eZ$$

Where $Z= b_0 + b_1 X_1 + b_2 X_2 + b_3 X_3 + \ldots\ldots\ldots + b_n X_n$   *where* $X_1, X_2, X_{3,\ldots\ldots}, X_n$ are independent variables. This function is also known as a sigmoid function. The value may be possible from 0 to 1. The curve is S-shaped as shown in the following figure:

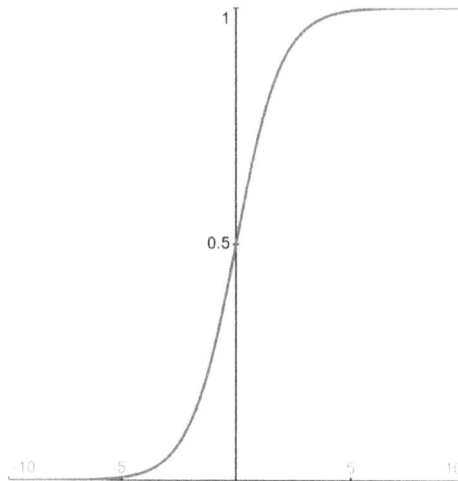

***Figure 2.10***: *Logistics function*
*Source: Image generated using Desmos*

The logistics function is basically a sigmoid function where input values range from $-\infty$ to $+\infty$. For very large positive values of z, $e^z \rightarrow \infty$ and *logistic* function $\rightarrow 1$. For very large negative values of z, $e^z \rightarrow 0$ and logistic function $\rightarrow 0$. So, output value is a probability value ranges from 0 to 1.

We will take the logarithm of both sides of logistic function to transform to linear form after rearranging the probability P:

$P = eZ \,/\, 1+ eZ$

$P(1+ eZ)= eZ$

$P+PeZ= eZ$

$P= eZ\text{-}PeZ \quad = eZ(1\text{-}P)$

$P/1\text{-}P = eZ$

$Ln(P/1\text{-}P) =ln(eZ)$

$Ln(P/1-P) = ln(eZ) = Z = b0 + b1\ X1 + b2\ X2 + b3\ X3 + \ldots\ldots\ldots\ldots + bn\ Xn$

$Ln(P/1-P) = b0 + b1\ X1 + b2\ X2 + b3\ X3 + \ldots\ldots\ldots\ldots + bn\ Xn$

*P/1-P* is known as the odd ratio. This is a ratio of the probability of success to the probability of failure. When odd ratio is one, then probability of success is equal to probability of failure. For an event with probability 0.75, the odds are as follows: *0.75/1−0.75=0.750/0.25=3*. This means that the event is three times as likely to occur than not. Log of P/1-P is known as log of odds.

Let us interpret the logistic regression model using R. ISLR package is installed, and the Default dataset is used in the following case study:

```
# ISLR package in R is a collection of datasets and functions:
install.packages("ISLR")
names(ISLR::Default)
[1] "default" "student"
[3] "balance" "income"
data_set<-ISLR::Default
summary(data_set)
 default     student         balance               income
 No :9667   No :7056    Min.    :    0.0     Min.    :   772
 Yes: 333   Yes:2944      1st Qu.:  481.7     1st Qu.:21340
                        Median:  823.6    Median :34553
                        Mean:   835.4    Mean    :33517
                        3rd Qu.:1166.3    3rd Qu.:43808
                        Max.    :2654.3    Max.    :73554
nrow(data_set)
[1] 10000
```

This dataset comprises information about 10,000 individuals as follows:

```
    default: Shows whether or not an individual defaulted.
    student: Shows whether or not an individual is a student.
    balance: Average balance carried by an individual.
    income: Income of the individual.
```

The following logistics regression model predicts that a given individual defaults. Bank balance, student status and income are used for building the model:

```
model_regress<-glm(default~balance+student+income, family="binomial",
data=data_set)
```

**Call**:

```
glm(formula = default ~ balance + student + income, family = "binomial",
data = data_set)
```

**Deviance residuals**:

```
    Min       1Q    Median       3Q       Max
-2.4691   -0.1418   -0.0557   -0.0203    3.7383
```

Coefficients:

```
                   Estimate    Std. Error    z value    Pr(>|z|)
(Intercept)    -1.087e+01    4.923e-01     -22.080     < 2e-16 ***
balance         5.737e-03    2.319e-04      24.738     < 2e-16 ***
studentYes     -6.468e-01    2.363e-01      -2.738     0.00619 **
income          3.033e-06    8.203e-06       0.370     0.71152
---
Signif. codes:  0 '***' 0.001 '**' 0.01 '*' 0.05 '.' 0.1 ' ' 1
(Dispersion parameter for binomial family taken to be 1)
Null deviance: 2920.6  on 9999  degrees of freedom
Residual deviance: 1571.5  on 9996  degrees of freedom
AIC: 1579.5
Number of Fisher Scoring iterations: 8
So, the null and residual deviance in result are as follows:
    Null deviance        : 2920.6 with df = 9999
    Residual deviance: 1571.5 with df = 9996
```

The null deviance states how well the dependent feature can be predicted with only an intercept term. The residual deviance states how well the dependent feature can be predicted by a model with the p predictor features. The lower the value, the better the model is able to predict the value of the dependent feature. To know if a model is useful, we can compute the chi-square statistic, as follows, with p degrees of freedom:

$$X2 = Null\ deviance - Residual\ deviance$$

We can then find the p-value associated with the chi-square statistic. The lower the p-value, the better the model is able to fit the dataset compared to a model with just an intercept term.

The preceding values can be used to calculate the X2 statistic as follows:

$X2 = Null\ deviance - Residual\ deviance$

$X2 = 2910.6 - 1579.0$

$X2 = 1331.6$

Here, the p value is quite less than .05 with 3 degree of freedom. So, we can say in this case study that this logistics regression model is useful for predicting that a given individual defaults.

# Other classification techniques

Each classification technique has many advantages and limitations. Apart from logistics regression and decision tree techniques discussed previously, there are many more techniques like Bayesian Belief Network, Naïve Bias Classification method, Artificial Neural Network, Support Vector Machines, and K-NN.

The Bayesian Belief Network applies the Bayesian theorem to a complex problem. This network is a probabilistic graphical model that portrays relationships between variables or features. These techniques are quite useful for modeling uncertainty and complexity. Basically, this technique narrates joint probability distribution for a set of features. Acyclic-directed graphs are used to represent a set of features and their conditional dependence through probabilities. There are numerous applications of this technique in business applications like credit risks, deriving the best strategy for customer engagement, treatment plans of patients, and prediction of disruption in supply chains. Similarly, the Naïve Bias Classification model is also built based on the principles of the Bayesian theorem. However, the underlying assumption is based on strong independent assumptions between variables or features. Popularly, this technique is used in classifying text, detecting spam and sentiment analysis. A few other applications of this technique are useful in fraud detection, prediction of stock performance, detecting diseases based on symptoms, and segmenting high-value customers based on their past purchase behavior. The Naïve Bias classification model is simple to implement and interpret with less training time.

Artificial neural network is based on the principle of mimicking the functioning of the human nervous system. They comprise interconnected nodes or neurons which process information in multiple layers. Each neuron of a layer is connected to all the neurons above and below it. Each connected link carries a weight. These neurons are usually exponential functions. The output of the network is compared with the expected output and the loop continues till the gap of error is negligible. ANNs have the capability to learn large datasets to accomplish complex tasks. Applications of ANNs are applied to be useful in credit scoring, predicting stock prices, detecting diseases, drug discovery, and recommending products and services.

Support Vector Machine is used to solve both regression and classification tasks. This technique tries to find out the best decision boundaries that separate observations of different classes. SVM is effective for high dimension datasets and can handle nonlinear relationships with easy visualization of decision boundaries. Usually, SVMs are applied in text classification, image classification, prediction of protein structure, document classification and predict machine failures.

**K nearest neighbour** (**k-NN**) technique is applied to both regression and classification tasks. Eucledian distance measure is usually adopted to measure similarity within k-NN. The value of k is guessed to proceed. Counting of number of similar categories within k data points are assigned to a class. In regression, the average of neighbors is taken. Like other classification techniques, K-NN is applied in examining the credit risk of borrowers, retention of customers, recommendation of various categories of products and detecting diseases.

There are various factors that need to be analyzed before the selection of a classification technique. For example, the size of the dataset, complexity, linear or nonlinear nature of data, and features engineering aspects should be examined to determine correct number of features required for applying to a model. As discussed in the preceding section, there should be a tradeoff between bias and variance. It is quite crucial to optimize bias and variance before the dataset is applied to the selected classification model. There are also various techniques available to deal with high-dimensional data. No single technique can be considered best for all kinds of problems and criteria. Selecting the correct classification technique depends on a specific problem at hand, the characteristics of the dataset, and computing resources. Sometimes, a few are combined for better performance, which is discussed in the section *Ensemble Learning*. Similarly, tuning of hyperparameters is also crucial, which is explained in the next section.

The following are simple R codes illustrating two classification techniques that are k-NN and **Support Vector Machine** (**SVM**) as discussed as follows:

- **k-NN classifier:**

```
# Load necessary library
library(class)
# Use the built-in iris dataset
data(iris)
# Split the dataset into training and testing sets
set.seed(123)
index <- sample(1:nrow(iris), 0.7 * nrow(iris))
train_data <- iris[index, ]
test_data <- iris[-index, ]
# Apply k-NN with k = 3
pred_knn <- knn(train = train_data[, -5], test = test_data[, -5],
cl = train_data$Species, k = 3)
# Evaluate the model with a confusion matrix
confusion_matrix <- table(Predicted = pred_knn, Actual = test_
data$Species)
print(confusion_matrix)
```

o **Explanation of R codes**: The iris dataset is split into training (70%) and testing (30%) sets to evaluate the k-NN classifier. The k-NN function from the class package classifies the test data based on the training data using the 3 nearest neighbors. A confusion matrix compares the predicted species with the actual species, assessing the classifier's performance.

- **SVM classifier:**

```
# Load necessary library
library(e1071)
# Use the built-in iris dataset
data(iris)
# Split the dataset into training and testing sets
set.seed(456)
index <- sample(1:nrow(iris), 0.7 * nrow(iris))
train_data <- iris[index, ]
test_data <- iris[-index, ]
# Build the SVM model
model_svm <- svm(Species ~ ., data = train_data, kernel = "linear")
# Predict on the test set
pred_svm <- predict(model_svm, test_data)
# Evaluate the model with a confusion matrix
confusion_matrix <- table(Predicted = pred_svm, Actual = test_data$Species)
print(confusion_matrix)
```

o **Explanation**: Using the e1071 package, we implement an SVM classifier with a linear kernel to predict the Species of iris flowers based on all features. The trained SVM model predicts the species on the test dataset. The confusion matrix displays the comparison between predicted and actual species, indicating the model's accuracy. These codes demonstrate how to implement k-NN and SVM classifiers in R using the iris dataset, which is a classic example for classification tasks. Both classifiers are fundamental techniques in machine learning and provide a foundation for analyzing and predicting categorical outcomes.

o **Packages used**:

- **class for k-NN**: Provides functions for classification, including the k-NN function.

- **e1071 for SVM**: Offers functions for SVMs and other ML methods.

○ **Dataset details**:

The iris dataset contains 150 observations of iris flowers, with four features (sepal length, sepal width, petal length, petal width) and one target variable (Species) with three classes (setosa, versicolor, virginica).

Hyperparameter tuning: Hyper parameters are defined before the learning process starts. These external parameters facilitate the control over the learning process. Tuning of these parameters are required to improve the performance of data mining algorithms. In particular, in decision trees, hyper parameters can be information gain, entropy, Gini index, maximum depth of tree, etc. In regression, lasso regression, ridge regression, and elastic net. There are various methods used for the tuning, like grid search, genetic algorithms, and Bayesian optimization. Tuning improves the performance of the model and generalizes the model for new data.

# Ensemble learning techniques

Ensemble learning, as a data mining technique, combines multiple learners to produce more accurate predictions than a single learner or model. For a layman, we can take a simple example of *Kaun Banega Crorepati*, an Indian reality show in television. Here, there is a concept of an Audience Poll. When a contestant fails to answer a question, the audience poll is a lifeline they can use. Usually, the audience response as a whole is a better prediction than an individual prediction, while the answer to a question is not known. Similarly, there are a few popular techniques in data mining to improve prediction through a combination of multiple models. Three common techniques for ensemble learning can be seen in the following figure:

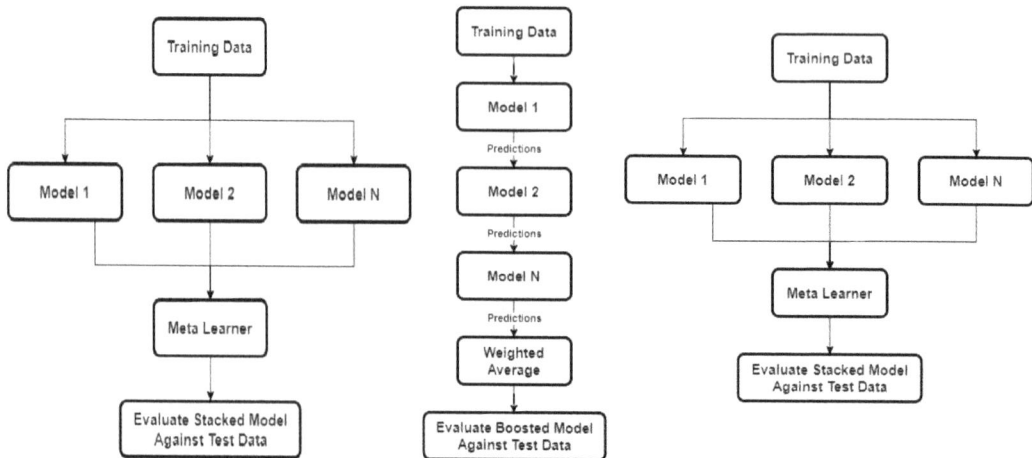

*Figure 2.11: Ensemble learning*

- **Bagging or bootstrap aggregating**: This is an ensemble learning technique where we divide the dataset into multiple subsets of datasets using random sampling with replacement. We try to improve prediction by reducing overfitting or variance. The final output is generated through the combination of the predictions of all models, which work in parallel. In case of regression models, the output of all models is averaged and in case of classification models, the final output is determined through majority voting. Monitoring performance metrics, hyper parameter tuning and selecting suitable base models are quite important to produce better predictions. Popular example of bagging is random forest.

- **Boosting**: This is an ensemble learning technique designed to create a strong classifier by combining weak classifiers in a sequential way. The initial model is constructed on a training dataset. The subsequent models are built based on the mistakes of previous models. Initially, equal weight is assigned to each data point of training dataset. Subsequently, the misclassified data points are given more weights to be trained to give scope to difficult cases in next models. The process is repeated for several rounds. Finally, predictions of all models are combined to get the final output.

- **Stacking**: Stacking inputs the prediction of multiple base models into a meta model which combines them to get final prediction. So, the meta model takes the outputs of the sub models as input and tries to learn how to best combine the predictions of the sub models to make a better prediction. This technique is also known as stacked generalization.

The following table narrates the comparison of bagging, boosting and stacking:

| | Bagging | Boosting | Stacking |
|---|---|---|---|
| Objective | Minimize variance | Minimize bias | Improve accuracy |
| Type of base learner | Homogeneous | Homogeneous | Heterogeneous |
| Base learner training | Parallel | Sequential | Meta model |
| Aggregation | Averaging for regression model<br>Voting for classification model | | |

*Table 2.3: Comparison of bagging, boosting and stacking*

**If you can't measure it, you can't manage it.**

*– Peter Drucker*

# Conclusion

In this chapter, we covered data pre-processing, regression and classification techniques. Examples of classification techniques and regression were explained using the R programming language. These techniques enable data driven decision making and predictions in business applications. So, business organizations can uncover hidden trends, optimize operations and drive strategic growth. For reliable results, specialists must take into consideration the effect of bias and variance. In the next chapter, we will learn about association rule mining as an unsupervised learning technique.

# Multiple choice questions

1. **Which is true about linear regression?**

   a. It is sensitive to outliers.

   b. It is an unsupervised learning model.

   c. Assumptions are not required in linear regressions.

   d. None of these.

2. **A student plotted a scatter plot between the residuals and predicted values in linear regression. He discovered that there is a relationship between them. Which of the following is true?**

   a. This dataset is not suitable for a linear regression model.

   b. This dataset is suitable for linear regression model.

   c. Decision cannot be taken with limited information.

   d. None of these.

3. **Imagine that you are working for a business school and want to develop a data mining algorithm which predicts the number of views on an article. Your analysis is based on features like the author's name, number of articles written by the same author in the past and a few other features. Which of the following evaluation metrics would you choose in that case? 1. Mean Square Error, 2. Accuracy, or 3. F1 score.**

   a. 2

   b. 3

   c. 1

   d. 1,2 and 3

4. **Adding a non-important feature to a linear regression model may result in 1. Increase in adjusted R-square, or 2. Decrease in adjusted R-square.**

    a.   1

    b.   2

    c.   Cannot be determined

    d.   None of these

5.   **Classification problems are distinguished from estimation problems in that:**

    a.   Classification problems require the output attribute to be numeric.

    b.   Classification problems require the output attribute to be categorical

    c.   Classification problems do not allow an output attribute.

    d.   Classification problems are designed to describe features.

6.   **Which of the following is a fundamental difference between bagging and boosting?**

    a.   Bagging is used for supervised learning. Boosting is used with unsupervised clustering.

    b.   Bagging gives varying weights to training instances. Boosting gives equal weight to all training instances.

    c.   Bagging does not take the performance of previously built models into account when building a new model. With boosting, each new model is built based upon the results of previous models.

    d.   Boosting is used for supervised learning. Bagging is used with unsupervised clustering.

7.   **Which of the following is true for a decision tree?**

    a.   A decision tree is an example of a linear classifier.

    b.   The entropy of a node typically decreases as we go down a decision tree.

    c.   Entropy is a measure of purity.

    d.   An attribute with lower mutual information should be preferred to other attributes.

8.   **A dataset comprises 9 positive and 5 negative classes. The entropy of this dataset with respect to this classification is what?**

    a.   0.940

    b.   0.06

    c.   0.50

    d.   0.22

# Answers

1.  a

2.  a

3.  c

4.  b

5.  b

6.  c

7.  b

8.  a

# Practice exercises

1.  You are developing a linear regression model to forecast the monthly sales of retail stores based on factors like advertising expenditure, location size, and number of employees. Before finalizing your model, it is vital to verify that the important assumptions of linear regression are satisfied:

    a.  List the main assumptions of linear regression and briefly explain each one.

    b.  Describe how you would test these assumptions using your dataset.

    c.  If you discover that multicollinearity exists among the independent variables, what steps can you take to address this issue?

2.  A researcher fits a linear regression model to forecast student test scores based on the number of study hours. Upon plotting the residuals against the predicted scores, she observes a U-shaped pattern:

    a.  What does this pattern indicate about the suitability of the linear regression model?

    b.  Suggest methods to improve the model based on this observation.

3.  You are working on predicting the annual income of individuals based on their education level, years of experience, and job sector. You have developed a regression model for this purpose.

    a.  Explain why Mean Squared Error is an appropriate evaluation metric for this regression task.

    b.  Why would classification metrics like accuracy or F1 score be inappropriate in this context?

4. In the process of refining your linear regression model for predicting car prices, you consider adding a new variable that shows minimal correlation with the price (e.g., the color of the car):

   a. Discuss how adding this non-important feature is likely to affect the adjusted R-squared value of your model.

   b. Should you include this variable in your final model? Provide justification for your decision.

5. Bagging and Boosting are both ensemble techniques used to enhance the performance of machine learning models, but they operate differently.

   a. Explain the key differences between bagging and boosting in terms of how they construct ensemble models.

   b. Provide one advantage and one limitation for each technique.

# Join our book's Discord space

Join the book's Discord Workspace for Latest updates, Offers, Tech happenings around the world, New Release and Sessions with the Authors:

**https://discord.bpbonline.com**

# CHAPTER 3
# Concept and Application of Association Rule Mining Algorithm

## Introduction

Association rule mining is a powerful unsupervised learning technique that uncovers hidden relationships between items that frequently occur together. For example, a grocery store might find that customers who buy brown bread often also purchase double-toned milk to reveal a pattern that can boost marketing strategies and product placement. Deciphering patterns like customers who buy brown bread often also purchase double-toned milk provides valuable insights to improve business strategies and decision-making.

This chapter delves into the fundamentals of association rule mining to focus on market basket analysis as a popular application of this technique. Key metrics such as support, confidence, and lift will be explored to quantify and validate the strength of associations between items. An in-depth examination of the Apriori algorithm is illustrated to discuss its methodology, advantages, and limitations. Practical examples using the R programming language show how to implement this algorithm effectively. At the same time, advanced algorithms like Eclat and FP-Growth are introduced, designed to efficiently handle very large datasets without compromising performance. By mastering these techniques, readers will be equipped to uncover meaningful patterns in complex data, leading to smarter decisions and significant improvements across various domains such as retail, marketing, recommendation systems and beyond. This chapter aims to provide a comprehensive understanding of association rule mining and its applications, setting a solid foundation for further exploration and innovation in data analysis.

# Structure

This chapter covers the following topics:

- Importance and evolution of association rule mining
- Fundamental concepts
- Popular algorithms and application in business domains
- Case study
- Challenges and future prospects

# Objectives

After going through this chapter, you will understand various applications of association rule mining algorithms in business. Readers will be familiar with metrics of association rule mining and algorithms like Apriori, Eclat and FP-Growth. Application of these algorithms in various functional areas like marketing, healthcare and telecommunication industry are discussed. Practical examples are specified using R programming language to explain these unsupervised learning algorithms. The challenges and future scope of these techniques are also highlighted.

# Importance and evolution of association rule mining

Association rule mining is a rule-based technique to decipher hidden relationships among variables within a dataset. The primary objective of this technique is to identify the strong rules in the dataset using a few metrics or measures. The rule has two parts—the antecedent or if part is a set of variables that must happen together. The consequent or then part is a set of variables that are likely to occur if the antecedent is present. For example, an association rule in a retail store can be as follows:

If a customer buys bread, then he is likely to purchase butter.

If the preceding rule is a strong rule, then there is a strong association between the purchase of bread and butter. Association rule mining is applied in a variety of applications like customer segmentation, personalized product recommendations, optimization of supply chains, fraud detection, credit scoring, cart abandonment analysis, network optimization in the telecommunication industry, and churn predictions. The initial application of association rules was mainly on the buying behavior of consumers, i.e., market basket analysis. The concept was introduced during the early 90s as an Apriori. Though it was popular, it was associated with issues like high computational costs and scalability issues. During the early 2000s, there was an effort to reduce the generation of candidates due to the introduction of advanced pruning techniques. More efficient algorithms like FP-

Growth were evolved during this time to deal with the Huse dataset and to manage memory efficiently.

# Fundamental concepts

Association rule mining is applied to datasets to uncover the hidden association between associated features, variables, or events. From a set of transactions of a dataset, association rules mining can predict the occurrence of an item based on the occurrence of another item. To understand and interpret these algorithms, one should be aware of the following terminologies:

- **Transactional database**: It comprises multiple transactions and each transaction is a subset of items. K = {R1, R2, ..., Rn} is a transactional database. Here, each Ri is a transaction. Each transaction Ri is a subset of items I = {i1, i2, ..., Ip}.

- **Itemsetd**: Itemset is a set of items. Each item is selected from a finite set of items. Itemset with p number of items is denoted as p-itemset. So, an itemset X is a subset of I (X ⊆ I). An example of an itemset can be {Sugar, Milk, Brown Bread}.

- **Association rule**: Expression $X \rightarrow Y$, where $X$ and $Y$ are item sets.

- **Rule Evaluation Metrics:**

  o **Support (s)**: Support of an itemset is the proportion of transactions containing the itemset. Let the itemset be $X$ and K be the transactional database. So, support is denoted as the following:

  $$\sigma(X) = |\{Ri \in K \mid X \subseteq Ri\}| \, / \, |K|$$

  Fraction of transactions that contain both $X$ and $Y$.

  o **Confidence (c)**: Confidence of a rule $X \mid Y$ is the likeliness of occurrence of the consequent given the antecedent is already available:

  $$Confidence \ (X \rightarrow Y) = \sigma \ (X \cup Y) \, / \, \sigma(X)$$

  Measures how often items in $Y$ appear in transactions that contain $X$.

  o **Lift(l)**: Lift measures the strength of association between the variables.

  $$Lift(X\text{-}>Y) = \sigma \ (X \cup Y) / \sigma \ (X) \, ^* \, \sigma \ (Y)$$

  The observed co-occurrence of $X$ and to what would be expected if they were independent, indicating how much more likely $Y$ is purchased when $X$ is purchased.

  o **Frequent itemset**: An itemset $X$ can be called a frequent itemset if *support(X) >= minsup*.

- ○ **Minimum confidence**: This is a threshold value set by the users which implies that the itemset with less than this confidence value is not interesting. This term is also known as **minconf**.

- ○ **Interesting association rule**: These rules are those whose support and confidence are more than minsup and minconf.

- ○ **Popular algorithms**: A few popular algorithms are Apriori, Eclat and FP-Growth algorithms.

Let us take an example to understand the basics of the metrics associated with association rules. There are ten transactions of a customer in a retail store. (milk curd) (bread chips):

| Transactions | Items in transaction |
|:---:|:---|
| 1 | Curd, Chips, Eggs |
| 2 | Curd, Juice |
| 3 | Juice, Butter |
| 4 | Curd, Chips, Eggs |
| 5 | Coffee, Eggs |
| 6 | Coffee |
| 7 | Coffee, Juice |
| 8 | Curd, Chips, Cookies, Eggs |
| 9 | Cookies, Butter |
| 10 | Curd, Chips |

*Table 3.1: Transactions cases of customer*

Let us calculate the support of the itemset {Curd, Chips} from the 10 transactions. Support is nothing but the total number of transactions in which the itemset or item is available, divided by the total number of transactions.

*Support of {Curd, Chips} = Number of transactions containing {Curd, Chips} / Total number of transactions*

So, *Support {Curd, Chips} =   4/10= 0.4 or 40%*

So, *in 40% cases, the customer is purchasing Curd and Chips.*

Let us calculate the confidence of {Curd, Chips}. Here, we have a dataset of 10 transactions, and the itemset {Curd, Chips} appears in 4 out of 10 transactions. Curd is present in 5 transactions. The confidence of the rule "If a customer buys Curd, he/she will also buy Chips" would be calculated as follows:

*Confidence ("If a customer buys curd, they will also buy chips") = Number of transactions containing {Curd, Chips} / Number of transactions containing {Curd}*

So, *Confidence of {Curd, Chips} = 4/5 = 0.8 or 80%*

80% of the time, the customer buys Chips along with Curd. We can also say, 20% of the time, the person is not purchasing Chips along with Curd.

Let us now calculate lift of {Curd, Chips}.

*Lift of {Curd ->Chips} = Support of {Curd, Chips}/ Support of {Curd} * Support of {Chips}*

So, *Lift of {Curds -> Chips} = 0.4/0.2 * 0.4 = 5*

If lift < 1, then the antecedent and consequent are substitutes for each other. That means the increase in frequency of an antecedent leads to a decrease in the frequency of consequent and vice versa. If lift is >1, then the antecedent and consequent are dependent on each other. That means that an increase in frequency of antecedent leads to an increase in the frequency of consequent and vice versa. If lift =1, then the frequency of antecedent and consequent are independent. That means the frequency of the antecedent does not affect the frequency of the consequent.

In our example, Lift of {Curd->Chips} is greater than one. So, the increase in the frequency of Curd will lead to an increase in the frequency of Chips.

# Popular algorithms and applications in business domains

There are several association rule mining algorithms with multiple applications like customer buying behavior analysis, web mining, text mining, social network analysis, and bioinformatics. Popular algorithms are Apriori, FP-Growth, and Eclat algorithms. Each of these algorithms has its own advantages and limitations.

## Apriori algorithm and business applications

Frequent itemset algorithms like Brute Force generate all possible itemset. Here, Support and confidence are calculated for all rules. Say, there are k distinct items. The number of itemset possible is $2^k-1$. Let us see an example. L= {Tomato, Potato, Brinjal, Onion, Eggs}. Here, there are five items. The maximum number of itemset possible is $2^5-1$, that is, 31. Similarly, the maximum number of association rules that are possible from a set containing k items are $3^k-2^{(k+1)} +1$. If the number of items in a set is 5, the maximum rules extracted are $3^5-2^6+1$, that is, 180 rules. If number of items increases, the number of rules also increases significantly. This process is very expensive. Then, the minimum support and minimum confidence cutoff is applied, in which many rules are discarded. Of course, computation effort is also wasted. The computation required to calculate support and confidence can be eliminated once these rules are pruned. Decoupling the requirement of both of these metrics can improve the performance of the algorithms. So, initially, we can calculate the support of the itemset. Then, based on the minimum support criteria, the items may be discarded which do not satisfy this constraint. This process is followed to get the frequent item sets. Further, association rules are generated from these frequent item sets. Subsequently, the minimum confidence criterion is applied to prune the association rules that are below this confidence threshold. The rules above the threshold value of confidence are strong association rules. The basic principle of Apriori algorithm is quite simple. It states that *If an item set is infrequent, then the superset of the item set is also infrequent. Similarly, if an item set is frequent, it's subset is also frequent.* Let us understand the algorithm in detail. Apriori principle holds due to the following property of the support measure:

$$\forall \ X, Y : (X \subseteq Y) \Longrightarrow s(X) \geq s(Y)$$

**Example 1**: Suppose, minsup of the following transactions is set as 0.2. The distinct items and their support are given in the following table with reference to *Table 3.2*:

| TID | Items in transaction |
|-----|----------------------|
| 1 | Curd, Bread, Eggs |
| 2 | Curd, Juice |
| 3 | Juice, Butter |
| 4 | Curd, Bread, Eggs |
| 5 | Coffee, Eggs |
| 6 | Coffee |
| 7 | Coffee, Juice |
| 8 | Curd, Bread, Cookies, Eggs |
| 9 | Cookies, Butter |
| 10 | Curd, Bread |

*Table 3.2: Customer transactions*

Seven items are unique out of ten transactions specified in example 1:

1. Support of all the unique items are calculated based on the principle of Apriori algorithm. Support of all the unique items is calculated to be more than or equal to 0.2. So, no itemset will be discarded in the first stage:

| Items | Count | Support |
|-------|-------|---------|
| Curd | 5 | 0.5 |
| Bread | 4 | 0.4 |
| Eggs | 4 | 0.4 |
| Juice | 3 | 0.3 |

| Items | Count | Support |
|---|---|---|
| Butter | 2 | 0.2 |
| Coffee | 3 | 0.3 |
| Cookies | 2 | 0.2 |

*Table 3.3: Distinct one item output*

2. Itemset whose support is less than 0.2 are discarded:

| Items | Count | Support |
|---|---|---|
| Curd, Bread | 4 | 0.4 |
| Curd, Eggs | 3 | 0.3 |
| Curd, Juice | 1 | 0.1 |
| Curd, Cookies | 1 | 0.1 |
| Bread, Eggs | 3 | 0.3 |
| Bread, Cookies | 1 | 0.1 |
| Eggs, Coffee | 1 | 0.1 |
| Eggs, Cookies | 1 | 0.1 |
| Juice, Butter | 1 | 0.1 |
| Juice, Coffee | 1 | 0.1 |
| Butter, Cookies | 1 | 0.1 |

*Table 3.4: Two items output*

3. The process of the algorithm stops at stage three with items: curd, Bread, and Eggs:

| Items | Count | Support |
|---|---|---|
| Curd, Bread, Eggs | 3 | 0.3 |

*Table 3.5: Three items output*

So, we will now generate all possible rules possible with these three items. Confidence of all the rules will also be calculated. The rules whose confidence is less than 0.8 confidence values will be rejected.

Now, to find all the association rules with support >= 0.2 and confidence >= 0.8:

- Association rules for {Curd, Bread, Eggs}:

  *{Curd, Bread} -> {Eggs}*

  o Support = 3/10 = 0.3, Confidence = 3/4 = 0.75

*{Curd, Eggs} -> {Bread}*

o   Support = 3/10 = 0.3, Confidence = 3/3 = 1

*{Eggs, Bread} -> {Curd}*

o   Support = 3/10 = 0.3, Confidence = 3/3 = 1

- Association rules for {Curd, Bread}:

*{Curd} -> {Bread}*

o   Support = 4/10 = 0.4, Confidence = 4/5 = 0.8

*{Bread} -> {Curd}*

o   Support = 4/10 = 0.4, Confidence = 4/4 = 1

- Association rules for {Curd, Eggs}:

*{Curd} -> {Eggs}*

o   Support = 3/10 = 0.25, Confidence = 3/5 = 0.6

{Eggs} -> {Curd}

o   *Support = 3/10 = 0.3, Confidence = 3/4 = 0.75*

- Association rules for {Bread Eggs}:

*{Bread} -> {Eggs}*

o   Support = 3/10 = 0.25, Confidence = 3/4 = 0.75

*{Eggs} -> {Bread}*

o   Support = 3/10 = 0.3, Confidence = 3/4 = 0.75

Strong association rules which satisfy the minsup and minconf condition are as follows:

*{Curd, Eggs} -> {Bread} (support=0.3, confidence=1)*

*{Eggs, Bread} -> {Curd} (support=0.3, confidence=1)*

*{Curd} -> {Bread} (support=0.4, confidence=0.8)*

*{Bread} -> {Curd} (support =0.4, confidence =1)*

**Example 2**: Support of an itemset never exceeds the support of its subset. This is known as the anti-monotone property of the metrics, i.e., support. Suppose the minsup of the transactions, shown in the following table, is set as 0.6 0r 60%:

| T. No. | Items |
|--------|-------|
| 1 | Bread, Milk |
| 2 | Bread, Diaper, Beer, Eggs |

| T. No. | Items |
|---|---|
| 3 | Milk, Diaper, Beer, Coke |
| 4 | Bread, Milk, Diaper, Beer |
| 5 | Bread, Milk, Diaper, Coke |

*Table 3.6: Customer transactions*

The distinct items from *Table 3.6* and their support are given as follows:

1. From five customer transactions mentioned previously, six items are found to be unique. Calculation of the support for each six individual items will be calculated, and the items cut off values will be retained:

| Items | Count | Support |
|---|---|---|
| Bread | 4 | 0.8 |
| Coke | 2 | 0.4 |
| Milk | 4 | 0.8 |
| Beer | 3 | 0.6 |
| Diaper | 4 | 0.8 |
| Eggs | 1 | 0.2 |

*Table 3.7: Distinct one item cases*

As cut off for support is 0.6, coke and eggs are discarded here as per the principle of Apriori.

2. Now, we will take all possible pairs as specified as follows:

| Items | Count | Support |
|---|---|---|
| {Bread, Milk} | 3 | 0.6 |
| {Bread, Beer} | 2 | 0.4 |
| {Bread, Diaper} | 3 | 0.6 |
| {Milk, Beer} | 2 | 0.4 |
| {Milk, Diaper} | 3 | 0.6 |
| {Beer, Diaper} | 3 | 0.6 |

*Table 3.8: Two items set*

Here, {Bread, Beer} and {Milk, Beer} are less than the cut-off value of support. So, we will eliminate these transactions.

3. Triplet or 3-item sets are specified as follows:

| Items | Count | Support |
|---|---|---|
| {Beer, Diaper, Milk} | 2 | 0.4 |
| {Beer, Bread, Diaper} | 2 | 0.4 |
| {Bread, Milk, Diaper} | 2 | 0.4 |
| {Beer, Bread, Milk} | 2 | 0.4 |

*Table 3.9: Triplet*

The following rules can be generated from the triplet seen previously:

1. **Bread, Milk -> Diaper:**
   a. Confidence of this rule is:
      i. *Support (Bread, Milk, Diaper)/Support (Bread, Milk) = (2/5)/(3/5) =2/3 or 0.67*

2. **Bread, Diaper-> Milk:**
   a. Confidence of this rule is:
      i. *Support (Bread, Milk, Diaper)/Support (Bread, Diaper) = (2/5)/(3/5) =2/3 or 0.67*

3. **Milk, Diaper-> Bread:**
   a. Confidence of this rule is:
      i. *Support (Bread, Milk, Diaper)/Support (Milk, Diaper) = (2/5)/(3/5) =2/3 or 0.67*

4. **Bread-> Milk, Diaper:**
   a. Confidence of this rule is:
      i. *Support (Bread, Milk, Diaper)/Support (Bread) = (2/5)/(4/5) =1/2 or 0.5*

5. **Milk-> Bread, Diaper:**
   a. Confidence of this rule is:
      i. *Support (Bread, Milk, Diaper)/Support (Milk) = (2/5)/(4/5) =1/2 or 0.5*

6. **Diaper-> Bread, Milk:**
   a. Confidence of this rule is:
      i. *Support (Bread, Milk, Diaper)/Support (Diaper) = (2/5)/(4/5) =1/2 or 0.5*

Apriori algorithm is simple to apply and scalable for medium sized dataset. Usually, the dataset is clean, human-readable, and readily available. However, for large datasets, time and space overhead create issues. Since it requires multiple scans to calculate support to generate an itemset. Similarly, the usage of high memory, computational complexity and there are issues to handle sparse data. If a lower support value is taken as threshold, the algorithm generates many frequent itemset. However, Apriori is a popular algorithm that is widely used in market basket analysis, social network analysis, web mining, bioinformatics, recommendation systems, network traffic analysis, and e-commerce applications.

# FP-Growth and Eclat algorithm in business applications

Apriori algorithm involves multiple scans. However, FP-Growth reduces the number of scans to improve performance so that large datasets can be handled. This algorithm creates a tree data structure from the dataset while generating frequent item sets. The dataset is scanned twice, only to construct tree and produce a conditional pattern base. As it compresses the database, this algorithm requires less memory. Still, for large datasets, memory utilization can be considerable and difficult to implement in real-life applications. Commonalities of Apriori and FP-Growth is that both use horizontal data format or breadth-first search approach. Though FP-Growth faces implementation complexity, it is efficient and suitable for large datasets. The **Equivalent Class Clustering and bottom-up Lattice Traversal (Eclat)** algorithm uses a vertical data format or depth-first approach for frequent itemset. This is comparatively more scalable and faster compared to Apriori. Due to depth first search approach, it uses less memory compared to Apriori. Eclat is quite suitable for dense data with good scalability. At the same time, Eclat is more suitable for text-mining applications.

# Data visualization and modeling using R

Data visualization on metrics of association rules and Apriori modeling can be accomplished using R. The interpretation of the result facilitates business leaders across industries like finance, HR, healthcare, retail, and operations. In business, this visualization can help to formulate marketing strategies. For example, from customer transactions, retailer can analyze to discover that a customer who buys milk often buy diapers also. In finance, credit risk can be detected. Similarly, in HR, factors affecting employee performance can be deciphered through R data visualization and modeling. In healthcare, identification of diseases, recommendation of personalized medicines, and improvement of treatment effectiveness of patients is possible. There are two packages, arules and arulesViz packages, which are required to be installed for data visualization, Apriori, and FP-Growth implementations. Mostly, we will use the Groceries dataset built in arules package.

The following codes take five different transactions and generates an itemfrequency plot, which shows the support of each item that was purchased from the store:

1.  Install and load required packages:

    ```
    # Install the packages if they are not already installed
    install.packages("arules")
    install.packages("arulesViz")
    # Load the libraries
    library(arules)
    library(arulesViz)
    ```

    **"arules"** Package provides the infrastructure for representing, manipulating and analyzing transaction data and patterns. **"arulesViz"** package offers visualization techniques for association rules and frequent item sets.

2.  Create a list of transactions:

    Define a list containing the items purchased in each transaction.

    ```
    # Define a list of transactions
    transactions_list <- list( c("Tomato", "Onion", "Brinjal"),
    c("Tomato", "Onion"),  c("Tomato", "Onion", "Lemon"),c("Brinjal",
    "Chilly"), c("Tomato", "Onion", "Lemon", "Chilly"))
    ```

    The dataset consists of five transactions, each represented as a vector of items:

    Transaction 1: Tomato, Onion, Brinjal

    Transaction 2: Tomato, Onion

    Transaction 3: Tomato, Onion, Lemon

    Transaction 4: Brinjal, Chilly

    Transaction 5: Tomato, Onion, Lemon, Chilly

    This list simulates customer purchases at a store.

3.  Convert the list into a transactions object which is the required format for analysis using the **"arules"** package.

    ```
    transactions <- as(transactions_list, "transactions")
    ```

    Here, the **as()** function coerces the list into an object of class **"transactions"**. This object structure allows efficient processing and analysis of transactional data.

4.  Create the item frequency plot to visualize the support of each item:

    ```
    itemFrequencyPlot(transactions, topN = 5, type = "absolute")
    ```

    **"itemFrequencyPlot()"** function creates a bar plot of item frequencies. **"topN**

**= 5"** specifies that the top 5 items should be plotted. Type as **"absolute"** plots the absolute frequency counts. The plot displays how often each item appears across all transactions. After running the code, an item frequency plot is generated (as shown in *Figure 3.1*). The plot displays the support (frequency) of each item: Brinjal, Chilly, Lemon, Onion, and Tomato. Tomato and Onion have the highest support, appearing in 4 out of 5 transactions. The plot visually highlights the most frequently purchased items, aiding in decision-making processes regarding inventory and promotions:

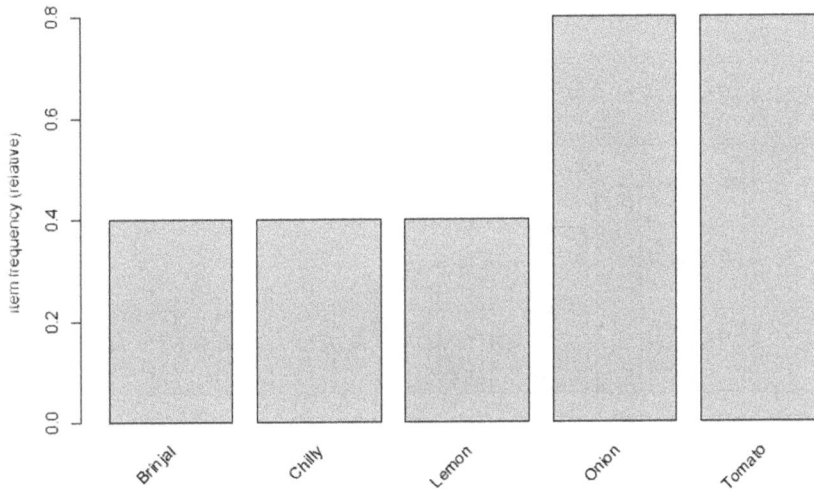

***Figure 3.1**: Item frequency plot*

In order to understand the metrics through visualization, any dataset either built-in in R or external dataset can be taken to understand the metrics of association rules. We can also generate best rules based on **apriori** algorithm application. So, proper marketing strategy like **cros** selling, upselling and product bundling decisions can be taken.

Let us take the Groceries built in dataset of **arules** package to generate an **itemfrequency** plot using R. We can take a few top products of Groceries. Here, let us take top 15 products:

1. Load required packages:

```
library(arules)
library(arulesViz)
```

Load the **arules** package for association rule mining and the **arulesViz** package for visualization.

2. Load the groceries dataset:

```
data("Groceries")
```

Load the **"Groceries"** dataset which comprises 9,835 transactions and 169 items.

3. Generate the item frequency plot:

```
itemFrequencyPlot(Groceries, topN = 15)
```

An item frequency plot is created displaying the top 15 items by support. The item frequency plot provides a visual representation of the most commonly purchased items. Items are displayed in ascending order based on their support values. This visualization helps identify popular products to aid in inventory management and marketing strategies.

The top 15 items with support values in ascending order are displayed in *Figure 3.2*:

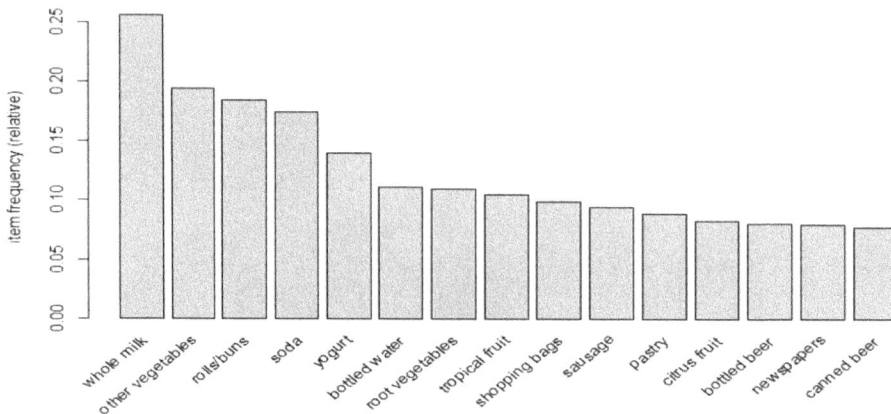

*Figure 3.2*: *Top 15 items of item frequency plot*

Now, R codes will be used to generate strong rules based on cut off values of support and confidence. The application of Apriri algorithm using R eliminates the manual calculation to generate strong rules.

Let us take minsupp=0.001, minconf=0.9 and maximum length of rules as 4 to eliminate rules with length more than 4 and focus on interpreting visualization and modeling using R:

```
rules=apriori(Groceries, parameter = list(supp = .001, conf = .9 ,
maxlen=4))
```

```
rules
```

**Output: 67 number of rules**

So, 67 rules are filtered using Apriori whose support cut off is 0.001 and confidence cut off is 0.9. Here, the transactions with four items are also filtered as maxlen parameter is set as 4.

We can display strong association rules using **inspect()** function. To display first five strong association rules, we can write R code as follows:

```
Inspect(rules[1:5])
```

| lhs | rhs | support |
|---|---|---|
| [1] {liquor, red/blush wine} | => {bottled beer} | 0.001931876 |
| [2] {curd, cereals} | => {whole milk} | 0.001016777 |
| [3] {soups, bottled beer} | => {whole milk} | 0.001118454 |
| [4] {whipped/sour cream, house keeping products} => {whole milk} | | 0.001220132 |
| [5] {pastry, sweet spreads} | => {whole milk} | 0.001016777 |

|  | confidence | coverage | lift | count |
|---|---|---|---|---|
| [1] | 0.9047619 | 0.002135231 | 11.235269 | 19 |
| [2] | 0.9090909 | 0.001118454 | 3.557863 | 10 |
| [3] | 0.9166667 | 0.001220132 | 3.587512 | 11 |
| [4] | 0.9230769 | 0.001321810 | 3.612599 | 12 |
| [5] | 0.9090909 | 0.001118454 | 3.557863 | 10 |

The following command will plot a graph with support in x axis and confidence in y axis. The concertation of the color of the bar in right size of the graph indicates the intensity of lift.

**plot(rules)**

This is a scatter plot using R where association rules are indicated as points. Support is placed in the X-axis, and confidence is shown in the Y-axis. The grey color points shown in the following figure indicate the strength of the rules:

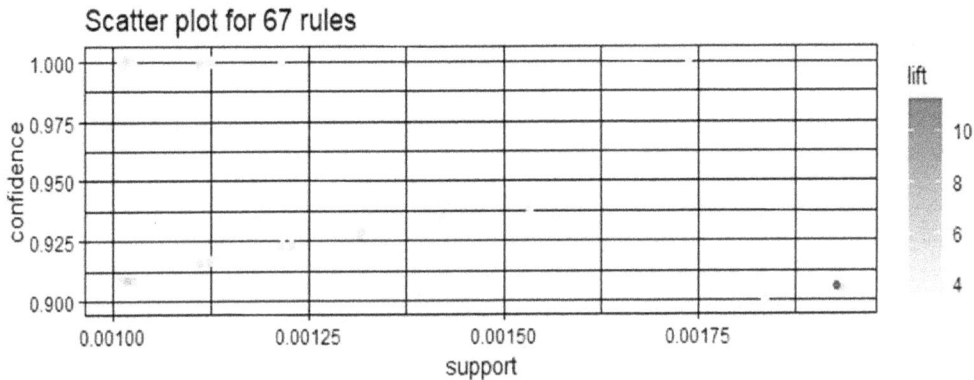

*Figure 3.3: Scatter plot of 67 rules*

*Figure 3.3* is a scatter plot of the 67 rules:

**plot (rules, method = "Grouped")**

This plot generates a grouped matrix visualization of association rules. Rules are grouped as antecedents and consequents. Darker rules are stronger compared to less dark rules here. Row levels signify antecedent items, and the column level signifies consequent items. Similarly, darker cells indicate high-confidence rules:

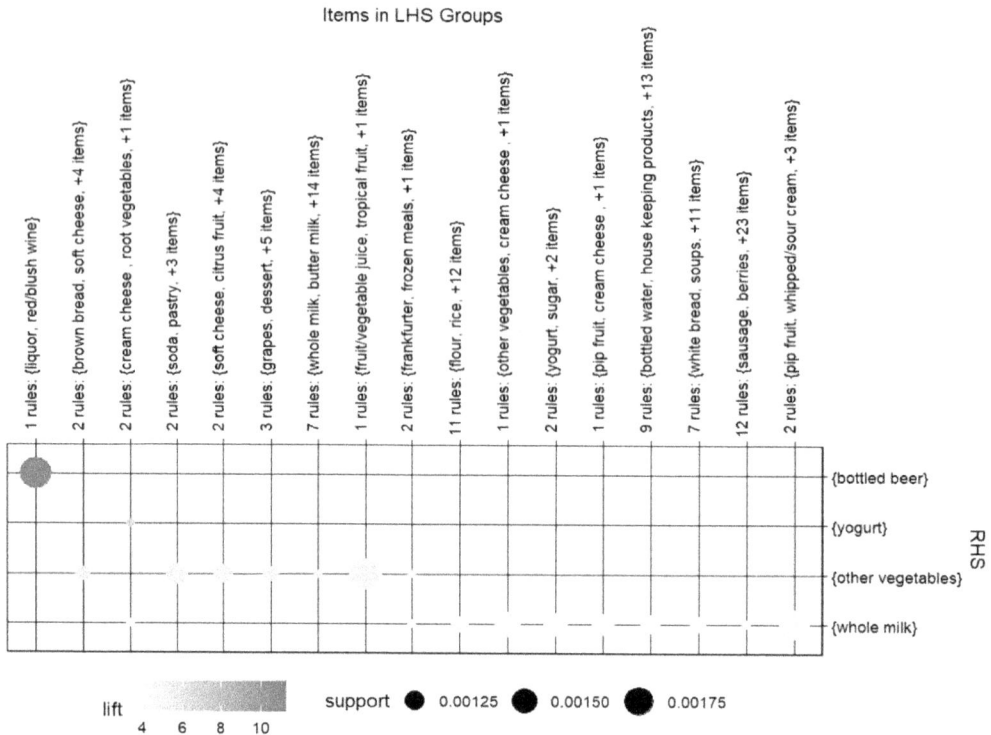

*Figure 3.4: Grouped visualization plot*

Let us limit the rules to know more about another visualization example.

To limit the number of rules and further understand an interesting plot, let us see the following example:

```
rules1=apriori(Groceries, parameter = list(supp = .0011, conf = .9 ,
maxlen=3))
rules1
```

**Output: set of 8 rules**

```
plot(rules1,method="graph",engine = "html")
```

This plot generates an interactive **html** graph visualization:

Select by id ▼

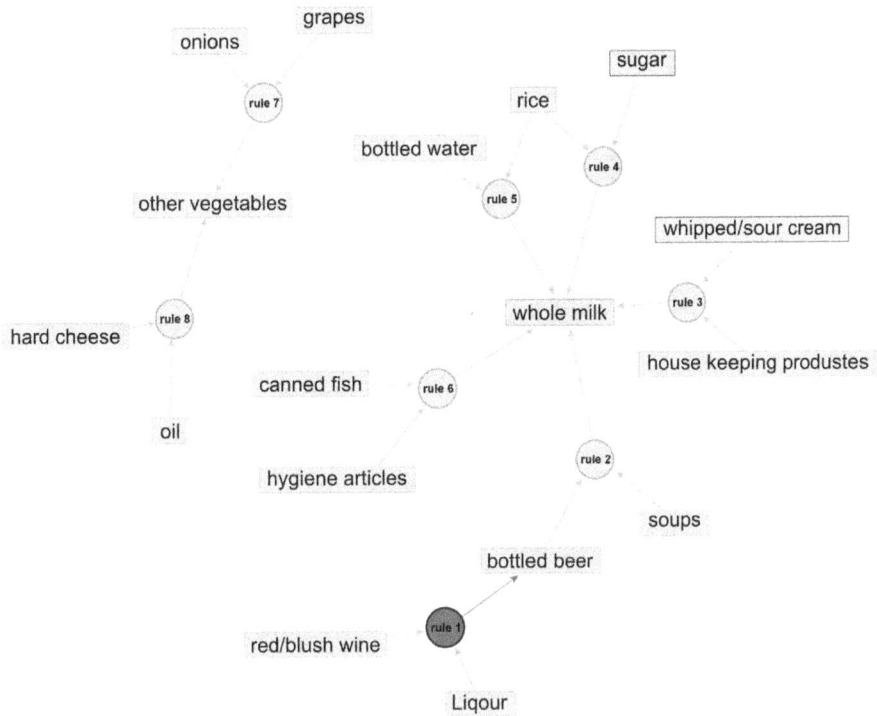

**Figure 3.5:** *Interactive visualization plot*

Let us see the following plot:

```
plot (rules, method = "matrix")
Itemset in Antecedent (LHS)
[1] "{liquor, red/blush wine}"
[2] "{grapes, onions}"
[3] "{hard cheese, oil}"
[4] "{rice, sugar}"
[5] "{canned fish, hygiene articles}"
[6] "{whipped/sour cream, housekeeping products}"
[7] "{rice, bottled water}"
[8] "{soups, bottled beer}"
Itemset in Consequent (RHS)
[1] "{whole milk}"        "{other vegetables}" "{bottled beer}"
```

*Figure 3.6* is a visual representation of the matrix plot. Here, LHS is plotted on the x-axis and RHS is plotted on the y-axis. The items sets of LHS and RHS are specified previously:

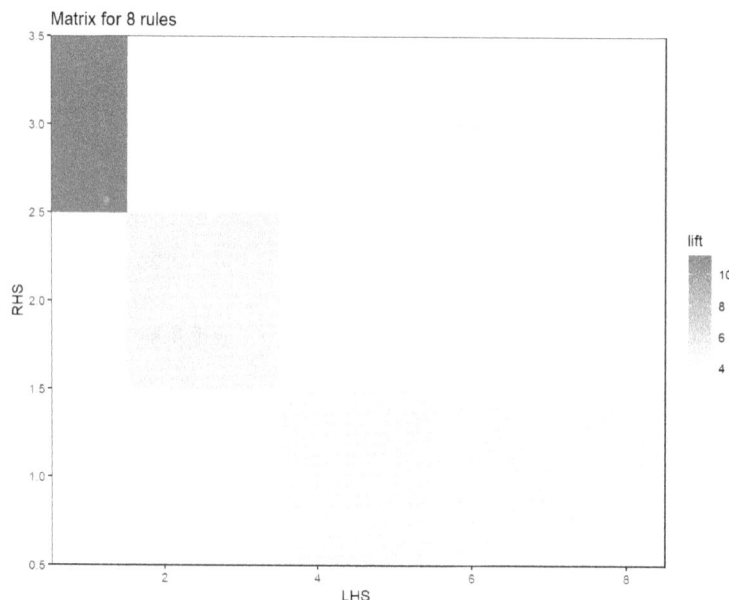

**Figure 3.6**: *Matrix plot of 8 rules*

# Case study

In the competitive retail landscape, understanding customer purchasing behavior is vital for optimizing marketing strategies, boosting product placement, and improving inventory management. Association rule mining is a powerful unsupervised learning technique that uncovers hidden relationships between items frequently purchased together. This case study analyzes the Apriori, FP-Growth, and ECLAT algorithms applied to the publicly available Groceries dataset, providing valuable insights into their performance and practical applications in retail analytics.

## Aims of the study

The aim of this case study is twofold. First, we apply the Apriori, FP-Growth and ECLAT algorithms to the Groceries dataset to identify frequent item sets and generate meaningful association rules. Second, we compare these algorithms based on execution time, computational complexity, and the number of association rules generated, providing rational explanations for the observed differences.

## Dataset description

The dataset for this case study is the Groceries dataset from the **arules** package in R. It comprises 9,835 customer purchase records featuring 169 unique grocery products, such as whole milk, bread, and yogurt. Characterized by sparsity, each transaction contains a varying number of items, reflecting real-world shopping behaviour in a retail setting.

# Methodology of the case study

This study portrays a clear and consistent way to analyze transactional data. By exploring the data in depth and testing different algorithms, it uncovers useful insights and shows how each method performs. This approach makes it easier to compare various association rule mining techniques and delivers trustworthy results that both students and professionals can easily understand.

# Data exploration

We began by loading the Groceries dataset and examining the distribution of items across transactions. This initial exploration helped us identify the most frequently purchased products, providing insights into baseline purchasing trends and the overall structure of the data.

# Algorithm implementation parameters

To ensure a fair comparison among the algorithms, we established consistent parameters:

- **Minimum support**: Set to 1%, meaning items must appear in at least 1% of transactions to be considered frequent.
- **Minimum confidence**: Set to 20%, indicating that the consequent must appear at least 20% of the time when the antecedent is present for a rule to be accepted.

The algorithms applied are as follows:

- **Apriori algorithm**: Generates candidate item sets of increasing length and iteratively prunes those that do not meet the support threshold. It has a time complexity of $O(2^n)$ in the worst case, where n is the number of unique items.
- **FP-Growth algorithm**: Constructs a compact FP-tree structure to represent frequent item sets, enabling it to mine frequent patterns without generating candidate item sets explicitly. Its time complexity is generally linear with the number of transactions but can vary depending on data structure.
- **ECLAT algorithm**: Utilizes a vertical data format, associating each item with a list of transaction IDs where it appears. Frequent item sets are found through efficient intersection operations of these lists. Time complexity depends on the computation of set intersections; it is particularly efficient with sparse data.

# Performance metrics

To evaluate and compare the algorithms effectively, we established the following performance metrics:

- **Execution time**: Measured using system time functions in R to capture the duration of each algorithm's execution.

- **Number of frequent item sets and association rules**: Counted after each algorithm's execution to determine the algorithms' effectiveness in uncovering meaningful patterns.

- **Validation**: Ensured consistency and reliability of results by performing multiple runs of each algorithm.

## Experimental setup

All analyses were conducted using the R programming language within the RStudio environment. We utilized the **arules** package for implementing both the Apriori and ECLAT algorithms, and the **Rcba** package for the FP-Growth algorithm. A system equipped with an Intel Core i7 processor and 16 GB of RAM ensured smooth execution without computational bottlenecks. The Groceries dataset required no additional preprocessing, as it was already appropriately formatted for transaction analysis. Execution times were measured using R's system time functions, and multiple runs were performed to validate the consistency of results. This setup enabled a fair comparison of the algorithms' performance.

## Results and analysis

To evaluate the performance of the algorithms, we executed each one under the same conditions and recorded their execution times, the number of frequent item sets identified, and the number of association rules generated:

- **Apriori algorithm:**
  - **Analysis**: The Apriori algorithm exhibited the longest execution time among the three algorithms. This is due to its process of generating and testing numerous candidate item sets, which increases computational complexity, especially as itemset length grows.
  - **Sample association rule:**

    Rule: If a customer buys whole milk, they also buy other vegetables.

    Support: 7.3%

    Confidence: 29.7%

    Lift: 1.58

    This rule suggests that customers who purchase whole milk are 1.58 times more likely to buy other vegetables compared to the average customer.

- **FP-Growth algorithm:**

- o **Analysis**: FP-Growth outperformed Apriori in execution time due to its use of the FP-tree structure, which compresses the dataset and eliminates the need for candidate generation.

- o **Sample association rule**:

  Rule: Customers buying root vegetables and other vegetables often purchase whole milk.

  Support: 1.7%

  Confidence: 37.5%

  Lift: 1.90

  This indicates a strong association, with customers who buy both types of vegetables being 1.90 times more likely to purchase whole milk.

- **ECLAT algorithm**:

  - o **Analysis**:

    ECLAT's execution time was moderate, benefiting from its vertical data format and efficient intersection operations. However, it requires additional steps to generate association rules.

| ECLAT | 1.5 seconds | 606 | 463 |

  - o **Sample association rule**:

    Rule: Customers who buy yogurt often also buy whole milk.

    Support: 5.6%

    Confidence: 40.2%

    Lift: 2.03

    This suggests that yogurt buyers are twice as likely to purchase whole milk compared to the general customer base.

  - o **Representation of results**: To enhance comprehension, we present the results in the following table and bar chart:

| Performance metric | Apriori | FP-Growth | ECLAT |
|---|---|---|---|
| Execution time (seconds) | 2.1 | 1.2 | 1.5 |
| Frequent item sets identified | 606 | 606 | 606 |
| Association rules generated | 463 | 463 | 463 |

*Table 3.10: Summary result of three algorithms*

The following figure presents the bar chart:

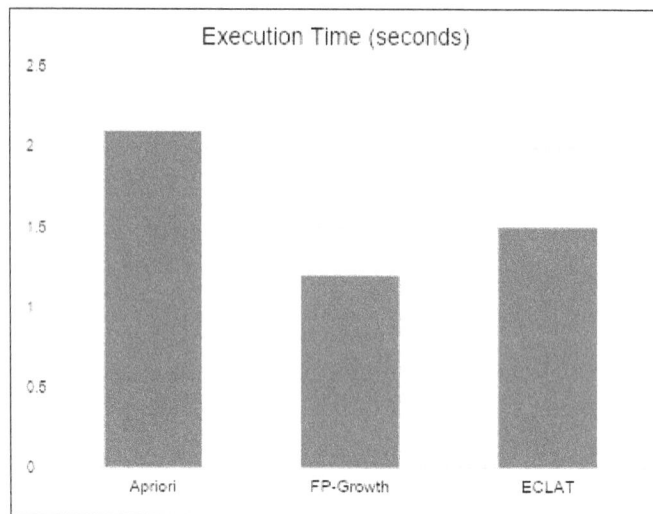

*Figure 3.7*: *Execution time comparison*

- Discussion:
    - **Execution time differences**:
        - **Apriori algorithm**: Slower due to extensive candidate generation and multiple database scans.
        - **FP-Growth algorithm**: Faster by avoiding candidate generation and utilizing an efficient tree structure. ECLAT Algorithm: Moderate performance, efficient with sparse data but requires extra steps for rule generation.
    - **Time complexity considerations**:
        - **Apriori**: Exponential time complexity $O(2^n))$ less scalable.
        - **FP-Growth**: Generally linear time complexity, better scalability.
        - **ECLAT**: Time complexity depends on intersection operations, efficient with sparse datasets.
    - **Number of association rules**: All algorithms generated the same number of rules due to identical support and confidence thresholds. The consistency validates the algorithms' effectiveness in identifying meaningful patterns given the parameters.

- **Practical implications**:
    - **Algorithm selection**: FP-Growth is preferable for larger datasets. Apriori suits smaller datasets or educational purposes. ECLAT is effective with sparse data.

- **Business applications**: Insights from the association rules can inform marketing strategies, product placement, and inventory management.

## Summary

This case study demonstrates that while all three algorithms effectively identify frequent item sets and generate meaningful association rules, their performance varies due to inherent design differences. FP-Growth offers superior execution speed and scalability, making it suitable for larger datasets. Apriori, although slower, is straightforward and useful for smaller datasets. ECLAT provides a balance but may require additional processing for rule generation. Understanding these differences allows practitioners to select the most appropriate algorithm based on the specific characteristics of their dataset and analytical needs.

## Key learnings

- **Algorithm efficiency**: FP-Growth is the most efficient in terms of execution time.
- **Data characteristics**: Sparse datasets benefit from ECLAT, while dense datasets may favor FP-Growth.
- **Parameter influence**: Support and confidence thresholds significantly impact the number of rules generated and computational requirements.

## Practical application

Association rules derived can directly influence retail strategies, enhancing decision-making processes.

# Challenges and future prospects

Association rule algorithms are integral to business applications. However, they face significant challenges that limit their effectiveness. Issues like noise, missing data, and outliers can compromise accuracy, which makes it difficult to extract reliable insights. Processing real-time data with high dimensionality adds another layer of complexity and concerns about transparency, bias, and data privacy which further complicate their implementation. At the same time, traditional association rules often neglect customer ratings, the likes and dislikes that are crucial for understanding purchasing behavior.

Advancements in artificial intelligence and big data technologies present promising solutions to these obstacles. AI techniques can more effectively handle noisy and incomplete data to improve the quality and precision of analyses. Big data tools enable the efficient processing of vast amounts of high-dimensional, real-time information to allow organizations to manage complex datasets with greater ease. By integrating customer ratings into the analysis, organizations can gain deeper insights into consumer preferences and buying patterns that lead to more personalized and effective marketing strategies.

Embracing these technological advancements allows association rule mining to reach new heights across various sectors, including retail, healthcare, supply chain, finance, sports and marketing. Collaboration among data scientists, business analysts and domain experts are crucial to effectively harness these techniques that drive business growth and uncovering valuable insights. As AI and big data continue to evolve, the potential applications of association rule mining will expand to revolutionize how organizations understand and leverage data in our rapidly evolving digital world.

# Conclusion

In this chapter, the power of association rule mining in modern business has been explored to reveal the algorithms that drive it and to address the challenges that shape its development. Using R programming, association rules have been visualized and modeled, their metrics understood, and the Apriori algorithm studied as a key tool for finding meaningful patterns in large datasets. Reflecting on the difficulties and future possibilities, there are many opportunities for applications in specific fields. Personalized recommendation systems are growing quickly and can transform how businesses connect with customers in today's data-driven world. In the next chapter on clustering, another technique that finds hidden patterns in data, these analytical tools will expand and the understanding of data mining will deepen. Association rule mining has vast potential and as technology advances, its applications will continue to grow.

# Multiple choice questions

1. **What is the primary objective of frequent pattern mining?**
   a. Regression
   b. Clustering
   c. Pattern discovery
   d. Classification

2. **A grocery store uses an association Rule Mining algorithm to identify frequent itemset and discovers that {sugar, tomatoes, onion} is a frequent itemset. They want to create marketing campaigns based on this insight. Which of the following actions should they consider?**
   a. Create a bundled sale or discount for purchasing sugar, tomatoes and onions together.
   b. Place sugar at the front of the store and cucumbers at the back to increase store navigation.
   c. Reduce the price of unrelated items to attract more customers.
   d. Conclude that customers are unlikely to purchase these items together and take no action.

3. **What is a major challenge of Apriori algorithm in association rule mining?**

    a. Difficulty in interpretation

    b. Difficult to handle categorical data

    c. Scalability issues

    d. All of the above

4. **Which association rule can handle large datasets efficiently?**

    a. Apriori

    b. FP-Growth

    c. Eclat

    d. DB Scan

5. **What are the number of frequent items sets possible from the dataset with 6 items?**

    a. 64

    b. 63

    c. 32

    d. 31

6. **What are the number of association rules possible out of a set of 5 items?**

    a. 120

    b. 121

    c. 180

    d. 181

7. **A grocery store uses frequent pattern mining and finds that {milk, cereal} is a frequent itemset with high support. However, the store observes that the confidence of the rule {milk} □ {cereal} is low. What can the store infer from this finding?**

    a. Milk and cereal are rarely purchased together.

    b. Many customers buy milk without buying cereal.

    c. Customers who buy cereal often buy milk.

    d. There is a strong positive correlation between milk and cereal.

8. **Which association algorithm requires multiple scans of data?**

    a. Apriori

    b. FP-Growth

    c.  Eclat

    d.  Decision tree

9.  **When we say that an association rule is interesting, what does it mean?**

    a.  If it only satisfies minimum support

    b.  If it only satisfies minimum confidence

    c.  If it satisfies both minimum support and minimum confidence

    d.  None of the above

10.  **In Association Rule Mining, what does a lift value greater than 1 indicate?**

    a.  Items are negatively correlated.

    b.  Items do not have any relationship.

    c.  Items are positively correlated.

    d.  Items occur together less frequently than expected by chance.

# Answers

1.  c

2.  a

3.  c

4.  b

5.  b

6.  c

7.  b

8.  a

9.  c

10. c

# Practice exercises

1.  Calculate the support, confidence, and lift for association rules using a following dataset:

The Student Performance Dataset contains information about students, including their demographic details, academic performance, and other relevant attributes.

Link: (**https://archive.ics.uci.edu/dataset/320/student+performance**)

Identify the support, confidence, and lift for the following association rules and interpret the results:

a.   {higher education} → {internet access}

b.   {extra-curricular activities} → {higher grades}

c.   {study time} → {good performance}

2.   Apply the Apriori algorithm to discover frequent item sets and association rules:

Students will use Online Retail dataset from the UCI Machine Learning Repository. This dataset contains transactional data about online retail purchases.

Link: **https://archive.ics.uci.edu/ml/datasets/online+retail?form=MG0AV3**

Implement the Apriori algorithm using the arules package in R. Set a minimum support threshold of 0.01 and a minimum confidence threshold of 0.5.

a.   Identify the top 5 frequent item sets and their corresponding association rules.

b.   List the top 5 association rules based on confidence.

3.   Implement the FP-Growth algorithm to find frequent patterns in a dataset.

Use the Online Retail dataset from the UCI Machine Learning Repository. This dataset contains transactional data about retail purchases which makes it ideal for analyzing frequent patterns.

Link: **https://archive.ics.uci.edu/dataset/352/online+retail**

a.   Use the arules package in R to implement the FP-Growth algorithm and identify frequent item sets with a minimum support threshold of 0.02.

b.   Compare the results with those obtained using the Apriori algorithm.

Use the ECLAT algorithm to mine frequent item sets in a dataset:

Apply the Student Performance dataset from the UCI Machine Learning Repository, which is also used in question one. This dataset contains information about students, including their demographic details, academic performance.

a.   Implement the ECLAT algorithm using the arules package in R to find frequent item sets with a minimum support threshold of 0.01.

b.   Analyze the efficiency of the ECLAT algorithm compared to the Apriori and FP-Growth algorithms.

4.   Visualize the association rules obtained from a dataset using various visualization techniques:

Apply the Online Retail dataset which is also applied in question 3. This dataset contains transactional data about retail purchases which is also ideal for data visualization.

a.  Apply an association rule mining algorithm such as Apriori or FP-Growth using R to find association rules.

b.  Create a scatter plot of support versus confidence for the association rules. This will help you understand the distribution and strength of the rules.

c.  Generate a heatmap showing the lift values of the top 10 association rules. This visualization will highlight the most significant associations.

d.  Create a bar chart of the top 5 frequent item sets. This will give you a clear view of the most commonly occurring groups of items.

# References

1.  *Agrawal, R., Imielinski, T., & Swami, A. (1993). Mining association rules between sets of items in large databases. In Proceedings of the 1993 ACM SIGMOD International Conference on Management of Data .pp. 207–216.*

2.  *Borgelt, C. (2005). An implementation of the FP-growth algorithm. In Proceedings of the 1st International Workshop on Open-Source Data Mining: Frequent Pattern Mining Implementations .pp. 1–5.*

3.  *Goethals, B., & Zaki, M. J. (2004). Advances in frequent itemset mining implementations: Introduction to FIMI 2004. In Proceedings of the IEEE ICDM Workshop on Frequent Itemset Mining Implementations.*

4.  *Hahsler, M., Grün, B., & Hornik, K. (2007). Introduction to arules – A computational environment for mining association rules and frequent item sets. Journal of Statistical Software, 14(15), 1–25.*

5.  *Han, J., Pei, J., & Yin, Y. (2000). Mining frequent patterns without candidate generation. In Proceedings of the 2000 ACM SIGMOD International Conference on Management of Data (pp. 1–12).*

6.  *Kotsiantis, S., & Kanellopoulos, D. (2006). Association rules mining: A recent overview. GESTS International Transactions on Computer Science and Engineering, 32(1), 71–82.*

7.  *Srikant, R., & Agrawal, R. (1995). Mining generalized association rules. In Proceedings of the 21st International Conference on Very Large Data Bases (VLDB) (pp. 407–419).*

8.  *Tan, P.-N., Steinbach, M., & Kumar, V. (2006). Introduction to Data Mining. Addison-Wesley.*

9.  *Tanbeer, S. K., Ahmed, C. F., Jeong, B.-S., & Lee, Y.-K. (2009). Efficient single-pass frequent pattern mining using a prefix-tree. Information Sciences, 179(5), 559–583.*

10. *Zaki, M. J. (2000). Scalable algorithms for association mining. IEEE Transactions on Knowledge and Data Engineering, 12(3), 372–390.*

# CHAPTER 4
# Clustering

## Introduction

In this chapter, we will discuss clustering as an unsupervised learning algorithm. This technique is used when we need to segment a dataset into subgroups based on similar characteristics. As a popular algorithm, k-means clustering, k-medoid, and hierarchical clustering are discussed. The chapter also introduces a few advanced algorithms, like DBSCAN and BIRCH algorithms. Data visualization on clustering with interpretation using R is also discussed.

## Structure

This chapter covers the following topics:

- Overview of clustering
- Distance metrics
- K mean clustering, applications and challenges
- Advanced clustering algorithms
- Data visualization on clustering using R

# Objectives

The interpretation of the clustering technique is based on an unsupervised learning algorithm. Here, there is no knowledge of the number of clusters in advance before running this model. The primary objective of clustering is to divide the observations into unique subgroups so that the data points belonging to the same cluster or subgroup are homogeneous. Based on the context, the similarity measure may be a correlation, distance-based or cosine similarity. Various applications can range from segmenting customers, classification of animals and plants, and allocating resources in logistics, the health and manufacturing sector, etc.

# Overview of clustering

In some cases, algorithms have knowledge of both input and output variables or features. In these cases, supervised learning algorithms are applied. However, in some situations, only the input variable or features are known to algorithms. Algorithms have no knowledge of output features or variables. Here, unsupervised algorithms are applied on the dataset. Clustering is a popular unsupervised learning approach. These techniques are applied to understand the behavior of customers, competitors and market conditions, so as to drive the growth of the firms. Clustering facilitates segmenting customers based on their tastes, design-customized marketing campaign plans, and cross-selling and upselling strategies. It is also possible to identify potential fraud customers and plan proper risk management strategies. There are various types of clustering techniques like partitioning, density based and hierarchical clustering, etc.

# Distance metrics

Similarly, the measure is calculated to know the distance between observations. If the distance between two observations is small, then there is a high degree of similarity between them. If the distance between two observations is large, then they are not close and may not belong to the same group. Of course, subjectivity is important to understand the similarity based on context:

## Euclidean distance measure

Euclidean distance measure is a quite popular and common metrics for computing similarity between observations. This measure is a straight-line distance between observations in Euclidean space. The Euclidean distance between two observations is as follows:

$$d = \sqrt{[(x_2 - x_1)^2 + (y_2 - y_1)^2]}$$

where two observations are (X1, Y1) and (X2, Y2). The distance between the two observations is d.

Let us take two customers, X and Y, with the following features:

*X: Age 30 years, Salary 60,000, Expenses 12,000*

*Y: Age 35 years, Salary 70,000, Expenses 15,000*

*So, Square of (30-35) = 25*

*Square of (60000-70000) = 10,00,00000*

*Square of (12000-15000) = 90,00000*

*Sum of the Squared difference is 25+100000000+9000000=1,09,000,025*

*So, Euclidian distance = sqrt (109000025) = 10,430.3 approx.*

Euclidean value can range from 0 to infinity. Interpretation depends on context and type of data. Sometimes, normalization is required to confirm that the features are on same scale. Based on context and functional knowledge, the similarity and dissimilarity are interpreted.

The measure is easy to interpret and can be calculated quickly for large datasets.

# Manhattan distance measure

Manhattan distance measure is the sum of the absolute differences of the coordinates. The Manhattan distance between two observations (X1, Y1) and (X2, Y2) in 2-dimensional space is as follows:

$$d = |X2\text{-}X1| + |Y2\text{-}Y1|$$

Say we want to compute the Manhattan distance between (4,5) and (2,10). Then:

$$|(\text{-}2)| + |(5)| = 2+5=7$$

This measure is less affected by outliers compared to the Euclidian measure and easy to interpret.

# Cosine similarity measure

This measure is computed using the dot product and the magnitude of two vectors:

*Cosine similarity (X, Y) = (X.Y)/ ( |X| |Y| )*

Here, X and Y are two vectors. X.Y is dot product of X and Y. $|X|$ and $|Y|$ are the absolute length of X and Y. The value of the measure remains between 0 and 1. If two vectors are of the same magnitude and direction, the cosine similarity value will be 1. If the magnitude of both vectors is the same but the direction is opposite, then the value will be -1. If the vectors have no similarity, then the cosine similarity value is zero and angle between the vectors is 90 degrees. If both vectors have some similarities, then the cosine similarity value will be between 0 and 1. This measure is widely used in text analytics applications. The measure is sensitive to the direction of vectors.

Let us take two vectors as follows:

$$X = [1,2] \text{ and } Y = [2, 3]$$

*Cosine similarity of X and Y = [1,2]. [2,3]/ | [1,2] | | [2,3] | = 1\*2+2\*3/ sqrt (1\*1+2\*2) \* sqrt (2\*2+3\*3)*

*Cosine Similarity = 8/sqrt (5) \*sqrt (13) =8/ sqrt (65) = 8/8.06=0.993*

So, the cosine similarity of X and Y is 0.993. It shows they are very similar.

# Jaccard coefficient measure

This measure is applied to compute the similarity between two clusters or sets:

*Jaccard coefficient = (Size of Intersection)/ (Size of Union)*

Values of the coefficient range from 0 to 1. Value 0 indicates no similarity between clusters. Value 1 indicates perfect similarity between clusters. Usually, low similarity ranges from 0 to .3, moderate similarity is between .3 to .5, high similarity is between .5 to .7, and very high similarity is between 0.7 to 1.

Say, two users, Ram and Hari, have rated the following Hindi movies:

*Ram: {Don, Sholay, Hera Pheri}, Hari: {Don, Hera Pheri, Parvrish}*

*Intersection: {Don, Hera Pheri}, Union: {Don, Sholay, Hera Pheri, Parvarish}*

So, Jaccard coefficient = (2)/(4) =0.5, So, there is moderate similarity of preference of these two users.

# K-means clustering, applications and challenges

In the case of the partitioning technique, the clusters are not overlapped. Observations of a cluster is confined to that cluster only. Usually, clusters are separately placed. K-means clustering is a popular example of the partitioning technique. Say, for example, a bank is interested in knowing its high-value customers so as to cross-sell any personalized services to retain them for the long run. So, variables or features like account balance, customer demographics, and other related features of customers are selected to apply the k means clustering to identify them into high-value, medium-value, and low-value clusters. Then, it is easy for the bank to target the high value customers to cross sell home loan, car loan or any other services. Let us take an example to understand the mechanism of k means clustering.

More generally, you:

- Select k number of clusters. K is a guess like 2,3, 4, etc.

- Choose k points, which are actual observations as cluster mean

- Compute the distance between each observation and the centroids chosen in *step 2* and assign each data point to the closest cluster.

- Compute the centroid, which is the mean position for each cluster.

- Repeat *steps 3* and *4* until the clusters do not change or the maximum number of iterations is reached.

We will apply k-means clustering on the following dataset with three features:

| Roll no. | Grade point average | Hours studied | % of attendance |
|----------|---------------------|---------------|-----------------|
| 1 | 3.5 | 20 | 90 |
| 2 | 3.2 | 15 | 85 |
| 3 | 3.8 | 25 | 95 |
| 4 | 2.9 | 10 | 80 |
| 5 | 3.1 | 12 | 88 |
| 6 | 3.6 | 22 | 92 |
| 7 | 3.3 | 18 | 89 |
| 8 | 3.9 | 28 | 96 |
| 9 | 2.8 | 8 | 78 |
| 10 | 3.4 | 20 | 91 |

*Table 4.1: Example dataset*

Let us take k= 3 as the initial guess to divide the dataset into three clusters:

- **First iteration**: First of all, three students are chosen as centroids. Let us select the following three students as three centroids:

    o 1st Cluster – GPA 3.5, hours studied 20, and attendance is 90%

    o 2nd Cluster – GPA 2.9, hours studied 10, and attendance is 80%

    o 3rd Cluster – GPA 3.8, hours studied 25, and attendance is 95%

  Students closest to the respective clusters are as follows, based on Euclidian distance discussed in the previous section.

    o 1st Cluster – 1st, 4th, 5th,7th and 10th student

    o 2nd Cluster – 2nd and 9th student

       o   3rd Cluster - 3rd, 6th and 8th student

Now, after re-computation of centroids:

       o   1st Cluster – GPA 3.34, hours studied 18.2 and attendance is 89.2

       o   2nd Cluster – GPA 2.85, hours studies 9.0 and attendance is 79.0

       o   3rd Cluster – 3.77, 25.0, 94.3

- **Second iteration**: Students closest to the new centroids are as follows:

       o   1st Cluster – 1st, 4th, 5th, 7th and 10th student

       o   2nd Cluster – 2nd and 9th student

       o   3rd Cluster – 3rd, 6th and 8th student

Again, after updating the centroids:

       o   1st Cluster – GPA 3.32, hours studies 18.5 and attendance is 89.5

       o   2nd Cluster – GPA 2.83, hours studies 9.2 and attendance is 79.2

       o   3rd Cluster – GPA 3.79, hours studies 25.2 and attendance is 94.5

- **Third iteration**: Students closest to the new centroids are as follows:

       o   1st Cluster – 1st, 4th, 5th, 7th and 10th student

       o   2nd Cluster – 2nd and 9th student

       o   3rd Cluster – 3rd, 6th and 8th student

After three iterations, the clusters remain the same. So, finally:

       o   $1^{st}$ cluster can be identified as students with good attendance and reading habits.

       o   $2^{nd}$ cluster contains students with poor attendance and poor reading habits.

       o   $3^{rd}$ cluster comprises students with excellent reading habits and attendance.

Some advantages of the K-mean algorithm is that it is easy to understand and apply and is quite flexible and robust. This algorithm is also efficient, robust, and flexible. However, there are a few disadvantages also. One has to guess the value of k or the number of clusters. The initial guess may result in complex iterations. The algorithm will create issues for outliers and noisy data. If the dataset is very large, computational time will be high.

# K-medoids clustering for data partitioning, applications and challenges

Here, grouping is accomplished with a central point, which is known as a medoid. In k means, an average of data points is calculated to make centroids. However, k-medoid takes actual observations as centroids of clusters. So, k-medoids are capable of dealing with outliers and noises in a better way. Let us take an example of grouping students into study groups. Say, the instructor of the students is planning to divide the students into groups so that the students can complete group projects. The location of the students is taken as a reference:

- **Stage one**: Let the number of groups(K) be selected as two.

- **Stage two**: Let us select two medoids, as Snigdha and Rujul.

- **Stage three**: Then, assign each student to the group of the nearest medoid. The students' location data are as follows:
    - Snigdha - (1, 2)
    - Shatabdi - (2, 2)
    - Ruparna- (2, 3)
    - Rujul - (8, 7)
    - Divyanshi - (8, 8)

Now, let us calculate the distance of each student from Snigdha and Rujul using the Manhattan measure as discussed in the previous section. Then, we will assign them to their nearest medoid.

**Initial assignment**:
- Group one (Snigdha's cluster): Snigdha, Shatabdi and Ruparna
- Group two (Rujul's cluster): Rujul and Divyanshi

- **Stage four**: Update group centers (medoids) for each group and find a new medoid that minimizes the total distance to all other students in the group. This is done to make the group centers more representative of their members.

**For group one**:
- Total distances if Snigdha is the medoid: $0 + 1 + 1.41 = 2.41$
- Total distances if Bob is the medoid: $1 + 0 + 1 = 2$
- Total distances if Ruparna is the medoid: $1.41 + 1 + 0 = 2.41$

So, Shatabdi becomes the new medoid for Group one because it has the minimum total distance.

**For group two**:
- Rujul and Divyanshi already have the minimum distance, so no change is needed.

New medoids:

- o **Group one**: Shatabdi (2, 2)
- o **Group two**: Rujul (8, 7)

- **Stage five**: Repeat Reassign students to the nearest medoid again and update the medoids. Repeat this until the medoids do not change.

Iteration one:

- o **Group one (Shatabdi's group)**: Snigdha, Shatabdi, Ruparna
- o **Group two (Rujul's group)**: Rujul, Divyanshi

Here, we can see that the algorithm converges as there are no further changes. So, we see that K-Medoids facilitate the search for the best locations for centroids by using actual observations instead of average locations.

K-Medoids clustering is an efficient algorithm applied in customer segmentation, gene expression analysis, and image compression. Its capability to handle noisy data and outliers makes it essential in real-world applications. For example, in customer segmentation, k-medoids can help identify unique customer groups based on demographic and transactional data which facilitates targeted marketing strategies. Additionally, in gene expression analysis, k-medoids can aid in identifying co-regulated genes and understanding their functional relationships. However, medoids clustering can be computationally expensive for large datasets, and the choice of initial medoids can significantly impact the clustering results.

# Hierarchical clustering, applications and challenges

Let us take with student example:

- **Initiate with individual students**: Say, there are five students in a class—Miku, Rimun, Somu, Guddu, and Eva. Each student starts as their own group.

- **Let us check for similarities**: Each student has different interests and skills. Miku likes drawing. Rimun likes writing. Somu likes both drawing and writing. Guddu likes math. Jinu likes science. We have to decide about how similar or different they are based on their interests.

- **Calculate distances**: In the current context, we see who has similar interests. Somu is similar to Miku because they both like drawing. Rimun is quite different from Guddu, who likes math.

- **Group the closest students**: First, we can group Miku and Somu together since they both enjoy drawing. So now we have the following:

- o **Group one**: [Miku, Somu]
- o **Individual groups**: [Rimun], [Guddu], [Jinu]

- **Update distances**: Now, we look at the groups again. Somu (in the group with Miku) has some similarity with Rimun since she likes writing, so let us group them next.

- **Repeat the process**: Now we merge Rimun with Miku and Somu because Somu's interests connect her to Rimun:
  - o **Group two**: [Miku, Somu, Rimun]
  - o **Individual groups**: [Guddu], [Jinu]

Next, Guddu and Jinu are different but let us say they find common ground in their subjects because Guddu's good at math and Jinu is good at science.

- **Final merging**: Guddu and Jinu can be considered for later projects. So, we can move as follows:
  - o **Group one**: Miku, Somu and Rimun
  - o **Group two**: Guddu and Jinu

- **Creation of Dendrogram**: At the outset, we can draw a small "tree" to portray how students are grouped. At the top, we have two big groups that are Group one (Art and Writing) and Group two (Math and Science). We can visually check that Miku, Somu, and Rimun are all connected because of their common interests whereas Guddu and Jinu are a separate group.

So, based on the analysis, the dendrogram is portrayed as follows:

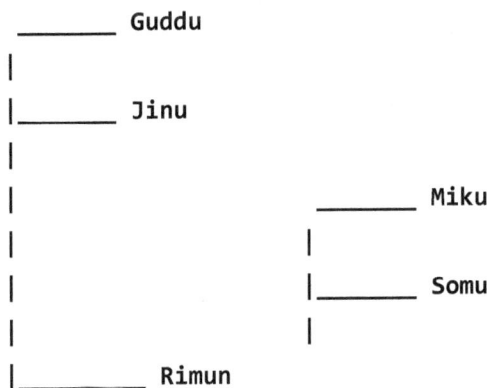

```
  _____ Guddu
 |
 |
 |_____ Jinu
 |
 |                       _____ Miku
 |                      |
 |                      |_____ Somu
 |                      |
 |_____ Rimun
```

In this way, hierarchical clustering works in a classroom setting. Students can cluster together based on their interests and skills. It facilitates them to unite themselves for teamwork in a way that everyone works with others who have similar interests, making it easier and more enjoyable to work together. Hierarchical clustering is a versatile and widely used algorithm in data analysis. It is applied in social network analysis, text mining and bioinformatics. The dendrogram represents the hierarchical relationships between clusters. This clustering is particularly useful in identifying nested patterns and relationships within the data. For example, in social network analysis, hierarchical clustering can help identify clusters of densely connected individuals and communities. However, hierarchical clustering can be challenging to interpret, especially for large datasets and the choice of linkage criterion and distance metric can significantly impact the clustering results. Furthermore, hierarchical clustering can be computationally expensive and may not be suitable for very large datasets.

# Advanced clustering algorithms

To handle very large datasets in clustering, a few algorithms like DBSCAN and BIRCH algorithms are popularly used:

- **Density-Based Spatial Clustering of Applications with Noise (DBSCAN)**: For very large datasets with varying densities, unknown numbers of clusters and the presence of noise and outliers, DBSCAN is a suitable algorithm to use. DBSCAN is applied in various fields like anomaly detection and segmentation of customers to make clusters of gene based on their levels of expression, segmenting customers, and deciphering congestion hotspots. DBSCAN is quite suitable for large datasets with high noise levels. However, the algorithm may be slow while the size of the large data set significantly increases. To handle high-dimensional data, DBSCAN requires parameter tuning.

- **Balanced Iterative Reducing and Clustering using Hierarchies (BIRCH algorithm):** To handle large datasets of varying densities, it is unusually advised to apply BIRCH algorithm in data mining applications. This algorithm is based on a hierarchical approach. The algorithm is more scalable compared to DBSCAN as it can handle datasets of even larger sizes. For high-dimensional data, this algorithm is suitable with additional computing resources. The BIRCH algorithm is more suitable to recommend to customers based on their past purchasing habits in recommendation systems. Similarly, this algorithm is more suitable to judge the creditworthiness of customers compared to DBSCAN.

# Data visualization on clustering using R

This section delves into the application of data visualization techniques in clustering analysis using the R programming language. Here, we start by exploring k-means clustering. The optimal number of clusters is determined using the elbow method and gap statistics. The Elbow Method involves plotting the within-cluster sum of squares against the number of clusters and identifying the point where the curve bends. Gap statistics, on the other hand, compares the total within-intra-cluster variation for different numbers of clusters with their expected values under a null reference distribution of the data. Once the optimal k value is determined, we utilize R to create a cluster plot to visually represent the k-means clustering results. This is illustrated using the built-in USArrests dataset. This dataset comprises crime statistics for various US states. In addition to k-means clustering, k-medoids clustering is also examined a more robust version of k-means that reduces the influence of outliers. Using the IRIS built-in dataset, which contains measurements of iris flowers, we perform k-medoids clustering and produce visualizations that highlight data partitioning into clusters. Furthermore, we explore hierarchical clustering, which creates a tree-like structure, i.e. dendrogram representing nested clusters at various levels of similarity. This is applied to the IRIS dataset using R to generate a dendrogram that provides valuable insights into the data's structure and the relationship between different clusters. By applying these clustering methods and visualization techniques, readers can gain valuable insights into the underlying structure of their data, ultimately informing data-driven decision-making processes.

# K-means clustering application

Here, we will use the USArrests dataset built-in into R. USArrests comprises information on arrests per 100,000 citizens for assault, murder, and rape in each of the 50 US states in 1973. This dataset also contains the percentage of the population living in urban areas. All four variables are numeric in nature. **factoextra** and **cluster** packages are installed to perform various k-means clustering functions. The following codes will be executed stepwise. Initially, the USArrests dataset is loaded, and the missing data are eliminated. Data scaling operation is performed with the standard deviation 1 and mean 0:

```
install.packages("cluster")
install.packages("factoextra")
library(factoextra)
library(cluster)
df <- USArrests
df <- na.omit(df) # Eliminates rows with missing data
df <- scale(df)    # Standardization  of variables is done
dim(df)
[1] 50   4
```

50 observations are there with 4 variables.

To find out the optimal number of clusters, we will use the following two different methods:

- **Elbow method**: This method facilitates the creation of the plot of sum of squared error against number of clusters. Optimal number of clusters is chosen from the elbow curve. Here, the addition of a further cluster does not change the explained variance significantly.

The following R codes will solve the purpose in creating the elbow graph:

```
fviz_nbclust(df, kmeans, method = "wss")
```

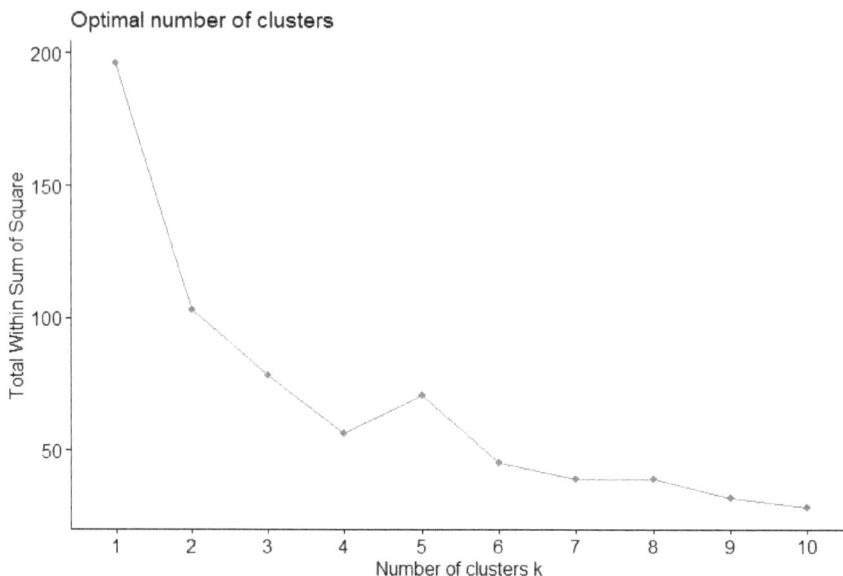

*Figure 4.1*: *Optimal number of clusters using elbow method*

It is clear from the graph that the optima value of k=4.

- **Determination of optimum number of clusters using gap statistics**: Gap statistics is a frequently used method for determining optimum number of clusters. The quality of the cluster solution is evaluated through this method. The gap statistics explains how well the clustering algorithm performs for each number of clusters. This gap statistic is plotted against a number of clusters. The optimal number of clusters corresponds to the largest gap statistics. Using the **clusGap** function, the gap statistic is calculated across a range of cluster counts from 1 to 10. K-means clustering is applied with multiple starting points (**nstart = 25**) and 50 bootstrap samples (**B = 50**) for reliability. The resulting gap statistics are visualized using **fviz_gap_stat** to plot the statistic for each potential cluster count. The peak indicates the optimal number of clusters that reflects the largest difference between observed clustering and random chance.

```
gapstats <- clusGap(df,FUN = kmeans,nstart = 25,K.max = 10,B = 50):
#plot number of clusters vs. gap statistic
fviz_gap_stat(gapstats)
```

The following graph shows optimal number of clusters. Here, no clusters are taken in the x-axis, and gap statistics are taken in the y-axis:

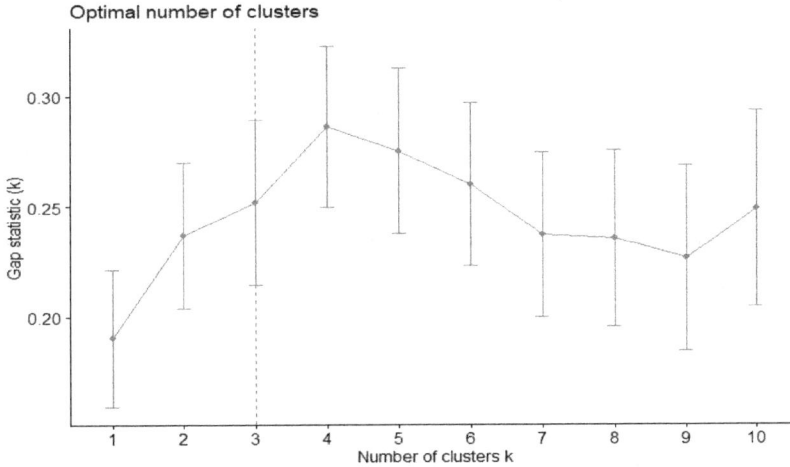

*Figure 4.2: Optimal clusters determination using gap statistics*

From the graph, it is clear that gap statistics is maximum at k=4. The value of k in Elbow method is also 4.

# K-means clustering using R

We will use the value of k=4 based on the preceding method.

We can interpret from the result that sixteen states are allocated to the 1st cluster, thirteen states are allocated to the 2nd cluster and 3rd cluster and eight states are allocated to the 4th cluster. A scatter plot can be displayed based on initial 2 components as follows:

**Fviz_cluster(km, data=df)**

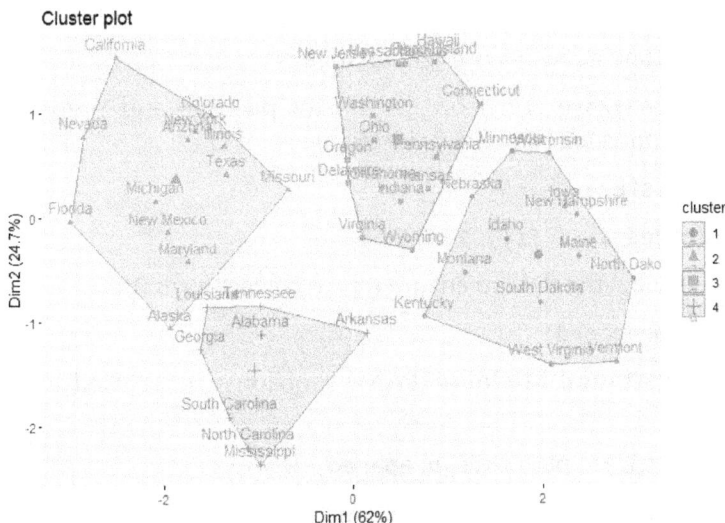

*Figure 4.3: Cluster plot*

The mean of the features of each cluster can be used:

```
Aggregate(USArrests, by=list(cluster=km$cluster), mean)
```

| Cluster | Murder | Assault | UrbanPop | Rape |
|---|---|---|---|---|
| 1 | 3.60000 | 78.53846 | 52.07692 | 12.17692 |
| 2 | 10.81538 | 257.38462 | 76.00000 | 33.19231 |
| 3 | 5.65625 | 138.87500 | 73.87500 | 18.78125 |
| 4 | 13.93750 | 243.62500 | 53.75000 | 21.41250 |

The interpretation of the result is as follows:

- The average number of murders per one lakh people among the states in cluster one is 3.6.

- The average number of assaults per one lakh people among the states in cluster one is 78.5.

- The average number of UrbanPop per one lakh people among the states in cluster one is 52.07.

- The average number of Rape per one lakh people among the states in cluster one is 12.17.

# K-medoid application

Take an example with the IRIS dataset for k-medoids clustering in R. We will check through R codes about the characteristics of the groups of the IRIS dataset. Let us load the IRIS dataset in RStudio:

- **data(iris)**: The IRIS dataset contains 150 observations of IRIS flowers. Four features are described: sepal length, sepal width, petal length and petal width.

  Now, let us view a few rows to get an idea:

  **head(irisThen)**, we will load the cluster package and prepare the data with numeric columns for K medoid clustering:

  ```
  library(cluster)
  ```

  ```
  iris_prepared <- iris[, 1:4]
  ```

  Now, let us view the data to ensure it is in correct format:

  ```
  head(iris_prepared)
  ```

  The **Partion Around Medoids (PAM)** function will be used to apply k-medoid with k=3:

  ```
  kmedoids_final <- pam(iris_prepared, k = 3)
  ```

  Here, we set k=3 which means we expect to find three clusters in the data.

The clustering results are stored in the **kmedoid_final** object. We can print the medoids which represent the central points of each cluster:

```
print(kmedoids_final$medoids)
```

- **Medoids**:

| ID | Sepal.Length | Sepal.Width | Petal.Length | Petal.Width |
|----|----|----|----|----|
| [1,] | 8 | 5.0 | 3.4 | |
| 1.5 | 0.2 | | | |
| [2,] | 79 | 6.0 | 2.9 | |
| 4.5 | 1.5 | | | |
| [3,] | 113 | 6.8 | 3.0 | |
| 5.5 | 2.1 | | | |

These medoids represent the characteristic features of each cluster. For example, the first medoid (ID 8) has sepal length and width values of 5.0 and 3.4, respectively, which may indicate a specific type of iris flower.

- **Clustering vector**: The clustering vector displays the cluster assignments for each observation:

```
[1] 1 1 1 1 1 1 1 1 1 1 1 1 1 1 1 1 1 1 1 1 1 1 1 1 1 1 1 1 1 1 1 1
1 1 1 1 1 1 1 1

[42] 1 1 1 1 1 1 1 1 1 2 2 3 2 2 2 2 2 2 2 2 2 2 2 2 2 2 2 2 2 2
2 2 2 2 3 2 2 2 2

[83] 2 2 2 2 2 2 2 2 2 2 2 2 2 2 2 2 2 2 2 3 2 3 3 3 3 2 3 3 3 3 3 2
2 3 3 3 3 2 3 2 3

[124] 2 3 3 2 2 3 3 3 3 3 2 3 3 3 3 2 3 3 3 3 2 3 3 3 2 3 3 2
```

This vector indicates which cluster each observation belongs to. For example, the first 20 observations are assigned to cluster 1.

- **Objective function**: The objective function value is a measure of the quality of the clustering:

```
build     swap :0.6709391  0.6542077
```

The objective function value represents the sum of the distances between each observation and its assigned medoid. A lower value indicates better clustering quality.

- **Available components**: The **kmedoids_final** object contains several components that can be accessed for further analysis:

```
[1] "medoids"    "id.med"     "clustering" "objective"  "isolation"
```

```
"clusinfo"
```

```
[7] "silinfo"     "diss"        "call"        "data"
```

These components include:

o   **medoids**: The medoids of the clusters

o   **id.med**: The IDs of the medoids

o   **clustering**: The cluster assignments for each observation

o   **objective**: The objective function value

o   **isolation**: The isolation of each cluster

o   **clusinfo**: Additional information about the clusters

o   **silinfo**: Silhouette information for each cluster

o   **diss**: The dissimilarity matrix

o   **call**: The call used to create the **kmedoids_final** object

o   **data**: The original data used for clustering

Analysis and visualization of the clusters are as follows: The clustering results are stored in the **kmedoids_final** object. The medoids can be printed, which represent the center points of each cluster.

```
print(kmedoids_final$medoids)    # Print the medoids
         Sepal.Length  Sepal.Width  Petal.Length  Petal.Width
[1,]          5.0          3.4          1.5          0.2
[2,]          6.0          2.9          4.5          1.5
[3,]          6.8          3.0          5.5          2.1
```

We can also print the cluster assignments for each observation.

```
print(kmedoids_final$clustering) # Print the cluster assignments
[1]   1 1 1 1 1 1 1 1 1 1 1 1 1 1 1 1 1 1 1 1 1 1 1 1 1 1 1 1 1 1 1 1 1 1 1 1 1 1 1 1
1 1 1 1 1 1
[42]  1 1 1 1 1 1 1 1 1 2 2 3 2 2 2 2 2 2 2 2 2 2 2 2 2 2 2 2 2 2 2 2 2 2 2 2 2 2 2 2
2 3 2 2 2 2
[83]  2 2 2 2 2 2 2 2 2 2 2 2 2 2 2 2 2 3 2 3 3 3 3 2 3 3 3 3 3 3 2 2 3 3
3 3 2 3 2 3
[124] 2 3 3 2 2 3 3 3 3 3 2 3 3 3 3 2 3 3 3 2 3 3 3 2 3 3 3 2 3 3 2
```

Cluster can be visualized using a plot as follows.

```
plot (kmedoids_final, main = "K-Medoids Clustering") # Plotting of  the
clusters
```

**K-Medoids Clustering**

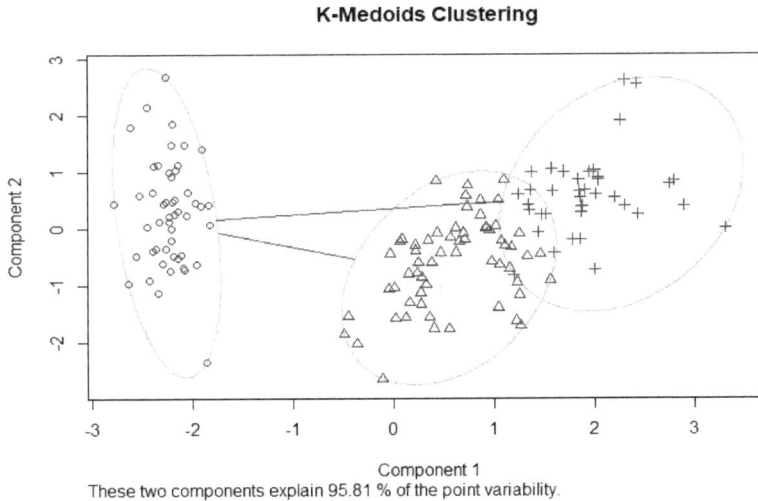

Component 1
These two components explain 95.81 % of the point variability.

*Figure 4.4*: *K-medoid clustering*

This algorithm grouped the flowers into three clusters based on their similarities. The clustering result indicates the medoids and the cluster assignments for each observation. In the business sense, based on these segments or clusters, proper marketing plans can be tailored.

# Hierarchical clustering application

This is a technique of grouping observations into clusters based on their similar characteristics. Hierarchical clustering does not need to specify the number of clusters in advance. It creates a dendrogram that shows the relationships among the observations and clusters at various levels of similarity.

Let us use the Iris dataset in R to show hierarchical clustering.

Load the Iris dataset and view the first few rows:

```
data(iris)
head(iris)
```

|   | Sepal.Length | Sepal.Width | Petal.Length | Petal.Width | Species |
|---|---|---|---|---|---|
| 1 | 5.1 | 3.5 | 1.4 | 0.2 | setosa |
| 2 | 4.9 | 3.0 | 1.4 | 0.2 | setosa |
| 3 | 4.7 | 3.2 | 1.3 | 0.2 | setosa |
| 4 | 4.6 | 3.1 | 1.5 | 0.2 | setosa |
| 5 | 5.0 | 3.6 | 1.4 | 0.2 | setosa |
| 6 | 5.4 | 3.9 | 1.7 | 0.4 | setosa |

The Iris dataset contains measurements of sepal length, sepal width, petal length, and petal width for three species of iris flowers.

Now, prepare the data with only numeric columns:

```
iris_hierarchy <- iris[, 1:4]
# View the prepared data
head(iris_hierarchy)
```

|   | Sepal.Length | Sepal.Width | Petal.Length | Petal.Width |
|---|---|---|---|---|
| 1 | 5.1 | 3.5 | 1.4 | 0.2 |
| 2 | 4.9 | 3.0 | 1.4 | 0.2 |
| 3 | 4.7 | 3.2 | 1.3 | 0.2 |
| 4 | 4.6 | 3.1 | 1.5 | 0.2 |
| 5 | 5.0 | 3.6 | 1.4 | 0.2 |
| 6 | 5.4 | 3.9 | 1.7 | 0.4 |

Now, calculate the distance matrix, which will show the pairwise distances between all observations.

```
distance_matrix <- dist(iris_hierarchy)  # distance matrix using Euclidean distance

head(as.matrix(distance_matrix))   # first few values of the distance matrix
```

Now, let us perform hierarchical clustering. The function **hclust** is used for the same.

Perform hierarchical clustering using the complete linkage method:

```
hc <- hclust(distance_matrix, method = "complete")
print(hc)  # View the hierarchical clustering result
Call:
hclust(d = distance_matrix, method = "complete")
Cluster method   : complete
Distance         : Euclidean
Number of objects: 150
```

Now, we will plot the dendrogram:

```
plot (hc, main = "Dendrogram", xlab = "Sample Index", ylab = "Height", sub = "")
```

A dendrogram is a tree-like diagram that shows how the data points are clustered together. The height at which two observations are joined indicates the distance (or dissimilarity) between them. Each leaf represents an observation. Each branch represents a cluster.

The height of the branches indicates the distance between clusters. In a business sense, hierarchical clustering can be used for various purposes like customer segmentation, market research, and inventory management, etc.

```
clusters <- cutree(hc, k = 3) # Here, we choose 3 clusters
pairs(iris_hierarchy, col = clusters, pch = 20, main = "Hierarchical
Clustering on IRIS Data set")
```

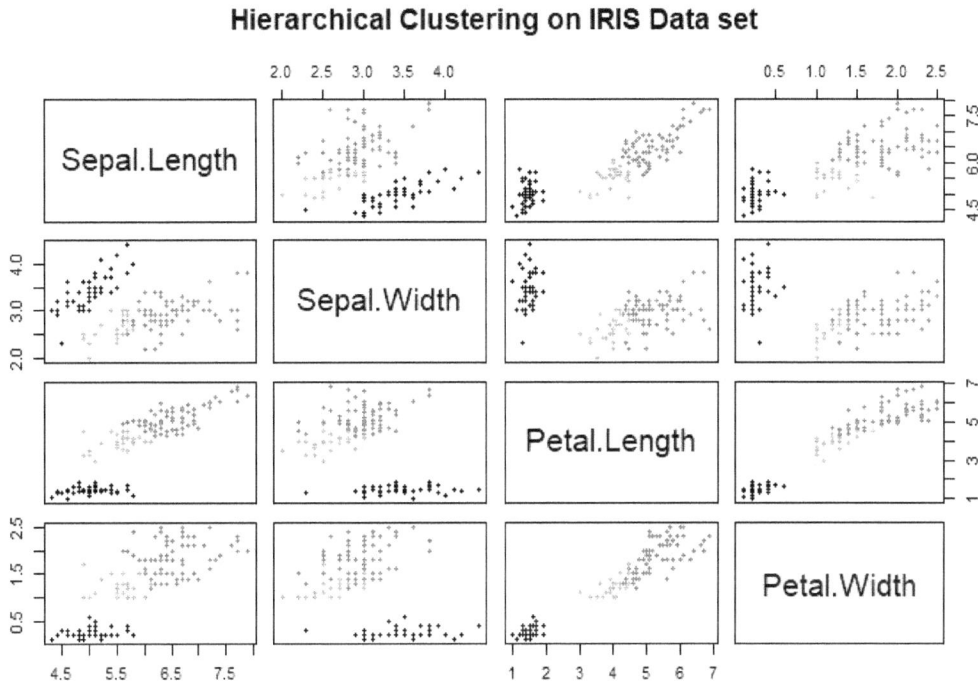

*Figure 4.5: Hierarchical clustering on Iris dataset*

# Conclusion

This chapter started with an overview of clustering to understand the grouping of similar observations to uncover the pattern. Subsequently, the concept of distance metrics is discussed, which determines the similarity between observations. Further, k-means clustering was discussed as a popular method for partitioning data into k clusters, along with its practical applications and challenges, such as selecting the right number of clusters. Then, an introduction to advanced clustering algorithms like hierarchical clustering, DBSCAN, and BIRCH algorithms are presented with proper scenarios of their applications. In the current context, the importance of data visualization using R was demonstrated with the R dataset to understand and interpret R's robust functionality. By mastering these concepts and tools, the readers will be able to analyze complex datasets, facilitating informed decision-making in various business applications. The next chapter is based on Introduction to Business Intelligence.

# Multiple choice questions

1. **Which of the following algorithms is most sensitive to outliers?**

   a. K-means

   b. DBSCAN

   c. K-medoids

   d. K-modes

2. **Scaling of variables is an important step before administering k-mean algorithm because?**

   a. In distance calculation, it will give the same weights for all variables.

   b. You always get the same clusters. If you use or do not use variable scaling.

   c. In Manhattan distance, it is an important step but in Euclidian, it is not.

   d. None of the above.

3. **The key difference between k-means clustering and k-medoid is?**

   a. K-means is used for hierarchical clustering, while k-medoids is for density-based clustering.

   b. K-means is density-based and k-medoid is partitional.

   c. K-means uses centroids as cluster centers, while k-medoids uses actual data points.

   d. K-means is supervised and k-medoid is unsupervised.

4. **The density-based clustering algorithm is?**

   a. DBSCAN

   b. Agglomerative hierarchical clustering

   c. K-medoid

   d. K-means

5. **Which of the following method is used for finding optimal of cluster in k-means?**

   a. Elbow method

   b. Manhattan method

   c. Euclidian method

   d. All of the above

6. **K-means algorithm updates the cluster centroids during each iteration by doing what?**

    a. Computing the mean of all observations in each cluster.

    b. Selecting the data point closest to the centroid.

    c. Merging clusters with similar centroids.

    d. Selecting the most central data point.

7. **K-means clustering optimizes cluster centroids by?**

    a. Minimizing the sum of squared distances from points to centroids

    b. assigning points to clusters based on nearest observations

    c. creating a hierarchy of clusters using distance measures

    d. finding clusters of arbitrary shapes based on density of data points

8. **What is the major issue of hierarchical clustering?**

    a. Sensitive to noise and outliers in the data.

    b. Cannot handle datasets with a large number of variables.

    c. Requires specifying the number of clusters beforehand.

    d. Has a higher computational complexity compared to other algorithms.

9. **BIRCH algorithm is which of the following?**

    a. Agglomerative clustering algorithm.

    b. Hierarchical algorithm.

    c. Hierarchical-agglomerative algorithm.

    d. Divisive.

10. **Which one is finally produced by hierarchical clustering?**

    a. Final estimate of cluster centroids

    b. Tree showing how close things are to each other

    c. Assignment of each observation to clusters

    d. None

# Answers

1. a

2. a

3. c

4. **a**

5. **a**

6. **a**

7. **a**

8. **d**

9. **c**

10. **b**

# Practice exercises

1.  Use the following dataset and complete the following exercises.

    Dataset description

    The Palmer Penguins dataset provides measurements for penguins from three species (Adélie, Chinstrap, and Gentoo) in the Palmer Archipelago, Antarctica. It includes features such as bill length, bill depth, flipper length, body mass, sex and species, offering a rich context for clustering based on biological data

    ```
    [Hint: Instruction to access data as follows

    install.packages("palmerpenguins")

    library(palmerpenguins)

    data("penguins")]
    ```

    a.  Load the dataset into R and perform an **exploratory data analysis** (**EDA**).

    b.  Compute summary statistics and visualize distributions for key features, such as bill length, bill depth, and flipper length.

    c.  Standardize the features and apply k-means clustering to segment the penguins based on their measurements. Determine the optimal number of clusters using the elbow method.

    d.  Visualize the clustering results using scatter plots of bill length vs. flipper length, colored by cluster assignments. Add cluster centroids to the plot.

    e.  Interpret the characteristics of each cluster and discuss the potential biological significance.

2.  Use the following dataset and complete the following exercises.

    Dataset description

    The air quality dataset provides daily measurements of air pollutants and meteorological variables in New York City from May to September 1973. Key variables include Ozone (ozone concentration), Solar.R (solar radiation), Wind

(wind speed), and Temp (temperature). This dataset offers an excellent opportunity to explore environmental factors affecting air quality and to practice hierarchical clustering techniques.

    a. Load the dataset into R and perform initial EDA. Handle any missing values appropriately to prepare the data for clustering.

    b. Standardize the numerical features and compute distance matrices using both Euclidean and Manhattan distances. Discuss how each distance metric influences the measurement of similarity between observations.

    c. Perform agglomerative hierarchical clustering using complete linkage for each distance metric. Generate dendrograms for each case and determine the optimal number of clusters by analyzing the dendrograms.

    d. Visualize the clusters using scatter plots of Ozone vs. Temp, with points colored according to their cluster assignments. Interpret the clustering results in terms of air quality patterns and environmental factors, and discuss any insights gained regarding the relationships among the variables.

**3.** Go through the following exercise instructions before proceeding with your analysis:

Dataset description

The mtcars dataset comprises fuel consumption and ten aspects of automobile design and performance for 32 cars. Key variables include miles per gallon (mpg), horsepower (hp), displacement (disp) and weight (wt), providing an opportunity to cluster vehicles based on performance metrics and explore patterns in automobile design.

    a. Load the dataset into R and perform an EDA.

    b. Select relevant features such as mpg, hp, disp, and wt. Standardize these features.

    c. Apply k-medoids clustering (using the PAM algorithm from the cluster package) to segment the automobiles based on the selected features. Determine the optimal number of clusters using the silhouette method.

    d. Visualize the clustering results using pairwise scatter plots, with points colored by cluster assignments. Include cluster medoids in your plots.

    e. Interpret the characteristics of each cluster and discuss potential insights for automobile classification or marketing strategies.

## Join our book's Discord space

Join the book's Discord Workspace for Latest updates, Offers, Tech happenings around the world, New Release and Sessions with the Authors:

**https://discord.bpbonline.com**

# CHAPTER 5

# Introduction to Business Intelligence

## Introduction

In the fastest-growing and data-driven business environment of the twenty-first century, organizations are constantly pursuing ways to stay ahead of their competitors to make informed decisions. By leveraging **business intelligence (BI)**, organizations can improve decision-making processes, increase operational efficiency, and gain deeper insights into customer behaviors and market trends. Real-world applications span across industries such as retail, finance, healthcare, retail, and manufacturing, demonstrating the versatility and impact of BI applications. In this chapter, we will discuss the introductory concepts of BI. Readers will be able to grasp the scope, benefits, and application of BI. Four categories of business analytics, such as descriptive, diagnostic, predictive, and prescriptive analytics, will be discussed. BI applications across the industry will be presented at the end of this chapter. This fundamental overview is designed to equip students and professionals with the knowledge and tools essential for effectively utilizing BI in diverse business contexts.

## Structure

This chapter covers the following topics:

- Business intelligence
- From data to decisions in a transforming market
- Charting the landscape of business intelligence

- Understanding descriptive, diagnostic, predictive and prescriptive analytics
- Business intelligence applications across industries
- Transforming higher education with business intelligence
- Case study

# Objectives

After going through this chapter, readers will understand the fundamental concepts, techniques, and applications of BI in general. Readers will be familiar with basic BI tools and techniques to solve real-world business problems. Opportunities and challenges associated with implementing BI solutions will be presented. After completing this chapter, readers will be able to develop a foundation in BI and its application across industries.

# Business intelligence

In today's fast-paced world, different pieces of data often come together to reveal important insights. Turning raw numbers into clear strategies helps businesses grow over time. Every piece of data contributes to smart solutions that give companies an edge. With practical analytics, complex information becomes easy to understand and helps guide better business decisions.

# From data to decisions in a transforming market

BI is the key that unlocks meaningful insights from the data. BI started with basic number crunching but has evolved into powerful tools that help businesses predict trends and make smarter decisions. Understanding how BI has evolved and its impact on today's market is essential for anyone aiming to stay ahead. The following sections take readers on a journey through the development of BI and explore its vital role in shaping the future of business.

# Revolutionizing business intelligence for strategic advantage

In today's digital era, organizations are inundated with data. Yet, raw data alone holds little value until it is transformed into actionable insights that drive strategic decisions. BI stands at the forefront of this transformation, turning scattered data into compelling narratives that empower leaders to act with confidence. BI is more than just analysis—it is the art and science of making data comprehensible. At its core, BI integrates a variety of advanced tools, technologies, and methodologies to sift through complex datasets, revealing underlying patterns and trends. This holistic process equips decision-makers with the clarity they need to steer their organizations through rapidly changing business landscapes.

The journey of BI is a story of relentless innovation. In its nascent stages, organizations relied on mechanical calculators and basic computing systems to crunch numbers. As technology progressed, the introduction of file-based systems gave way to the first management information reports. The 1970s ushered in the era of database technologies, and by the 1990s, the foundations of modern BI were laid with the advent of data warehousing and decision support systems. These early systems evolved to incorporate **Online Analytical Processing (OLAP)**, enabling multidimensional reporting and a deeper analytical reach.

Today, modern BI harnesses a suite of essential components as follows:

- **Data warehousing**: Central repositories that consolidate information from diverse sources, providing a unified platform for analysis.

- **Extract, transform, load (ETL***)*: Processes that clean, standardize, and integrate data, ensuring it is ready for insightful analysis.

- **Data mining**: Techniques that delve into large datasets to uncover hidden patterns, associations, and anomalies.

- **Dashboards and reporting**: User-friendly interfaces that convert complex data into dynamic visual stories, making insights accessible at a glance.

- **Predictive analytics**: Utilizing statistical methods and machine learning to forecast future trends based on historical data, enabling proactive business strategies.

The evolution of BI is being accelerated by rapid technological advancements and an ever-increasing influx of data. Today's BI tools, such as Tableau, Power BI, and QlikView simplify the visualization of complex data and integrate real-time analytics and predictive capabilities fueled by artificial intelligence. This convergence of technologies means that organizations can now decode patterns faster, predict future trends more accurately, and make decisions that are both timely and impactful. As we explore the world of BI, it becomes clear that this field is more than a technical function. It is a strategic imperative. Embracing BI means equipping your organization with the foresight to navigate uncertainties and seize opportunities in an increasingly data-driven global economy.

# Empowering innovation through business intelligence

BI has evolved into a strategic pillar for organizations worldwide. Driven by the surge in digital transformation and the expanding volume of big data, BI has become indispensable in shaping agile, data-driven decision-making processes. This narrative explores both the global BI market and its rapid evolution within the Indian context.

# Global perspectives

In 2023, the international BI market was valued at approximately US $29.42 billion and is forecasted to nearly double, to US $63.76 billion, by 2032, reflecting a **compound annual growth rate (CAGR)** of around 9%. Leading the charge in innovation, North America remains the dominant market, where influential firms such as Microsoft, SAP, and Qlik are pushing the envelope. These industry leaders are integrating advanced analytics capabilities like predictive analytics, machine learning, and cloud-based solutions to deliver scalable and cost-effective insights.

# Key drivers in the global market

In today's interconnected economy, several significant trends are reshaping how businesses operate around the world. These factors influence everything from technology adoption to decision-making and strategic planning. The following key drivers illustrate the major forces behind this transformation:

- **Digital transformation**: Widespread adoption of digital technologies is reshaping entire industries.

- **Advanced analytics**: Integration of predictive and ML models is driving more informed decisions.

- **Cloud-based solutions**: Scalability and cost-efficiency are compelling businesses of all sizes to adopt these systems.

- **Crisis response**: The COVID-19 pandemic underscored the urgency for real-time data and agile strategies.

It is important to understand the momentum behind business intelligence today. The following figure illustrates the market size in USD billions from 2023 through 2034, offering insight into past performance and future growth potential in this dynamic industry:

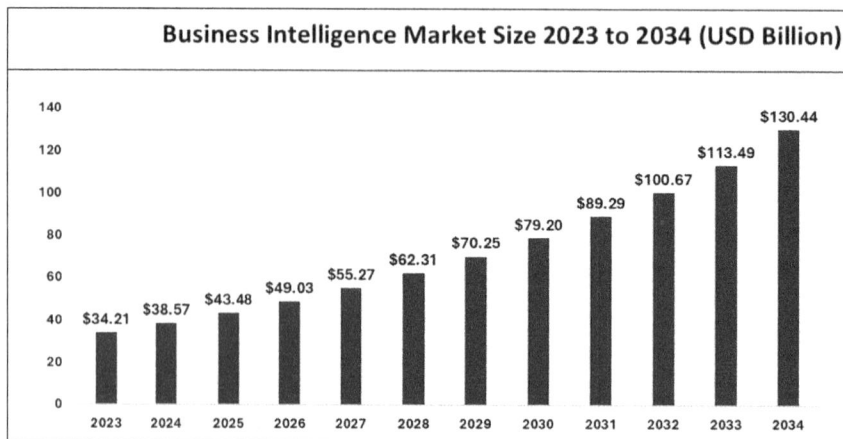

*Figure 5.1: Business Intelligence Market Size 2023 to 2034(USD Billion)*

*Source: Precedence research*

# Indian landscape

India is echoing the global BI momentum by leveraging data-driven insights to foster innovation and boost operational efficiency. The Indian BI market is projected to reach US $385.20 million in 2024, with a further rise to US $647.90 million by 2029—an indicator of a robust CAGR of nearly 11%.

Let us look at some catalysts in the Indian market:

- **Government initiatives**: Programs such as Digital India are pivotal in streamlining digital transformation and increasing BI adoption across sectors.

- **Local innovation**: Leading IT firms like **Tata Consultancy Services** (**TCS**) and Infosys are developing tailored BI solutions that directly address the unique requirements of the Indian market.

- **Enterprise innovation**: From large conglomerates to dynamic startups, Indian businesses are harnessing BI to streamline operations, enhance customer engagement, and maintain a competitive edge.

The following figure shows a bar chart displaying the BI software revenue in India measured in million USD from 2016 to 2028. It presents both historical data and future projections, offering a clear view of the market's growth trajectory. Digital transformation and an increasingly data-driven approach to decision-making are key drivers behind these trends:

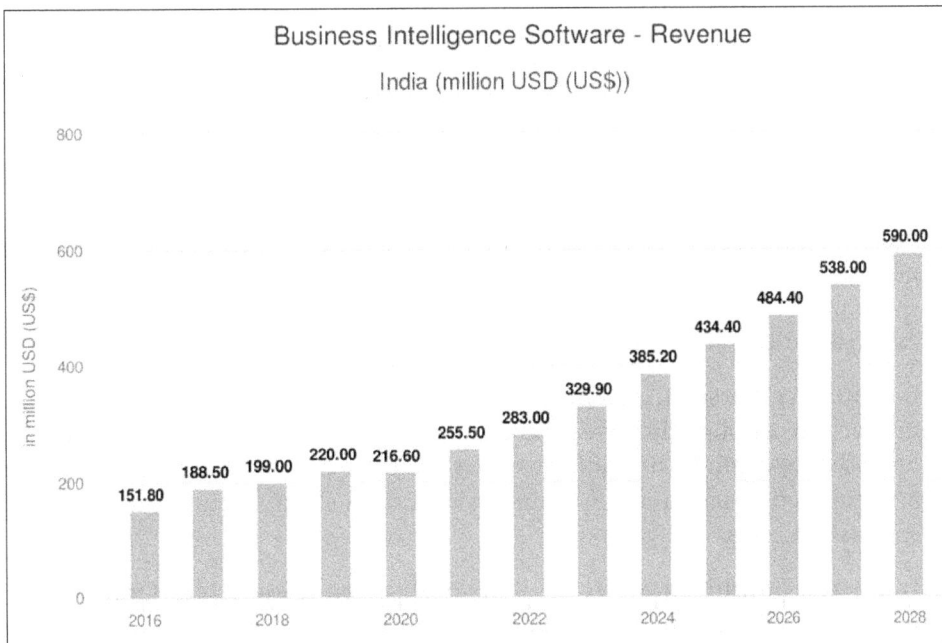

*Figure 5.2*: *BI Software Market Revenue*
*Reference: Statista*

# Charting the landscape of business intelligence

BI helps companies use data to make better decisions and find new opportunities. However, using BI effectively brings challenges that organizations must overcome to succeed.

# Embracing opportunities and confronting challenges

It is clear that BI is more than just a buzzword. BI is a transformative force reshaping the business world. It empowers organizations to make data-driven decisions and uncovers hidden market opportunities. BI plays a pivotal role in steering companies toward success, and its implementation is not without hurdles. The following sections explore how BI's vast scope offers immense benefits and the unique challenges businesses must navigate to stay ahead.

# Scope and benefits

Across industries, BI tools are transforming the way companies operate by fostering a data-centric culture and empowering informed decision-making through the following ways:

- **Retail innovation**: Retailers use BI to analyze sales trends and customer behavior, gaining deep insights into repeat purchase patterns and seasonal preferences. With these insights, they can optimize inventory, customize promotions, and strategically time marketing campaigns—resulting in increased sales and minimized surplus stock.

- **Financial efficiency**: Financial institutions leverage BI to monitor and analyze key performance indicators. By identifying cost drivers through expenditure analysis, companies can negotiate better terms with suppliers and refine operational expenses, ultimately boosting profitability and fiscal performance.

- **E-commerce personalization**: Online businesses rely on BI to decode customer interactions through clickstream analysis. By understanding browsing and purchase histories, e-commerce platforms can deliver personalized recommendations and tailored promotions that enhance customer satisfaction and drive higher conversion rates.

- **Industrial optimization**: In the industrial sector, leaders like Tata Steel harness BI to streamline production and supply chain operations. Continuous monitoring of production data helps identify inefficiencies and schedule timely maintenance, reducing downtime and boosting productivity. Likewise, companies such as

Amazon use real-time insights to refine their marketing strategies and elevate the overall customer experience.

This refined perspective on BI demonstrates not only its capacity to drive operational excellence but also its powerful role in shaping competitive strategies across a diverse range of industries.

# Challenges in implementing business intelligence

While BI offers transformative benefits, its widespread adoption is impeded by several persistent challenges:

- **Complex analytics**: Organizations face difficulties when integrating extensive data from multiple formats and sources. Even with advanced integration tools, inconsistent or poor-quality data can lead to misleading insights, complicating the analysis process.

- **Limited user adoption**: Many BI platforms are not designed with user experience at the forefront, resulting in a steep learning curve and low engagement from staff. When employees find the tools cumbersome or unintuitive, valuable insights remain underutilized.

- **Ineffective data visualization**: Even the most robust analytics can fall short if insights are not communicated effectively. Overly complex or poorly designed dashboards can obscure key trends, making it challenging for decision-makers to quickly grasp critical information.

- **Challenges in cultivating a data-driven culture**: Successful BI initiatives require more than just technology; they demand a shift in organizational mindset. Building a data-driven culture is difficult without strong leadership, effective change management, and comprehensive training. Resistance from employees and a lack of alignment between data practices and business objectives can stymie progress.

- **Management of self-service BI**: Self-service BI tools empower employees to explore data independently, but without proper governance and oversight, they can lead to fragmented efforts. This misalignment may result in information silos, where different teams generate inconsistent analyses that hinder cohesive decision-making.

- **Shortage of skilled manpower**: The rapid evolution of BI technologies has outpaced the availability of professionals with the necessary analytical and technical skills. This talent shortage poses a significant barrier to harnessing the full potential of BI.

- **Data silos**: When data is trapped within isolated departments or systems, organizations lose the ability to form a comprehensive view of their operations.

Breaking down these silos is essential to ensure that decision-makers have access to consistent and integrated information across the organization:

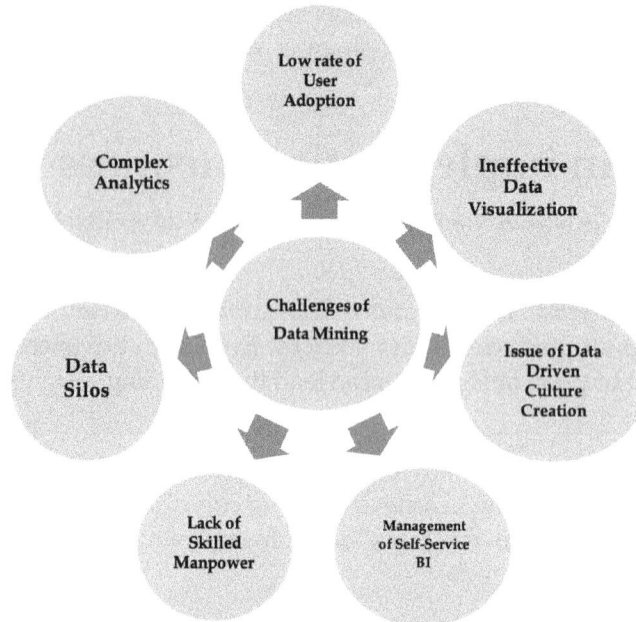

*Figure 5.3*: *Challenges of BI*

# Understanding descriptive, diagnostic, predictive and prescriptive analytics

Transforming data into actionable insights goes beyond mere technical tasks. It involves understanding and interpreting information from different angles. Descriptive, diagnostic, predictive, and prescriptive analytics each offer a unique perspective on data. They enable firms to see what happened, understand why it happened, predict what may happen next and determine the best recommended actions to take. Grasping the following four types of analytics is crucial for fully leveraging business intelligence:

## Descriptive analytics

Descriptive analytics is at the heart of data-driven decision-making. It provides a clear understanding of past business events by answering the pivotal question, *What happened*? This field harnesses both historical and current data to extract insights and serves as the foundation for strategic decision-making and operational improvement. By leveraging techniques such as EDA, data visualization, data aggregation, and comprehensive reporting, organizations can distill intelligence that drives strategic decisions and boosts overall performance.

At its core, descriptive analytics unfolds through the following key stages:

- **Data collection**: Gathers relevant information in a systematic manner.

- **Data cleaning**: Ensures accuracy and high quality of the data.

- **Data aggregation**: Compiles diverse data sources into a coherent format.

- **Data visualization**: Transforms raw data into clear, intuitive graphics that ease interpretation.

This structured approach empowers businesses to refine policies, streamline operations, and enhance customer satisfaction. Industries ranging from retail, healthcare, marketing, finance, and manufacturing increasingly adopt descriptive analytics as a means to drive sustainable growth and elevate operational efficiency. Modern advancements in technology have transformed the landscape of descriptive analytics. Emerging tools such as artificial intelligence and machine learning automate tasks like data cleaning and dynamic visualization. This evolution accelerates the analysis process and sharpens the ability to detect significant trends. When descriptive insights are integrated with predictive and prescriptive models, organizations obtain a comprehensive analytics strategy that bridges historical data with future possibilities and enables proactive, adaptable decision-making.

For example, in India, *Apollo Hospitals* employs descriptive analytics as a critical tool for monitoring and reducing hospital-acquired infections. By analyzing data on infection rates, demographic profiles and treatment outcomes, the institution discerns patterns that inform proactive infection control strategies. This approach improves patient care and contributes to broader efforts in shaping effective healthcare practices.

In summary, by blending historical insights with current data and advanced analytical techniques, descriptive analytics establishes a cornerstone for successful business strategy. It converts raw data into meaningful narratives that drive growth, operational excellence and customer satisfaction, ensuring organizations remain agile and competitive in today's dynamic environment.

# Uncovering business performance with diagnostic analytics

Diagnostic analytics goes beyond merely stating what occurred. It delves into the underlying logic behind business events and answers the pivotal question *Why did it happen?* By harnessing historical data alongside current operational insights, diagnostic analytics lays the groundwork for data-driven decision making and operational refinement. Techniques such as anomaly detection, root cause analysis, and holistic reporting empower organizations to unravel the root causes behind operational challenges and strategic shifts.

At its core, diagnostic analytics unfolds through several key stages:

- **Data assessment**: Systematically reviewing historical records and current metrics to identify anomalies and deviations from expected trends.

- **Anomaly detection**: Spotting irregularities in data, whether in performance metrics, customer behavior, or operational statistics, that signal underlying issues.

- **Root cause analysis**: Drilling into the identified anomalies to uncover the fundamental drivers that prompted the deviation.

- **Integrated synthesis**: Merging insights from various sources, such as customer feedback, market trends, and internal performance metrics, to construct a comprehensive narrative of the event.

This structured approach facilitates organizations to pinpoint inefficiencies, correct course and enhance overall performance. Industries ranging from retail and healthcare to manufacturing and finance increasingly rely on diagnostic analytics to ground their strategic discussions in robust and actionable data.

Modern advancements have transformed this discipline considerably. Real time data streaming, cloud-based dashboards and AI-powered analysis tools now boost processes, such as data collection, cleaning, and visualization. These innovations speed up the journey from data to insight and sharpen the precision of root cause determinations. When diagnostic insights are integrated with predictive and prescriptive models, businesses achieve an analytics strategy that not only understands the past but also anticipates future challenges and opportunities.

For example, in India's dynamic retail landscape, *Reliance Retail* employs diagnostic analytics to monitor inventory performance and assess the effectiveness of marketing campaigns. By integrating historical sales data with current customer behavior and seasonal trend analysis, the company can quickly determine why certain products underperform and which campaigns require recalibration. This targeted approach allows Reliance Retail to optimize inventory levels, avoid stockouts and fine tune promotional strategies, thereby enhancing customer satisfaction and driving sustainable growth.

In summary, by converting historical and real-time data into meaningful insights on why events unfold in particular ways, diagnostic analytics provides a critical foundation for effective business strategy. Its evolving integration with AI and cloud technologies ensures that organizations can remain agile, proactive and continuously oriented toward improvement in today's competitive environment. For further context and a deeper exploration of diagnostic analytics alongside descriptive techniques, consider how these two disciplines complement each other by providing a full spectrum of insights from *What happened* to *why it happened* and even *what should be done next*.

# Harnessing predictive analytics for future business insights

Predictive analytics is a powerful tool that transforms historical data into insights that forecast future trends. It has revolutionized the way organizations operate by providing valuable foresight that drives decision making across various functional areas. Key models within predictive analytics include regression models, classification models, clustering methods, and time series analysis. Each model offers distinct advantages and is selected based on the nature of the data being analyzed.

At its core, predictive analytics unfolds through several key components:

- **Regression analysis**: This technique is used to identify relationships between variables and predict continuous outcomes.

- **Classification techniques**: This technique is employed to categorize data into predefined groups.

- **Clustering methods**: This method groups similar data points together based on shared characteristics.

- **Time series analysis**: This technique analyzes data collected over time to forecast future values.

Modern predictive analytics has made its mark in a variety of industries. For example, in the streaming service sector, *Netflix* uses predictive analytics to recommend movies and television shows to its viewers by analyzing individual viewing histories and ratings. This approach enhances the viewing experience and drives higher engagement and customer loyalty. Similarly, companies like *General Electric* leverage predictive analytics for equipment maintenance by analyzing sensor data to anticipate potential failures. This proactive method reduces downtime, minimizes maintenance costs, and extends the lifespan of essential machinery. In the financial sector, institutions such as the *State Bank of India* utilize predictive analytics models to assess customer credit risk. By evaluating factors such as credit scores, payment histories, and account balances, the bank can estimate the likelihood of default and make informed decisions regarding loan approvals while mitigating risk.

By combining historical data with sophisticated models, predictive analytics empowers organizations to anticipate future trends and make proactive decisions. Its application across diverse sectors, from personalized content recommendations to predictive maintenance and credit risk management, is transforming business operations and driving efficiency and innovation. For further exploration, consider how the integration of predictive analytics with real-time data and emerging artificial intelligence techniques is opening new avenues for forecasting and strategic planning in today's rapidly evolving business landscape.

# Empowering decision making with prescriptive analytics

In today's rapidly changing data landscape, prescriptive analytics emerges as a dynamic tool that diagnoses problems and forecasts future outcomes to actively guide organizations toward optimal decision making. It goes beyond mere observation and synthesizes abundant data using sophisticated algorithms to recommend the best course of action. Rather than focusing only on past events or future predictions, it guides us in choosing the most effective next steps. Prescriptive analytics operates at the intersection of data and decision making by incorporating models from fields such as operations research and artificial intelligence to analyze complex situations and provide recommendations that are data-driven and contextually relevant. This approach uses historical data, real-time inputs, and algorithmic calculations to assess a wide range of possible scenarios. Its ultimate objective is to suggest the most effective actions based on an organization's objective.

Key applications of prescriptive analytics exist in several sectors, like the following:

- **Personalized customer experiences**: Companies use prescriptive analytics to deliver customized recommendations that match individual consumer preferences. For example, streaming services use viewing histories and user ratings to suggest content that enhances engagement and builds customer loyalty.

- **Predictive maintenance**: Organizations in the maintenance sector examine equipment performance data and operational conditions to anticipate potential machine failures. This proactive method allows for scheduling maintenance at the most appropriate times to reduce costs and ensure smooth operations.

- **Supply chain and logistics**: By analyzing logistics data traffic patterns and market trends, companies optimize inventory levels delivery routing, and resource allocation. Dynamic pricing models adjust prices in real time based on demand, competition, and market conditions to maximize profitability and create a competitive advantage.

- **Financial risk management and portfolio optimization**: Financial institutions analyze vast data sets to recommend investment strategies that balance risk and return. This approach helps in making informed decisions regarding asset allocation while dynamically adjusting investment portfolios in response to market fluctuations.

- **Healthcare improvement**: Healthcare providers leverage patient data, treatment outcomes, and clinical guidelines to develop personalized treatment plans that improve patient outcomes and promote cost-effective care.

A recent use case in the consumer goods sector involves large companies refining their marketing campaigns through prescriptive analytics. By analyzing comprehensive customer data, behavior patterns, sales histories, and current market trends, these companies design targeted marketing strategies for different customer segments. The prescriptive analytics approach identifies the most effective marketing channels and messaging tactics to ensure each campaign resonates with its intended audience. This strategy enhances campaign impact and drives significant sales growth. As organizations increasingly adopt prescriptive methodologies, the evolution from mere observational analysis to proactive decision support marks a fundamental shift in the way data is utilized. Companies can navigate complex challenges confidently by basing their decisions on rigorous data insights. The result is enhanced performance and sustained competitiveness across industries.

Prescriptive analytics forms a foundation for modern data-driven decision making. Its power lies in converting vast streams of data into clear guidance for strategic planning. As businesses continue to innovate and integrate real-time data and emerging artificial intelligence techniques, the future of decision-making promises to be more agile, informed, and responsive to the dynamics of an ever-evolving marketplace.

The four types of analytics are presented in *Table 5.1*. The table briefly describes their objective, techniques, tools, and snapshot of short examples to grasp a quick idea for readers:

| Type | Key question | Objective | Technique | Tools | Applications |
|---|---|---|---|---|---|
| Descriptive | What happened? | Summarization of past and current events | Data summarization, aggregation, data visualization, visualization and reporting dashboards | Microsoft Excel, Power BI, Tableau, Qlik, Google Data Studio, Python, R and SAS | Descriptive analytics can track business metrics and key performance indicators to get a clarity of the business heath of organizations |
| Diagnostics | Why did it happen? | Understanding the causes | Causal analysis, drill down, data discovery, drill-down analysis, data discovery and correlation analysis | Power BI, Tableau, SA, Qlik, R and Python | Diagnostics analytics find out the root cause of customer attrition and enhances customer retention plans |
| Predictive | What will happen? | Forecasting future outcomes | statistical modelling, regression analysis, time series modelling and machine learning | KNIME, RapidMiner, IBM SPSS, Orange datamining tool and Azure Machine Learning | Predictive analytics forecast demand of customers to optimize inventory level and enhance satisfaction of customers |

| Type | Key question | Objective | Technique | Tools | Applications |
|---|---|---|---|---|---|
| Prescriptive | What do we want to make happen? | Recommendation of actions | Scenarios analysis, optimization models and decision trees and simulation models | KNIME, MATLAB, AnyLogic, Gurobi and Alteryx | Recommendation of optimal pricing strategy to maximize profits while considering constraints like production costs, level of inventory and market conditions |

*Table 5.1: Overview of types of analytics*

Let us also go through the following case let to get a holistic idea about all the categories of analytics discussed previously.

# Case let

*IntelliMart* is a retail giant with chains over 150 locations across India. It is planning to improve its performance by leveraging business analytics across various domains. This case explores how *IntelliMart* uses descriptive, predictive, diagnostic, and prescriptive analytics to augment its operations:

- Descriptive analytics:

    **Objective:** Comprehend past sales performance and behavior of customers

    Analysis:

    - **Sales data**: Total sales of INR 400 million during the last festive season.
    - **Customer demographics**: 55% of customers aged 25-45, 45% of sales from online purchases.
    - **Popular products**: Electronics (30% of sales), Apparel (25%), Groceries (20%).

- Predictive analytics:

    **Objective:** Predict future sales and demand of customers

    Forecasting:

    - **Historical sales growth**: Average 8.5 % annual growth in the past three years.
    - **Market trends**: Increasing demand for smart home devices.
    - **Sales forecast**: Projected 12% increase in sales during the upcoming festive season, with a 15 % growth in online sales.

- Diagnostic analytics

    **Objective:** Identify reasons behind declining sales in certain stores.

    Data and analysis:

    - **Store performance**: Twelve stores in urban areas showed an 8% decline in sales.

    - **Customer feedback**: Common complaints about product availability and checkout times.

    - **Inventory records**: Frequent stockouts of popular items in underperforming stores.

    - **Root cause**: High competition, inventory management issues, and long checkout times.

- Prescriptive analytics

    **Objective:** Develop business plans to address identified issues and optimize operations.

    Recommendations:

    - **Targeted marketing**: Implement campaigns in urban areas, leveraging social media and local advertising.

    - **Inventory management**: Integrate automated replenishment systems to reduce stockouts.

    - **Checkout process improvement**: Introduce self-checkout kiosks and mobile payment options.

**Results**: 9% increase in overall sales, 20% reduction in customer complaints, and 28 % reduction in stockouts within six months.

# Business intelligence applications across industries

BI is a game changer across industries. In retail, BI is reshaping customer experiences and optimizing inventory management. Airlines are soaring to new heights with data-driven route planning and enhanced customer service. Agriculture is leveraging BI to become smarter and more efficient to boost yields and managing resources sustainably. In pharmaceuticals, it is accelerating research and improving patient care. The media and entertainment sector are tapping into BI to understand audience preferences and customize content effectively. Finally, education is innovating teaching methods and improving student outcomes through data insights.

# Business intelligence applications in the retail sector

The retail industry uses BI tools to boost sales, manage inventory, and gain a competitive edge through decisions based on data and customer satisfaction. Interactive reports and dashboards simplify complex data so that firms can easily track key performance indicators, trends, and metrics. For example, an Indian leather company, *Clarks India*, offers a wide range of products for children, men, and women. For men, it provides casual, formal shoes and sandals. For women, it offers heels, sandals, and ballerinas, while for children, it supplies casual shoes, bags, and school shoes. The company also produces custom offerings based on customer demand and seasonal collections. Clarks India applies BI across its operations, spanning design, production, sales, and customer service. Past data on customer preferences and seasonal trends help shape marketing campaigns for products like sandals. Likewise, sales history and customer reviews are carefully analyzed to refine the quality and design of heels.

Another example is *Reliance Digital*, which uses BI to analyze customer purchase data to understand preferences and trends. BI tools enable the segmentation of customers based on purchasing behavior, demographics, and tastes. This approach supports personalized campaigns and promotional efforts for long-term retention. Real time monitoring of inventory levels and demand forecasting minimizes stockouts and reduces carrying costs. In addition, dynamic pricing plans are implemented in real time by using data on competitor pricing, market demand, and customer preferences. BI also identifies fast-moving and slow-moving products along with top customers and best-performing suppliers. Finally, through analysis of customer feedback helps pinpoint weak areas so that product quality and service can be continuously improved.

# Analysis of business intelligence's impact on the airline industry

BI tools are fundamentally reshaping airline operations by enhancing efficiency, improving customer experience, and driving profitability. Operating in a market with volatile demand, unpredictable fuel costs, and strict operational constraints, airlines increasingly rely on BI to navigate these challenges. A prime example is *Indigo Airlines*, which has embraced BI to optimize its operations on multiple fronts.

One notable innovation is the implementation of a real-time dynamic pricing mechanism. By analyzing historical ticket data, competitor pricing, and customer behavior, *Indigo* adjusts fares in response to market conditions. This strategy not only maximizes revenue but also ensures competitive rates for customers.

Furthermore, BI dashboards play a critical role in monitoring operational performance. Real-time insights into crew management, maintenance scheduling, and flight operations enable the swift identification and resolution of inefficiencies, significantly reducing turnaround times. Additionally, targeted BI analytics help pinpoint delays in processes like baggage handling and boarding, allowing for prompt corrective actions.

Customer feedback is another area where BI tools prove invaluable. Through sentiment analysis of data gathered from sources such as social media, Indigo can proactively address customer concerns, fostering loyalty and enhancing satisfaction. Real-time integration with flight tracking APIs further allows the airline to monitor operational conditions, reducing cancellations and delays. Moreover, continuous sensor monitoring feeds into predictive maintenance models that preemptively flag potential issues, ensuring safety and minimizing downtime.

Indigo's migration of core systems to cloud platforms, supported by a hybrid infrastructure, has enhanced data processing and scalability. The creation of a dedicated BI center reinforces a data-driven culture by ensuring that timely insights reach decision makers across the organization. This strategic deployment of BI not only solidifies *Indigo's* leadership in the low-cost carrier segment but also exemplifies how evolving data technologies can shape the future of aviation.

# Business intelligence in agriculture

The agriculture sector is undergoing a transformation driven by the integration of BI tools. Advances in technology, such as drones and sensors, have enabled the continuous collection of data on environmental conditions and crop health. BI systems analyse this information and convert it into actionable insights that empower farmers to boost productivity and reduce waste.

Farmers use these insights to optimize resource allocation and refine farming practices. Through advanced data analysis, BI helps monitor soil conditions, water usage, and pest management. Predictive analytics compares historical climate data with current trends to forecast future yields accurately. This predictive power is essential for anticipating challenges such as weather fluctuations and soil degradation while planning effective interventions.

Several applications tailored for the agricultural landscape demonstrate the impact of BI. Platforms that assess product quality help farmers improve their offerings and secure better market prices. Other solutions offer marketplaces for comparing farm equipment, as well as consultancy services on soil evaluation and yield prediction. Interactive reports and real time dashboards simplify complex data so that farmers can make informed decisions regarding crop selection and irrigation strategies.

Overall, the adoption of BI not only improves current operations but also enables long-term strategic planning. With continuous monitoring and data analytics guiding resource management and decision-making, the agriculture sector is poised for more sustainable and profitable growth.

# Transforming pharmaceutical practices through business intelligence

A transformative change is underway in the pharmaceutical industry as companies adopt BI tools to convert large volumes of raw data into practical insights. In a field that demands adherence to complex regulatory frameworks and quick decision making, BI solutions are essential for supporting drug development, ensuring regulatory compliance, and optimizing supply chain operations.

Pharmaceutical organizations use BI to analyze data from clinical trials, research findings, and patient records. This analysis helps identify promising compounds and makes it possible to reduce the time and cost of bringing new drugs to market. Companies such as *Novartis, Roche,* and *Pfizer* use BI to support drug discovery and to monitor risks related to compliance with industry standards.

These tools also support safety and regulatory efforts. For example, data from clinical trials and manufacturing processes are continuously monitored to detect deviations from required guidelines. This real time review enables companies to take immediate corrective measures and generate comprehensive reports that reassure regulators and protect patient safety.

BI further assists in refining marketing strategies. By examining prescribing patterns and patient demographics, companies like *Johnson and Johnson* can focus their campaigns on areas with high demand. In addition, BI plays a critical role in managing inventory. Firms such as *Sun Pharmaceutical Industries* analyse inventory levels, supplier performance, and market demand to ensure the right balance of raw materials and finished products while reducing waste.

In clinical trials, continuous analysis of patient responses helps researchers detect side effects early and adjust dosages as needed. This proactive monitoring leads to safer trials and faster development of new drugs. Overall, BI is reshaping pharmaceutical practices by improving operational efficiency and ultimately enhancing patient outcomes.

# Transforming media and entertainment practices through BI

A transformative change is underway in the media and entertainment arena as organizations embrace BI tools to convert large volumes of raw data into actionable insights. In an industry marked by rapid technological evolution, fluctuating consumer preferences, and cutthroat global competition, BI solutions are essential for decoding audience behavior, optimizing content distribution strategies, and elevating engagement.

Media companies now harness BI to analyze data from diverse sources, such as social media interactions, online surveys and digital consumption patterns. This analytical effort provides a granular understanding of viewer demographics to enable organizations to tailor content and marketing approaches that resonate with their target audiences.

An illustrative example can be seen in the approach of platforms like *Hotstar*. By analyzing detailed viewer behavior, these platforms can identify the content that strikes a chord with varied audience segments. Such insights not only guide content curation but also refine marketing campaigns and power personalized recommendation systems that strengthen customer loyalty.

BI tools also empower media organizations to stay ahead in a swiftly shifting landscape. Continuous monitoring of real time data, including viewership metrics, social media feedback, and online reviews, allows companies to pinpoint emerging trends early and adjust their strategies accordingly. This proactive stance minimizes reaction delays and helps maintain relevance in a market where audience tastes can change overnight.

In addition to content strategy, BI plays a pivotal role in optimizing distribution. By examining region-specific viewership patterns and platform performance, media firms can schedule releases and promotions with precision. This targeted approach ensures that high-quality content reaches the right viewers at the optimal time, thereby enhancing both engagement and operational efficiency.

Moreover, BI enhances customer engagement through personalization. By mining individual viewing histories and consumption patterns, organizations can design personalized content suggestions that greatly elevate the overall user experience. This tailored approach deepens viewer loyalty and drives sustained subscription growth and overall audience satisfaction.

BI further supports revenue optimization by offering deep insights into subscription trends, advertising performance, and pricing models. Media organizations can evaluate the impact of various pricing strategies and promotional campaigns, ensuring that price points remain competitive while maximizing profit margins in a crowded marketplace.

On the whole, BI is reshaping media and entertainment practices by bridging creative vision with data-driven decision-making. By unlocking actionable insights and fostering agile responses to market dynamics, BI is setting the stage for sustained innovation and operational excellence across the industry.

# Transforming higher education with business intelligence

BI is reshaping higher education in India by delivering actionable insights that enhance decision-making and strategic planning. BI tools compile and analyze data, such as student grades, attendance, and participation to reveal performance trends and highlight areas for improvement. Educators use these insights to tailor their teaching methods and bolster academic achievement. Enrollment management benefits from BI as institutions can predict trends and plan resource allocation and marketing strategies effectively. Analysis of data related to classroom usage, faculty performance, and equipment utilization ensures that resources are deployed in the most efficient manner.

A standout example is the *Indian Institute of Management, Bangalore*. The institute employs BI tools to gain a deep understanding of student performance, enabling professors to identify areas where additional support is needed. BI systems also help forecast future enrollment trends and optimize resource allocation across classrooms, faculty, and facilities. In addition, the institute uses data insights to implement targeted interventions that boost student retention. Curriculum development is continuously refined by assessing course outcomes against student feedback and industry trends, ensuring that the curriculum remains current and competitive.

Beyond academic performance, BI also facilitates a comprehensive review of institutional operations. As more educational institutions adopt these technologies, the higher education sector is poised to benefit from improved decision making, more efficient resource management and enhanced student outcomes, paving the way for a data driven future in education.

# Case study

This case study analyses how the mid-sized retail chain *Hemalata Retail Dynamics* leveraged BI to transform raw data into strategic decisions. The company operates in key urban centers in India, including Mumbai, New Delhi, and Chennai, and is expanding its presence throughout the Asian subcontinent. Their journey, detailed as follows, offers valuable insights for businesses seeking to harness data for growth and innovation:

- **Evolving from data to decision***s*: Hemalata Retail Dynamics has long been a trusted name in urban retail. As India's digital revolution gains momentum and e-commerce competition intensifies, traditional decision-making methods are simply no longer enough to meet today's challenges. The company launched a digital transformation initiative to harness BI in a rapidly evolving market. Data, once scattered across sales records, inventory systems, and customer feedback channels, delayed timely decision-making. Increased mobile technology use and widespread internet access created a dynamic consumer landscape that demanded agile responses. Additionally, reliance on outdated legacy systems and inconsistent data practices underscored the need for a unified BI platform. By overcoming these challenges, Hemalata Retail Dynamics turned obstacles into opportunities and established BI as the foundation of its business strategy.

- **Charting the BI transformation**: The company aligned its BI initiatives with clear business objectives. Metrics such as daily sales, customer engagement and inventory turnover were customized to capture local market nuances. A robust data warehouse was deployed to consolidate information from both brick-and-mortar outlets and emerging e-commerce channels. This centralized repository streamlined data aggregation and provided real-time insights, empowering the organization to make better operational and tactical decisions.

Comprehensive training programs for store managers, regional supervisors and IT professionals bridged the gap between advanced analytics and day-to-day operations. These initiatives fostered a culture that values data-driven insights across the organization. Integrated BI dashboards offered immediate visibility into operations. Real-time data enabled leaders to detect trends and anomalies swiftly, adjust strategies, and optimize processes. Advanced analytics further supported the development of targeted marketing campaigns, improved forecasting, and enhanced inventory management. As a result, the company achieved both operational efficiency and long-term sustainable growth.

Challenges in this transformation included integrating modern BI technologies with legacy systems. This process required careful technical planning to manage complex data streams and ensure smooth interoperability. Shifting to a digital-first mindset required a cultural evolution, with employees moving from traditional practices to innovative methodologies supported by structured change management and continuous skill development. In addition, ongoing investments in training and technology were essential to maintain data security, protect privacy and comply with complex regulatory environments throughout Asia.

- **Scope, benefits, and challenges of BI**: By consolidating operational data into a unified view, Hemalata Retail Dynamics enhanced decision-making at every level. The company achieved tangible cost savings through improved forecasting, refined inventory management, and more effective customer engagement. This data-driven approach spurred innovation and enabled rapid adaptation to shifting market trends. Integration of insights also empowered teams to develop creative strategies that further strengthened the company's competitive edge.

  However, integrating data from diverse sources posed significant technical challenges. Robust IT frameworks and continuous refinement of integration methods were crucial to managing these complexities. Regular staff training ensured that every team member, from store managers to IT professionals, could fully leverage modern analytics tools. Maintaining data security, protecting privacy, and managing information ethically were critical when navigating complex regulatory environments, underscoring the importance of proactive risk management and resilient systems.

- **Empowering action through data insights**: Hemalata Retail Dynamics built its BI strategy on four key analytical approaches:

  a. **Descriptive analytics**: Customized dashboards offered real-time insights into sales, inventory levels, and customer footfall. Interactive reports allowed management to review historical data and identify performance trends. These tools converted complex data sets into clear and accessible information, promoting transparency and continuous improvement.

b. **Diagnostic analytics**: Detailed reports enabled the team to investigate issues such as stock-outs and unexpected sales drops by uncovering their underlying causes. Comparative analysis across urban regions provided localized insights that guided targeted strategies. In-depth examinations of historical data identified supply chain inefficiencies, leading to corrective actions and long-term operational enhancements.

c. **Predictive analytics**: Time series analysis and regression models forecast future sales cycles and seasonal demand, supporting proactive measures. Predictive clustering segmented the customer base into meaningful groups to enhance marketing effectiveness. This forward-looking approach allowed Hemalata Retail Dynamics to anticipate market shifts and prepare accordingly, turning data-driven foresight into a competitive advantage.

d. **Prescriptive analytics**: Simulation models provided actionable recommendations for optimal stock management and promotional timing. Enhanced decision support tools presented various scenario-based options for decision-makers. By exploring multiple *what if* scenarios, leaders could balance risks and rewards, reducing uncertainty and translating data insights into measurable business improvements.

- **BI Applications across industries**: The journey of Hemalata Retail Dynamics exemplifies how BI can drive innovation and efficiency across different sectors in Asia.

In healthcare, hospitals and clinics use BI to optimize patient care, streamline resource allocation, and enhance service delivery. Real-time analytics enable providers to identify trends that prompt proactive intervention, reduce wait times, and improve treatment outcomes. Integrating diverse data streams refines clinical workflows, boosts efficiency, and increases patient satisfaction.

In manufacturing, factories employ predictive maintenance and operational analytics to reduce downtime and increase efficiency. Advanced sensor data and machine learning help anticipate equipment failures, ensuring timely repairs and continuous production. Real-time monitoring and integrated quality control foster innovation and elevate product quality in a competitive industrial landscape.

In financial services, banks and insurance companies use BI for risk management, fraud detection, and personalized customer service. Analysis of extensive transactional data enables early detection of anomalies and timely interventions. Enhanced insights drive the development of tailored products and services, strengthen client relationships, and support regulatory compliance through transparent audit trails and continuous monitoring.

Overall, Hemalata Retail Dynamics demonstrates that business intelligence is a versatile tool that drives innovation and operational excellence across multiple sectors.

- **Conclusion**: The transformative journey of Metro Retail Dynamics demonstrates how embracing BI can revolutionize decision-making. By shifting from fragmented data to an integrated data centric strategy, using descriptive, diagnostic, predictive and prescriptive analytics, the company enhanced operational efficiency and improved customer engagement. This case study serves as a practical roadmap for businesses in India and across Asia that aspire to build robust BI capabilities and achieve sustainable growth.

- **Questions**:
    1. What strategies did Hemalata Retail Dynamics use to overcome fragmented data challenges, and how did the centralized data warehouse turn raw data into actionable business insights?

    2. How did targeted training programs for key stakeholders foster a data-centric culture, and why is this cultural shift essential for effective BI implementation?

    3. In what ways did descriptive, diagnostic, predictive, and prescriptive analytics individually contribute to strategic decision-making and how did they work together to create a competitive advantage?

    4. How can the BI strategies demonstrated by Hemalata Retail Dynamics be adapted to drive innovation and efficiency in sectors such as healthcare, manufacturing, and financial services?

# Conclusion

In this chapter, a foundational understanding of BI was established to trace its evolution from basic data reporting to today's sophisticated analytical systems that drive strategic decision-making. BI has significant importance and a wide scope. It offers benefits such as enhanced operational efficiency, improved customer insights, and the identification of new business opportunities. However, organizations may face challenges in implementation, such as data integration issues and cultural adaptation. An examination of the different types of analytics, such as descriptive, diagnostic, predictive, and prescriptive, provided insights into how each uniquely contributes to a comprehensive BI strategy. This demonstrates how businesses analyze past performances, uncover root causes of trends, forecast future events and recommend actionable strategies. By presenting applications of BI across various industries, the chapter demonstrated its versatility and impact on sectors like retail, healthcare, finance, and manufacturing, showcasing how BI tools address industry-specific challenges and facilitate informed decision-making. Equipped with this foundational knowledge, readers are now prepared to delve into the architectural aspects of BI systems in the next chapter, which will explore key concepts such as slicing, dicing, and pivoting and introduce Power BI, guiding through data modeling and the creation of interactive dashboards to effectively apply BI techniques and visualize data in support of strategic objectives.

# Multiple choice questions

1. **What fundamentally sets BI apart from traditional data reporting methods?**
   a. BI focuses exclusively on generating financial reports for large corporations.
   b. BI combines historical data analysis with predictive and prescriptive insights to support strategic decision-making.
   c. BI only processes real-time data without utilizing historical information.
   d. BI is limited to descriptive analytics and does not include advanced analytical techniques.

2. **Which of the following is not a typical benefit associated with implementing BI solutions in an organization?**
   a. Enhanced decision-making capabilities based on data-driven insights.
   b. Improved operational efficiency through process optimization.
   c. Automatic guarantee of increased profits without further strategic initiatives.
   d. Identification of new business opportunities through data analysis.

3. **In the retail industry, which of the following is a common application of prescriptive analytics within BI?**
   a. Generating detailed reports of past sales performance.
   b. Analyzing customer feedback to determine causes of reduced satisfaction.
   c. Forecasting future inventory requirements based on sales trends.
   d. Recommending optimal product placement and promotional strategies to maximize sales.

4. **What is one of the main challenges businesses face when implementing BI solutions?**
   a. Lack of data availability.
   b. Integrating BI tools with existing systems.
   c. Excessive initial cost.
   d. Overabundance of skilled personnel.

5. **Which type of analytics is most critical for providing actionable recommendations for immediate decision-making in complex business scenarios?**
   a. Descriptive analytics
   b. Diagnostic analytics
   c. Predictive analytics
   d. Prescriptive analytics

6. **In the context of BI, what is an OLAP cube used for?**

   a. To store massive amounts of unstructured data.

   b. To enable fast analysis of data from multiple perspectives.

   c. To perform real-time data processing.

   d. To visualize data through infographics.

7. **Which of the following is a significant trend in the BI market?**

   a. Decreasing interest in cloud-based BI solutions.

   b. Increased focus on real-time analytics and data streaming.

   c. Reduction in the use of artificial intelligence in BI.

   d. Decline in the adoption of self-service BI tools.

8. **In predictive analytics within BI, which technique is commonly used to identify patterns and make forecasts based on historical data?**

   a. Data cleansing

   b. Regression analysis

   c. Data encryption

   d. Cluster sampling

9. **What is a key advantage of utilizing cloud-based BI solutions compared to traditional on-premises systems?**

   a. Greater customization options due to dedicated in-house hardware.

   b. Enhanced flexibility and scalability to adjust resources according to demand.

   c. Increased control over data security and compliance measures.

   d. Simplified implementation process due to existing infrastructure.

10. **In which scenario would a company most appropriately employ diagnostic analytics as part of their BI strategy?**

    a. To predict customer purchasing trends for the next fiscal year.

    b. To determine the underlying causes of a sudden drop in product quality ratings.

    c. To develop a strategic plan for entering new markets.

    d. To provide a summary of annual financial performance to investors.

# Answers

1. b

2. c

3. d

4. b

5. d

6. b

7. b

8. b

9. b

10. b

# Practice exercises

1. A retail chain company experiences fluctuating sales throughout the year and wants to optimize inventory levels to meet customer demand without overstocking. How can this company apply descriptive, diagnostic, predictive and prescriptive analytics to address their inventory challenges? Briefly explain each type of analytics in the context of this scenario.

2. An online streaming service firm has amassed a large amount of user data but struggles to increase user engagement and retention. Identify the benefits and challenges the firm might encounter when implementing a BI solution. What strategies can they use to leverage BI for improving user experience?

3. A manufacturing company operates multiple factories and seeks to improve its supply chain efficiency and reduce operational costs. Explain how BI applications can help this company optimize its supply chain management. What key factors should they consider when integrating BI tools into their operations?

4. A financial institution aims to stay ahead in the competitive market by making informed decisions based on data insights. Discuss how the evolution of Business Intelligence has enabled organizations like this to boost decision-making processes. How can they utilize current BI technologies to gain a competitive advantage?

# CHAPTER 6

# Business Intelligence Architecture, Query and Reporting Practices

## Introduction

In this chapter, we will discuss the architecture of **business intelligence (BI)**, BI query tools for real-time, and ad hoc analysis. BI reporting practices will be discussed with a detailed understanding of the process, which involves collecting and interpreting data from various systems to generate insights for business decisions. The review of consolidated data, data modification, and presentation of data in user-defined report format are presented in this chapter. Data modelling and data visualization applications are explained in the last part of this chapter using Power BI.

## Structure

This chapter covers the following topics:

- Introduction to business intelligence architecture
- ETL process and data warehouse design
- OLAP and cube designs
- Data modelling applications using Power BI
- Dashboard design and data visualization using Power BI
- Case study

# Objectives

The objective of the chapter is to provide a comprehensive overview of the fundamental components and frameworks that underlie effective business intelligence systems. It aims to explore the architectural principles that guide the design and implementation of business intelligence solutions. It also delves into best practices for query generation and reporting. This chapter also aims to provide readers with an in-depth understanding of how to effectively utilize Power BI to consolidate, analyze, and visualize data. After going through the chapter, the readers will be familiar with the practical knowledge and skills necessary to leverage Power BI for data analysis. This effort will enable them to make informed and data-driven decisions through insightful reporting and visualizations.

# Introduction to business intelligence architecture

Data serves as the central nervous system that connects and integrates all sources. The strategic framework behind the raw data is the BI architecture. It transforms data into actionable insights. Gathering data is not enough; organizations need a system that organizes, analyzes, and delivers information in a meaningful way. BI Architecture is the backbone of decision-making processes. It enables efficient collection, storage, and analysis of data. Key components of BI work together to identify and integrate diverse data sources using **extract, transform and load** (**ETL**) processes to cleanse and standardize data. This architecture matters because it fuels informed decision-making, enhances operational efficiency, provides deep customer insights, and offers a competitive edge by revealing market trends and opportunities. BI Architecture has evolved with technological advancements. It has shifted from on-premises to cloud-based solutions, has embraced self-service models that empower users, and has integrated artificial intelligence and machine learning for advanced analytics. It has enabled real-time data processing to respond swiftly to market changes. However, implementing effective BI architecture comes with challenges like data silos, quality issues, scalability concerns and user adoption challenges. Best practices include defining clear objectives aligned with business goals. Ensuring data quality through rigorous cleansing is essential. Investing in user-friendly tools encourages widespread use. Prioritizing security and compliance are also important. Promoting a data-driven culture fosters collaboration between IT and business units. As firms navigate the complexities of the digital landscape, the role of BI architecture becomes ever more critical for survival in a data-centric world. It provides the roadmap for leveraging data as a strategic asset, guiding organizations toward innovation and growth. By transforming how we see data and unlocking its full potential, BI Architecture paves the way for businesses to thrive in an era where information is power.

# ETL process and data warehouse design

The ETL process is a key procedure to gather, clean, and consolidate structured data from varied sources into a data warehouse. The entire process can be divided into data extraction, data scrubbing, data transformation, and data loading. Let us go through the steps:

1. **Data extraction**: Initially, data is extracted from various sources like files, POS systems databases, and **application programming interfaces** (**API**). Data is loaded as static load and incremental load:

   a. **Static load**: The initial load where the entire dataset is extracted. This is usually a onetime process to gather all historical data. For example, extracting all customer records from a legacy system when setting up a new data warehouse.

   b. **Incremental load**: This involves extracting only the new or updated data since the last extraction. This ensures the data warehouse is up-to-date without reloading the entire dataset.

2. **Data scrubbing**: Data scrubbing or data cleansing involves detecting and correcting corrupt or inaccurate records from a dataset. It is vital to ensure data quality before further processing.

   a. **Validation and correction**: Validation involves verifying data types, formats, and completeness. Fixing errors includes correcting misspellings, filling in missing values, and removing duplicates.

3. **Data transformation, normalization and denormalization**: Transformation changes data into a format that is suitable for analysis. It involves modifying data to meet the target system's requirements. Adjusting data structures can reduce redundancy or optimize query performance. Normalization organizes data to minimize duplication, while denormalization might add duplication to improve performance. For example, splitting a full name into first and last names or combining related tables for faster querying.

   a. **Aggregation**: Summarizing detailed data. For instance, calculating total sales, average purchase values or other summary statistics.

   b. **Data enrichment**: Enriching data means making it more valuable by combining it from different sources. This can involve merging datasets, adding new calculated fields, or translating codes into more meaningful values. For example, adding demographic information to customer data can support to understand audience better. By enriching data in this way, one can gain deeper insights, make more informed decisions, and tailor strategies to meet specific needs. It is all about turning raw data into actionable knowledge that drives success.

4. **Data loading**: Loading is the final step in the ETL process, where the transformed data is moved into a data warehouse or a target system. This step must ensure data integrity and efficiency. Maintaining data integrity means the data remains accurate and clean during the loading process so that it reflects the true information without errors. Ensuring efficiency means the data is loaded in a timely manner without unnecessary use of resources. This step is vital because any problem here can compromise the entire data pipeline to affect the quality of analysis and decision-making that relies on data.

   a. **Static load**: Loading the entire dataset into the target system is typically performed once during the initial setup. This full data load initializes the system with all the necessary information to begin operations.

   b. **Incremental load**: Regularly updating the target system with new or changed data. This is done to keep the data warehouse current with minimal load time and resources. Apart from these structured steps in data reconciliation, auditing and error handling are also accomplished. Data auditing ensures the accuracy and consistency of data. Logs of data loading and transformation are maintained through logging and monitoring. All four steps of ETL process, systems failure, quality issues of data, and process failures, etc. are also validated.

# Data warehouse design

The design of the data warehouse organizes the data in a unified manner to make informed decisions. Dimensional modeling or star schema as a fundamental model is developed in this context. A star schema is a database structure where a central fact table is connected to multiple dimension tables. For example, consider a small retail chain. The sales table acts as the fact table. It is linked to dimension tables like period, store, and product. This arrangement of the fact table surrounded by dimension tables forms a star schema. The primary keys of Product, Store and Period dimension tables are Product_ID, Store_Code and Period_ID respectively. These are the foreign keys in sales fact table. Another important concept in star schema is granularity. Grain of a fact table explains the level of details. The selection of the grain depends on how much detail customers require when querying the tables. The finest grain includes detailed information of each sales transaction. So, the grain directly impacts the size of the fact table because finer grains result in larger tables. Estimation of all possible values for each dimension associated with the fact tables is required to estimate the size of the fact table. Understanding the granularity is vital because it balances the level of details with storage requirement and performance.

To make data easy to understand and analyze, it should be organized in a clear and intuitive way. The star schema offers a straightforward design that structures data for quick access and efficient querying. The following figure illustrates how a star schema or dimensional model connects different pieces of information in a simple and effective layout:

```
           Product                                                    Store
┌─────────────────────┐                                    ┌──────────────────────┐
│ Product_ID          │◄──┐                             ┌─►│ Store_Code           │
│ Prod_Description    │   │                             │  │ Store_Manager        │
│ Prod_Qty            │   │                             │  │ Store_Location       │
│ Product_Color       │   │                             │  │ Store_City           │
│ Size                │   │                             │  └──────────────────────┘
└─────────────────────┘   │                             │
                          │   Sales_Fact fact table     │
                          │ ┌─────────────────────────┐ │
                          │ │ Sales_ID                │ │
                          │ │ Store_Code     (FK)     │─┘
                          └─│ Product_ID     (FK)     │
                            │ Period_ID      (FK)     │
                         ┌──│ Sold_Qty                │
                         │  │ Cost__Rupees            │
                         │  └─────────────────────────┘
                         │
                         │         Period
                         │  ┌─────────────────────┐
                         └─►│ Period_ID           │
                            │ Year                │
                            │ Quarter             │
                            │ Month               │
                            │ Day                 │
                            └─────────────────────┘
```

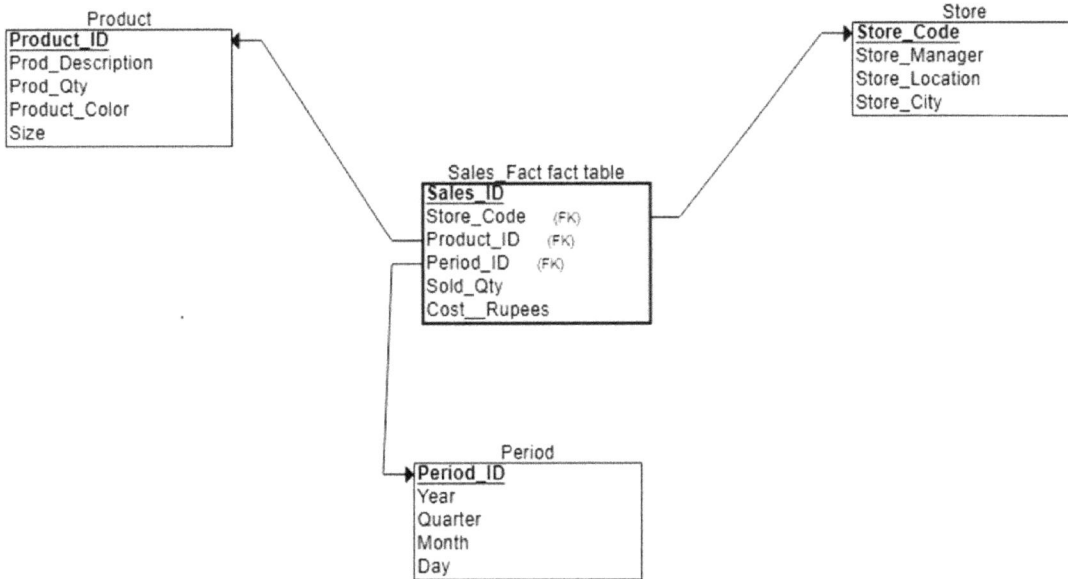

**Figure 6.1:** *Dimensional modeling*

# OLAP and cube designs

Business Intelligence systems transform raw data into actionable insights. **Online Analytical Processing (OLAP)** cubes allow users to interactively analyze multidimensional data from multiple perspectives, providing a robust framework for deep data exploration and decision support. OLAP systems enable users to perform multidimensional analysis of data, allowing them to explore data across multiple dimensions, such as time, geography, and product categories. OLAP cubes encapsulate data in a format that is optimized for query performance and allows users to retrieve and analyze data instantly and efficiently. Therefore, it is imperative for students and practitioners in the fields of business analytics, data science and information systems to comprehend the intricacies of OLAP cubes and the principles underlying their design. Now, we will understand the fundamental concepts of OLAP cubes and cube design methodologies and their roles in data analysis and reporting while providing practitioners with a structured approach to effectively architect OLAP solutions.

## Key components of OLAP

An OLAP cube is a data structure that facilitates fast and flexible data analysis. Key components of OLAP are specified as follows:

- **Dimensions**: Dimensions are groups or classes of data that end customers need to analyze. They describe the different aspects of the data. Examples can be Product, Time, Customer, Product dimensions, etc.

- **Hierarchies**: Hierarchies organize dimensions into different levels of granularity to allow users to drill down or drill up data.

  **Examples**:
    - **Time hierarchy**: Year → Quarter → Month → Day
    - **Geography hierarchy**: Country → Region → City
    - **Product hierarchy**: Category → Brand → Product Line

- **Measures**: Measures are the numerical data that users analyze within the dimensions. They represent the quantities and metrics of interest.

  **Examples**:
    - **Sales**: Total Sales, Revenue, Units Sold
    - **Finance**: Profit, Expense, Budget
    - **Inventory**: Stock Level, Reorder Quantity

- **Cubes**: A cube is a multidimensional dataset that contains dimensions, hierarchies and measures. It is the core structure for OLAP analysis.

  **Examples**:

  A sales cube that includes dimensions like Time, Geography and Product with measures like Total Sales and Profit. These components work together to enable complex, multidimensional analysis to make OLAP cubes powerful tools for business intelligence and decision support.

# Levels in OLAP hierarchies

Levels are distinct stages within a hierarchy, representing varying degrees of granularity for a particular dimension. They enable users to drill down or roll up to access data at different levels of detail. Levels are part of the hierarchical structure within dimensions that allow for detailed data analysis at different granularities.

Key points about levels

- **Hierarchies**: Dimensions are often organized into hierarchies, and levels are the building blocks of these hierarchies.

  **Example**: In a Time dimension, the hierarchy might include levels such as Year, Quarter, Month and Day.

- **Drill-down**: Moving from a higher, summarized level to a more detailed level.

- **Drill-up:** Aggregating data from a detailed level to a higher summarized level.

  **Example**: Drilling down from Year to Month and drilling up from Day to Month.

  Example of levels in a dimension hierarchy:
    - Time dimension:

- **Level 1**: Year (e.g., 2022, 2023)
- **Level 2**: Quarter (e.g., Q1, Q2)
- **Level 3**: Month (e.g., January, February)
- **Level 4**: Day (e.g., 1st, 2nd)
  - ○ Geography dimension:
    - **Level 1**: Country (e.g., USA, India)
    - **Level 2**: Region (e.g., East Coast, West Coast)
    - **Level 3**: City (e.g., New York, Los Angeles)

Levels are essential for providing the flexibility and depth required for comprehensive data analysis in OLAP systems. They empower users to view data from broad overviews down to fine details, supporting diverse analytical needs.

# OLAP operations

Let us take an example of a retail company to analyze its sales performance across product category, time and location dimensions. Say, the company deals with stores across cities of India. The company sells a wide range of products, including Organic Tea and Bread. To stay competitive, the retail company uses OLAP tools to analyze sales data and make data driven decisions.

To understand the performance of their products and stores to optimize inventory, improve sales strategies, and enhance customer satisfaction, the company will do the following:

- Analyze sales trends for specific product categories.
- Compare sales performance across different store locations.
- Identify seasonal patterns in sales.
- Gain detailed insights into daily sales trends for high-demand periods.

**Example**:

| Month | Product category | Store location | Sales (in RUPEES) |
|---|---|---|---|
| January | Organic Tea | Bhubaneswar | 150,000 |
| January | Organic Tea | Kolkata | 120,000 |
| January | Bread | Bhubaneswar | 90,000 |
| January | Bread | Kolkata | 100,000 |
| February | Organic Tea | Bhubaneswar | 130,000 |

| Month | Product category | Store location | Sales (in RUPEES) |
|---|---|---|---|
| February | Organic Tea | Kolkata | 110,000 |
| February | Bread | Bhubaneswar | 85,000 |
| February | Bread | Kolkata | 95,000 |
| March | Organic Tea | Bhubaneswar | 140,000 |
| March | Organic Tea | Kolkata | 115,000 |
| March | Bread | Bhubaneswar | 88,000 |
| March | Bread | Kolkata | 98,000 |

*Table 6.1: Real data for OLAP analysis*

# Application of OLAP operations

In the realm of business intelligence, OLAP operations are fundamental tools that empower users to perform multidimensional analysis of large datasets. These operations enable interactive exploration of data from various angles and perspectives to facilitate deeper insights and more informed decision-making processes. Before delving into specific OLAP operations such as slicing, dicing, and pivoting, it is crucial to appreciate how these techniques enhance analytical capabilities and contribute to extracting meaningful information from complex data structures:

- **Slicing:**
  - **Objective**: Analyze sales trends for Organic Tea.
  - **Operation**: GRS slices the data cube to extract sales data for the Organic Tea category across all stores and time periods.
  - **Output**:

| Month | Store location | Sales (in RUPEES) |
|---|---|---|
| January | Bhubaneswar | 150,000 |
| January | Kolkata | 120,000 |
| February | Bhubaneswar | 130,000 |
| February | Kolkata | 110,000 |
| March | Bhubaneswar | 140,000 |
| March | Kolkata | 115,000 |

*Table 6.2: Slicing operation*

- **Dicing:**
  - **Objective**: Compare sales performance for Organic Tea and Bread in Bhubaneswar and Kolkata during Q1 of 2024.
  - **Operation**: GRS dices the data cube to focus on sales data for Organic Tea and Bread categories in Bhubaneswar and Kolkata, during January to March 2024.
  - **Output**:

| Month | Product category | Store location | Sales (in Rupees) |
|---|---|---|---|
| January | Organic Tea | Bhubaneswar | 150,000 |
| January | Organic Tea | Kolkata | 120,000 |
| January | Bread | Bhubaneswar | 90,000 |
| January | Bread | Kolkata | 100,000 |
| February | Organic Tea | Bhubaneswar | 130,000 |
| February | Organic Tea | Kolkata | 110,000 |
| February | Bread | Bhubaneswar | 85,000 |
| February | Bread | Kolkata | 95,000 |
| March | Organic Tea | Bhubaneswar | 140,000 |
| March | Organic Tea | Kolkata | 115,000 |
| March | Bread | Bhubaneswar | 88,000 |
| March | Bread | Kolkata | 98,000 |

*Table 6.3: Dicing operation*

- **Pivoting**:
  - **Objective**: View sales data from different perspectives.
  - **Operation**: Pivoting the data cube transforms the view from sales by Time and Product Category to sales by Store Location and Product Category.
  - **Output**:

| Store location | Product category | Sales (in Rupees) |
|---|---|---|
| Bhubaneswar | Organic Tea | 4,20,000 |
| Bhubaneswar | Bread | 2,63,000 |
| Kolkata | Organic Tea | 3,45,000 |
| Kolkata | Bread | 2,93,000 |

*Table 6.4: Pivoting operation*

- **Drilling down**:
  - ○ **Objective**: Gain detailed insights into daily sales trends during January 2024.
  - ○ **Operation**: GRS drills down from monthly sales data to daily sales data for Organic Tea in Bhubaneswar for January 2024.
  - ○ Output (Example of daily sales for January 2024):

| Date | Sales (in RUPEES) |
|---|---|
| 2024-01-01 | 5,000 |
| 2024-01-02 | 6,000 |
| 2024-01-03 | 5,500 |
| ... | ... |
| ... | ... |
| 2024-01-31 | 4,800 |

*Table 6.5: Drilling through operation*

- **Drilling up:**
  - ○ **Objective**: Aggregate sales data to view overall monthly trends.
  - ○ **Operation**: GRS drills up from daily sales data to monthly sales data for Organic Tea in Bhubaneswar for Q1 2024.
  - ○ **Output:**

| Month | Sales (in Rupees) |
|---|---|
| January | 150,000 |
| February | 130,000 |
| March | 140,000 |

*Table 6.6: Drilling up operations*

- **Rolling up:**
  - ○ **Objective**: Aggregate data across product subcategories within Organic Tea.
  - ○ **Operation**: GRS rolls up sales data from product subcategories (e.g., green tea, black tea) to the overall Organic Tea category.
  - ○ **Output:**

| Product subcategory | Sales (in Rupees) |
|---|---|
| Green Tea | 200,000 |
| Black Tea | 150,000 |
| Herbal Tea | 170,000 |

*Table 6.7: Drilling up operations*

By leveraging OLAP operations such as slicing, dicing, pivoting, drilling down, drilling up, and rolling up, the company gains valuable insights into its sales data. These insights enable the company to make informed decisions, optimize inventory management, and develop effective sales strategies to enhance overall performance.

OLAP cubes serve as an essential component in the architecture of BI systems, enhancing querying and reporting capabilities for multidimensional data analysis. A thorough understanding of cube structures, dimensions, measures, and effective design methodologies ensures that organizations can efficiently harness their data for informed decision-making. As the complexity of data environments continues to expand, so must the sophistication of the OLAP solutions employed. Therefore, ongoing education and rigorous adherence to best practices in OLAP cube design are paramount for those committed to leveraging business intelligence effectively. OLAP cubes serve as a critical vehicle for facilitating advanced analytical capabilities within the broader framework of BI. Through systematic cube design and a deep understanding of underlying architectural principles, organizations can optimize their data environments to support informed decision-making processes. By selecting appropriate dimensions and measures, implementing hierarchies, optimizing for performance, and ensuring data integrity, businesses can harness the full potential of their data assets, leveraging OLAP for sustained competitive advantage. It is imperative that as the volume and complexity of data continue to evolve, so too must the strategies and methodologies employed in OLAP cube design, ensuring they remain relevant and robust in an increasingly data-driven landscape.

# Data modelling applications using Power BI

Power BI is a vital tool in data modeling. It provides a comprehensive set of features to structure and shape data for analysis and reporting for businesses to make informed and data-driven decisions. The Power Query Editor is a foundational component of Power BI which facilitates data transformation, cleansing, and preparation, and performs critical operations like duplicate removal, error correction, and data reconfiguration for analysis. This editor allows end users to connect to various data sources like relational databases, Excel/CSV files, cloud-based storage, and big data platforms to transform and manipulate data using an intuitive and user-friendly interface.

Power BI excels in integrating data from multiple sources and users to establish relationships between tables and enables cohesive analysis of heterogeneous data, which enhances insight interpretability and richness. This supports a unified view of data from various sources and enables organizations to gain a deeper understanding of their operations, customers and market trends. Power BI also incorporates the DAX language, which is useful for users to construct custom calculations, aggregations, and measures. DAX enables deeper analytical insights that transcend basic aggregations.

Proper data categorization and typing are essential practices in Power BI, which ensures calculation and visualization accuracy and master data modeling features like dimensional modeling and star schema principles to construct robust and efficient data models. By harnessing these capabilities, Power BI becomes an indispensable tool for data professionals, transforming raw data into actionable insights through intuitive interfaces and powerful analytical tools. The benefits of using Power BI for data modeling and analysis are numerous, including improved data accuracy, enhanced business intelligence, and faster decision-making. By leveraging Power BI's advanced features and capabilities, businesses can gain a competitive edge, drive innovation, and achieve their strategic objectives. Now, we will discuss DAX operations and Dimensional modeling using Power BI in the following discussions of data modeling.

# Introduction to Data Analysis Expressions

**Data Analysis Expressions** (**DAX**) is a powerful collection of functions, operators, and constants used in formulas or expressions to perform advanced calculations and return one or more values. DAX is primarily utilized in Power BI, Power Pivot, and SQL Server Analysis Services to enhance data modeling and reporting capabilities. It is an essential tool for data analysts and business intelligence professionals to enable them to create sophisticated data models and perform complex calculations.

DAX enables complex computations such as calculating year-to-date sales with the **TOTALYTD** function. For example, if one needs to know how much a company has sold from the start of the fiscal year until today, the **TOTALYTD** function will help to calculate this figure. This is particularly useful for tracking performance over time and making informed business decisions.

DAX also allows for custom aggregations. You can create measures that sum sales for specific products using the **CALCULATE** and **FILTER** functions. For instance, one can use these functions to sum the sales of only those products that belong to a specific category like electronics. This level of customization allows organizations to analyze their data in ways that are most relevant to their specific needs.

# Data types in DAX

DAX supports various data types, each serving a specific purpose in calculations and data modeling:

- **Whole number**: This data type is used for integers. For example, SUM(Sales[Units Sold]) calculates the total number of units sold.

- **Decimal number**: This data type is used for floating-point numbers. For example, AVERAGE(Sales[Price]) determines the average price of all products sold.

- **Boolean**: This data type represents true/false values. For example, `IF(Customer[Total Spend] > 10000, TRUE, FALSE)` checks if a customer's total spend is greater than ₹10,000.

- **Text**: This data type is used for strings. For example, Product Name.

# DAX operators

DAX includes a variety of operators that can be used in expressions to perform calculations and comparisons:

- **Arithmetic operators**: These operators perform basic mathematical operations. For example, Profit Margin = (Sales[Revenue] - Sales[Cost]) / Sales[Revenue] calculates the profit margin.

  Let us take this example and do the following exercise steps in Power BI:

  1. **Open Power BI desktop**: Launch Power BI Desktop on your computer.
  2. **Load data**: Import your sales.xlxs data specified in *Table 6.8* into Power BI. You can do this by clicking on the **Get Data** button and selecting the appropriate data source. Here, data is in Excel format.
  3. Create a new column.
  4. Go to the Modeling tab in the ribbon.
  5. Click on **New Column** for Profit Margin.
  6. In the formula bar, enter the following DAX expression:
  7. Profit Margin = ('Sales'[Revenue (₹)] - 'Sales'[Cost (₹)]) / 'Sales'[Revenue (₹)]
  8. Press Enter.
  9. Go through the output to see Profit Margin Calculated in Power BI:

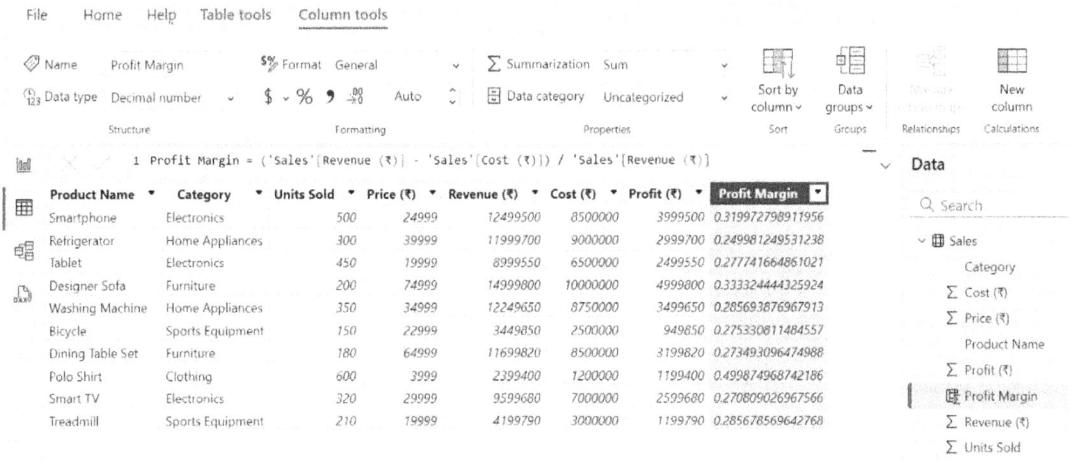


| Product Name | Category | Units Sold | Price (₹) | Revenue (₹) | Cost (₹) | Profit (₹) | Profit Margin |
|---|---|---|---|---|---|---|---|
| Smartphone | Electronics | 500 | 24999 | 12499500 | 8500000 | 3999500 | 0.319972798911956 |
| Refrigerator | Home Appliances | 300 | 39999 | 11999700 | 9000000 | 2999700 | 0.249981249531238 |
| Tablet | Electronics | 450 | 19999 | 8999550 | 6500000 | 2499550 | 0.277741664861021 |
| Designer Sofa | Furniture | 200 | 74999 | 14999800 | 10000000 | 4999800 | 0.333324444325924 |
| Washing Machine | Home Appliances | 350 | 34999 | 12249650 | 8750000 | 3499650 | 0.285693876967913 |
| Bicycle | Sports Equipment | 150 | 22999 | 3449850 | 2500000 | 949850 | 0.275330811484557 |
| Dining Table Set | Furniture | 180 | 64999 | 11699820 | 8500000 | 3199820 | 0.273493096474988 |
| Polo Shirt | Clothing | 600 | 3999 | 2399400 | 1200000 | 1199400 | 0.499874968742186 |
| Smart TV | Electronics | 320 | 29999 | 9599680 | 7000000 | 2599680 | 0.270809026967566 |
| Treadmill | Sports Equipment | 210 | 19999 | 4199790 | 3000000 | 1199790 | 0.285678569642768 |

***Figure 6.2**: Calculated profit margin column*

*Source: Author's Power BI Desktop Output*

- **Comparison operators**: These operators compare values. For example, IF(Sales[Revenue] > 100000, TRUE, FALSE) checks if the revenue is greater than ₹100,000.

  o **Logical operators**: These operators perform logical operations. For example, IF(Sales[Revenue] > 5000 && Sales[Units Sold] > 100, TRUE, FALSE) checks if both conditions are true.

  o **Text operators**: These operators manipulate text strings. For example, Sales[Product Name] && " - " && Sales[Category] concatenates the product name and category.

# DAX calculation types

DAX supports different types of calculations, each serving a specific purpose in data modeling:

- **Calculated columns**: These are columns added to a table using a DAX formula. For example, Total Cost = Sales[Units Sold] * Sales[Unit Cost] calculates the total cost by multiplying the units sold by the unit cost.

- **Calculated tables**: These are tables created using a DAX formula. For example, FILTER(Sales, Sales[Revenue] > 50000) creates a new table that includes only products with revenue greater than ₹50,000.

- **Measures**: These are calculations used in data analysis. For example, SUM(Sales[Revenue]) sums the revenue for all sales to provide the total revenue.

Creating calculated columns and tables in Power BI is straightforward. The steps to create calculated columns and tables are as follows:

- **Calculated columns**: Open the Data Model in Power BI, select the Sales Table, and enter the formula in the formula bar. For example, to create a calculated column for total cost, you would enter Total Cost = Sales[Units Sold] * Sales[Unit Cost].

- **Calculated tables**: Go to the Data Modeling Tab in Power BI, select New Table, and enter the DAX expression. For example, to create a calculated table for top products, you would enter Top Products = FILTER(Sales, Sales[Revenue] > 50000).

DAX includes a variety of functions that can be used to perform calculations and data analysis:

- **Aggregation functions**: These functions perform calculations on a set of values. For example, SUM(Sales[Revenue]) sums the total sales revenue.

- **Time intelligence functions**: These functions perform calculations on date and time data. For example, TOTALYTD(SUM(Sales[Revenue]), Sales[Date]) calculates the total sales revenue from the beginning of the year to the current date.

- **Filtering functions**: These functions filter data based on specific criteria. For example, CALCULATE(SUM(Sales[Revenue]),Sales[Category]="Electronics"). This function calculates the total sales revenue for the "Electronics" category.

- **Logical functions**: These functions perform logical operations. For example, IF(Sales[Price] > 1000, "Yes", "No") checks if a product's price is greater than ₹1,000, returning "Yes" if it is and "No" otherwise.

# Sales table

Here is an example of a sales table based on the DAX expressions mentioned:

| Product name | Category | Units sold | Price (in rupees) | Revenue (in rupees) | Cost (in rupees) | Profit (in rupees) |
|---|---|---|---|---|---|---|
| Smart-phone | Electronics | 500 | 24,999 | 1,24,99,500 | 85,00,000 | 39,99,500 |
| Refriger-ator | Home appliances | 300 | 39,999 | 1,19,99,700 | 90,00,000 | 29,99,700 |
| Tablet | Electronics | 450 | 19,999 | 89,99,550 | 65,00,000 | 24,99,550 |
| Designer sofa | Furniture | 200 | 74,999 | 1,49,99,800 | | 49,99,800 |
| Washing machine | Home appliances | 350 | 34,999 | 1,22,49,650 | 87,50,000 | 34,99,650 |
| Bicycle | Sports equipment | 150 | 22,999 | 34,49,850 | 25,00,000 | 9,49,850 |
| Dining table Set | Furniture | 180 | 64,999 | 1,16,99,820 | 85,00,000 | 31,99,820 |
| Polo shirt | Clothing | 600 | 3,999 | 23,99,400 | 12,00,000 | 11,99,400 |
| Smart TV | Electronics | 320 | 29,999 | 95,99,680 | 70,00,000 | 25,99,680 |
| Treadmill | Sports equipment | 210 | 19,999 | 41,99,790 | 30,00,000 | 11,99,790 |

*Table 6.8: Sales table for DAX exercises*

This table includes columns for product name, category, units sold, price, revenue, cost, and profit. Readers can use DAX expressions to calculate these values, as shown in this subsection.

# Calculating total revenue in Power BI example

Let us see a step-by-step guide:

1. **Open Power BI Desktop**: Launch Power BI Desktop on your computer.

2. **Load data**: Import your sales data into Power BI. You can do this by clicking on the Get Data button and selecting the appropriate data source. Here, the data is in Excel format.

3. **Create a new measure**:
   a. Go to the Modeling tab in the ribbon.
   b. Click on New Measure.
   c. In the formula bar, enter the following DAX expression: Total Revenue = SUM(Sales[Revenue])
   d. Press Enter.

4. **Visualize the measure**:
   a. Drag the Total Revenue measure from the Fields pane to the Values area of a visual chart.
   b. Power BI will automatically calculate and display the total revenue based on the data in the Sales table.

In this example, the DAX expression SUM(Sales[Revenue]) calculates the total revenue by summing up the values in the Revenue column of the Sales table. This measure can be used in various visuals to provide insights into the total revenue generated by the company.

# Dimensional modelling using Power BI

Here, we will refer to the fact and dimension tables explained in the previous section. Data will be populated into these tables to show the basic dimensional modeling exercises using Power BI:

- Data preparation
  o **Sales table** :

| Sales_ID | Product_ID | Store_Code | Period_ID | Sold_Qty | Cost_Rupees per unit |
|----------|-----------|-----------|-----------|----------|----------------------|
| 1 | P101 | S001 | T001 | 10 | 500 |
| 2 | P102 | S002 | T002 | 5 | 600 |
| 3 | P103 | S003 | T003 | 8 | 700 |
| 4 | P104 | S001 | T001 | 12 | 800 |

*Table 6.9: Sales Table (Fact Table)*

  o **Product table** :

| Product_ID | Product_Desc | Prod_Qty | Color | Size |
|-----------|-------------|----------|-------|------|
| P101 | Widget Pro | 100 | Red | Medium |
| P102 | Widget Max | 150 | Blue | Large |
| P103 | Widget Mini | 200 | Green | Small |
| P104 | Gadget Ultra | 80 | Black | Medium |

*Table 6.10: Product table (Dimension Table))*

o   **Period table**:

| Period_ID | Year | Quarter | Month |
|---|---|---|---|
| T001 | 2023 | Q1 | January |
| T002 | 2023 | Q1 | February |
| T003 | 2023 | Q1 | March |

*Table 6.11: Period Table (Dimension table)*

o   **Store table**:

| Store_Code | Manager | City | Location |
|---|---|---|---|
| S001 | Alice Smith | New York | Downtown |
| S002 | Bob Johnson | Los Angeles | Uptown |
| S003 | Carol Davis | Chicago | Midcity |

*Table 6.12: Store Table (Dimension table)*

# Importing data into Power BI

Refer to the following steps:

1.   Open Power BI Desktop.

2.   Let us Start by importing  data into Power BI:

   a.   Get Data:

      i.   Click Get Data and select the data source.

      ii.   Import four tables (Sales, Product, Period and Store)

      iii.   Import the four tables: Sales, Product, Period, and Store.

   b.   Load data:

      i.   Select four tables(Sales,Product,Period and Store) from the data source.

      ii.   Click Load to import the data into Power BI.

3.    Transform and Clean Data

   a.   Open Power Query Editor:

      i.   Click "Transform Data" to launch the Power Query Editor.

   b.   Review Tables:

      **i.   Sales Table**: :Check that Product_ID, Store_Code, and Period_ID match the keys in the dimension tables.

      ii.   Data Types: Set sales_ID, sold_qty, and cost_rupees as whole numbers or decimals and ensure Year, Quarter, Month, and Day are correctly typed (e.g., Year as a whole number).

  c. Close and apply:

    i. Click "Close & Apply" to save changes and load the cleaned data.

4. Create Relationships between tables

    a. Switch to Model View:

     i. Click on the Model icon on the left sidebar.

  a. Establish relationship:

    i. Drag Sales [Product_ID] onto Product [Product_ID].

    ii. Drag Sales [Store_Code] onto Store [Store_Code].

    iii. Drag Sales [Period_ID] onto Period [Period_ID].

  b. Check relationships:

    i. Ensure relationships are Many-to-One with the Sales table on the many sides.

    ii. Set Cross-filter Direction to Single to avoid ambiguous paths.

Let us see the Start Schema generated in the Power BI Model:

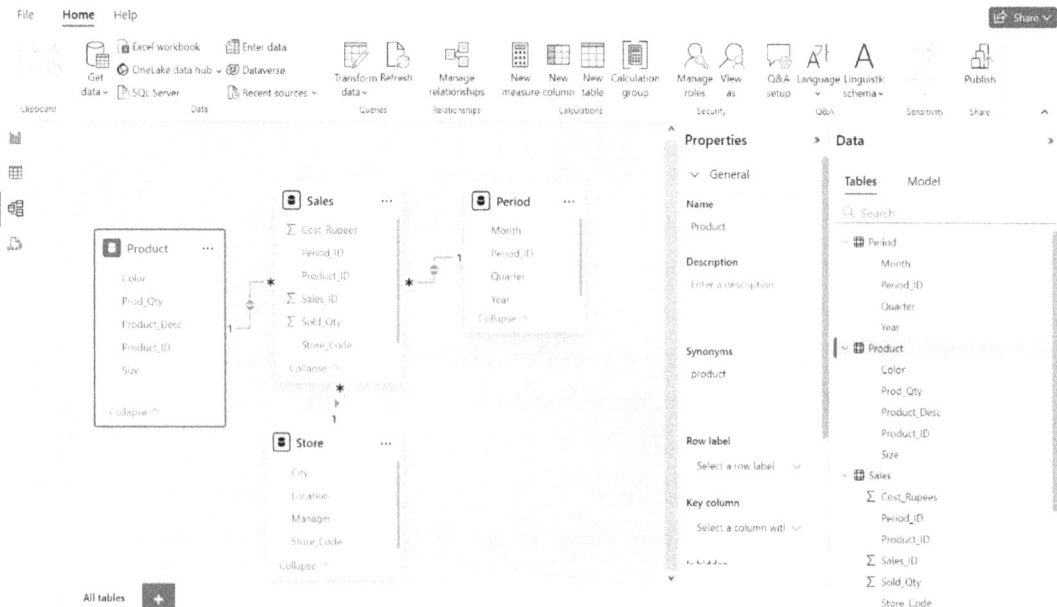

*Figure 6.3*: *Star Schema in Power BI Model*

*Source: Author's Power BI Software*

Refer to the following steps:

1. **Create Calculated Columns and Measures:**

    a. Calculated Columns

    **Total Cost in Sales Table:**

    *Total Cost (Rupees) = Sales[sold_qty] \* Sales[cost_rupees]*

    **Total Inventory Value in Product Table**

    *Inventory Value (Rupees) = Product [Prod_Qty] \* AVERAGE(Sales[cost_rupees])*

    **Measures**

    **Total Quantity Sold**

    *Total Sold Quantity = SUM(Sales[sold_qty])*

    **Total Revenue and Average Selling Price**

    *Total Revenue = SUM (Sales [Total Cost (Rupees)])*

    *Average Selling Price = [Total Revenue] / [Total Sold Quantity]*

2. **Building of visualizations**: Switching to the Report view to create visualizations:

    a. **Sales Over Time**: Line Chart:

      **Axis**: Period [Month]

      **Values**: [Total Revenue]

      Shows revenue trends over months.

    b. **Sales by Product**: Bar Chart:

      **Axis**: Product [Product_Desc]

      **Values**: [Total Sold Quantity]

      Compares quantities sold for each product.

    c. **Revenue by City**: Map Visualization:

      **Location**: Store [City]

      **Size**: [Total Revenue]

      Visualizes revenue distribution across cities.

    d. **Inventory Status**: Table Visual:

      **Columns**: Product [Product_Desc], Product [Prod_Qty], Product [Inventory Value (Rupees)]

      Provides insight into stock levels and inventory value.

    e. **Sales by Manager**: Pie Chart:

      **Legend**: Store [Manager]

      **Values**: [Total Revenue]

      Illustrates sales contribution by each manager.

   f.  **Add Interactive Filters**:

      **Slicers**:

      **Year Slicer**: Use Period [Year] to filter data by year.

      **Product Color Slicer**: Use Product [Color] to filter based on product color.

      **Store Location Slicer**: Use Store [Location].

   g.  **Format the Report**:

      **Visual Consistency**: Apply a uniform theme or color palette.

      **Titles and Labels**:

      Add clear titles to visuals.

      Label axes and data points for clarity.

      **Tooltips**: Customize tooltips to show additional details when hovering over data points.

   h.  **Validate the Model**

      **Check Calculations**:

      Verify that measures and calculated columns display expected results.

      **Test Filters**:

      Interact with slicers to ensure they filter visuals correctly.

   i.  **Set Up Data Refresh**

      **Configure Data Refresh (if applicable)**:

      If you are using live or periodically updated data sources, set up scheduled refreshes in Power BI Service.

   j.  **Publish and Share**

      **Publish the Report**:

      Click Publish and select your Power BI workspace.

      **Set Permissions**:

      Decide who can view or edit the report.

      **Share the Report**:

      Share the report with team members or stakeholders.

# Dashboard design and data visualization using Power BI

Power BI is a cloud-based tool provided by Microsoft to analyze and visualize data from a variety of sources, such as cloud and on-premises. It transforms the way users visualize data. The tool changes raw figures into interactive visual descriptions that are easy to understand and interpret. The Power BI platform is quite user-friendly. It is a drag-and-drop interface that empowers users to effortlessly design varieties of charts like bar charts, line charts, pie charts, etc. End users can dynamically explore data from multiple perspectives using features like dashboards, filters, and drill-throughs. The consistent formatting and themes available in Power BI ensure that all visuals adhere for a cohesive and professional look that aids in making visually appealing reports which are easy to analyze. Furthermore, the accessibility of Power BI across various devices, including desktops, tablets, and mobile phones ensures that users can stay connected to their data, facilitating real-time and informed decision-making regardless of their location. As the tool is scalable across organizations, it is one of the popular data visualization and modelling tools in the market.

Power BI dashboards and data visualizations facilitates organizations to monitor performance, decipher trends and make informed decisions. Here, readers can go through and practice basic import data and data preparation. We will explore various data visualizations and focus on best practices in dashboard design and data visualization. For the following exercises, please refer to **Sales.xlsx** in *Table 6.8.*

# Importing data into Power BI

Here, we will focus on importing datasets into Power BI Desktop:

1. **Preparation of the dataset**: The dataset represents sales figures for various products across different categories:

    a. **Launch Power BI desktop**: Open Power BI Desktop on your computer.

    b. Load the Data.

    c. Navigate to Get Data:

       i. On the Home ribbon, click on the Get Data button.

       ii. From the dropdown, select Excel.

    d. Select the Excel File:

       a. Browse to the location of **Sales.xlsx**.

       b. Select the file and click Open.

    e. Choose the Worksheet:

       i. In the Navigator window, you will see a list of worksheets.

       ii. Select the worksheet containing the data.

       iii. A preview of the data will appear on the right.

       iv. Ensure the data is correctly displayed.

    f. Load the Data:

       i. Click Load to import the data into Power BI.

The dataset will appear in the Fields pane on the right under the name of your Excel file.

2. Verify the data:

   a. Expand the dataset to view all columns.

   b. Confirm that the data types (e.g., text, whole number, decimal number) are correctly assigned.

3. **Creating visualizations**: With the data loaded, we can now create visualizations to explore and present our data effectively.

4. **Bar chart—Units sold by category:** A bar chart is useful for comparing quantities across categories.

The following clustered bar chart illustrates key data points for easy comparison:

Step-by-step guide:

   a. Insert a Clustered Bar Chart:

      i. In the Visualizations pane, click on the Clustered Bar Chart icon .

   b. Set Up the Data Fields:

      Drag Category from the Fields pane to the Y-axis field.

   c. Drag Units Sold to the X-axis field.

   d. Format the Bar Chart:

      i. Click on the chart to select it.

      ii. Navigate to the Format pane (paint roller icon).

      iii. Expand Data Labels and turn them On to display the values on the bars.

      iv. Customize colors under Data Colors for visual appeal.

      v. Add a chart title under Title, e.g., Units Sold by Category.

An insightful bar chart showcasing the total units sold for each product category and allow for easy comparison across categories. One hands on snapshot follows for reference of readers here.

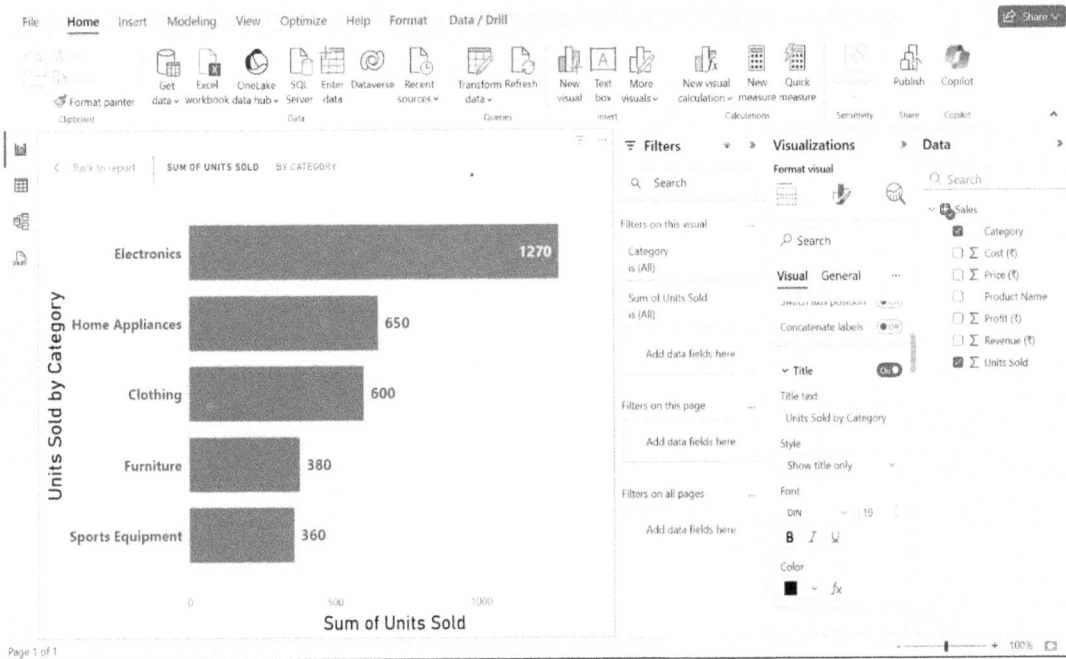

*Figure 6.4*: Clustered bar chart

5. **Pie chart—Profit distribution by product:** Pie charts are ideal for displaying proportions among parts of a whole.

   Step-by-step guide:

   a. Insert a Pie Chart:

      i. Select the Pie Chart icon in the Visualizations pane.

   b. Set Up the Data Fields:

      i. Drag Product Name to the Legend field.

      ii. Drag Profit (₹) to the Values field.

   c. Format the Pie Chart:

      i. Enable Data Labels to show profit values on each slice.

      ii. Adjust the Detail labels to display both category and percentage.

      iii. Title the chart Profit Distribution by Product.

A pie chart illustrating each product's contribution to the total profit, highlighting the most profitable products. The chart is generated in a Power BI software as follows:

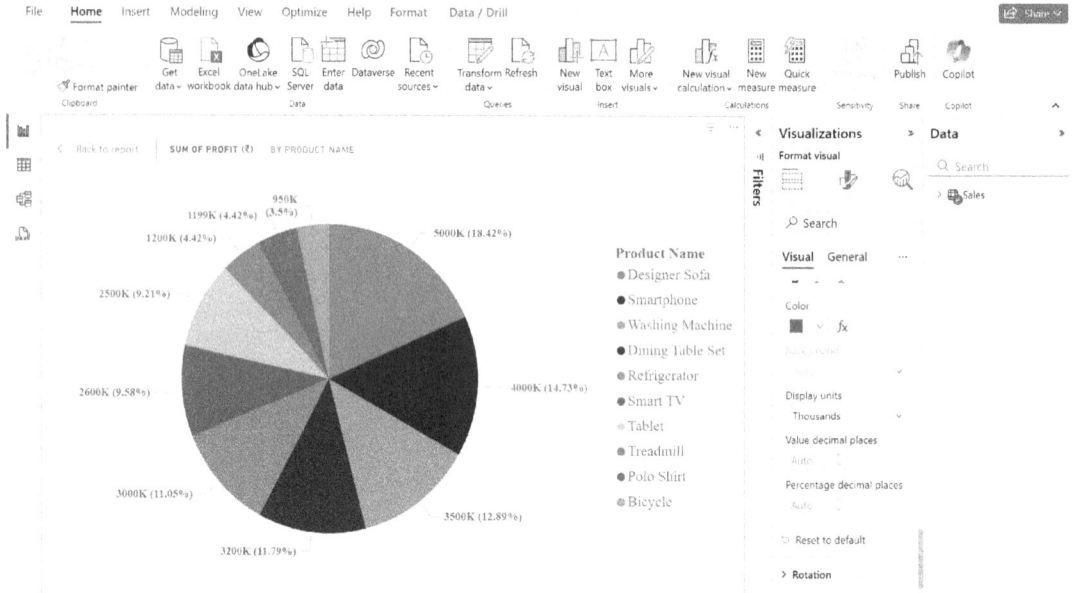

*Figure 6.5*: Pie chart

6. **Clustered column chart—revenue across products**: Clustered column charts are ideal for comparing values across categories, making them perfect for visualizing revenue for each product.

   Step-by-step guide

   a. **Insert a clustered column chart**: Click on the Clustered Column Chart icon.

   b. **Set up the data fields**: Drag Product Name to the Axis field.

      Drag Revenue (₹) to the Values field.

   c. **Format the Clustered Column Chart**:

      i. Under Format, enable Data Labels for precise values.

      ii. Adjust the X-axis to sort products in a logical order if necessary.

      iii. Title the chart Revenue Across Products.

A clustered column chart displaying revenue generated by each product, clearly comparing the performance of products side by side.

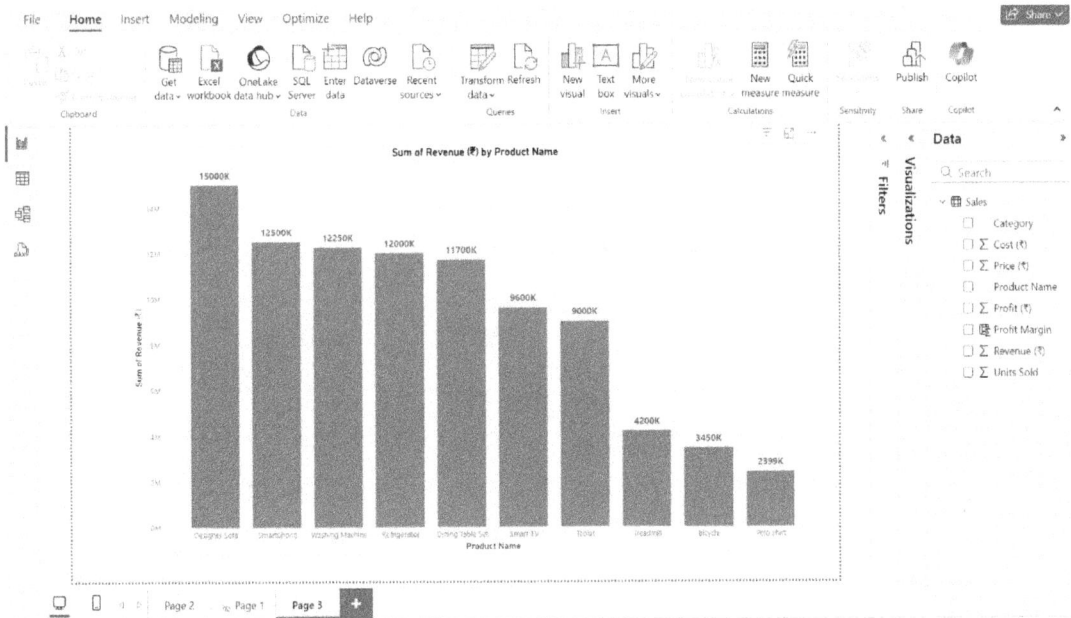

*Figure 6.6: Line Chart*

# Designing an interactive dashboard

An interactive dashboard brings together multiple visualizations to allow users to interact with the data dynamically. The dashboard can be developed through the following steps:

1. Assembling the dashboard:
   a. Arrange visualizations
      i. Resize and position the three visualizations created in the previous section on the report canvas.
      ii. Aim for a clean layout that is easy to navigate.
   b. **Add Slicers for data filtering**: Slicers enable users to filter data on the dashboard interactively.
2. Adding a Category Slicer:
   a. Insert a Slicer:
      i. Click on the Slicer icon in the Visualizations pane.
   b. Set Up the Slicer:
      i. Drag Category to the Field of the slicer.
   c. Format the Slicer:
      i. Choose Dropdown or List under 'Selection controls'.

        ii.     Enable Single select or Multi-select based on preference.

    d.  Test dashboard interactivity:

        i.     Interact with the slicer by selecting different categories.

        ii.     Observe how the visualizations update in response, reflecting only the data for the selected category.

1. Boosting Dashboard aesthetics and usability:

    a.  Apply a Theme:

        i.     Go to the View tab.

        ii.     Select a pre-defined theme or customize your own under Customize current theme.

    b.  Add Titles and Text Boxes:

        i.     Use Text boxes to add descriptive titles or instructions.

        ii.     Ensure that each visualization is clearly labelled.

2. Company labelling:

    a.  Insert images such as company logos using the Image icon.

    b.  Position branding elements appropriately to maintain professionalism.

Expertise in these skills is essential for any professional seeking to leverage data in a business context. By following this step-by-step process, a real-world dataset is transformed into an interactive and insightful dashboard. The preceding process to import data, clean, and prepare for the creation of various visualizations and implementation features in Power BI are quite useful for gaining insights for competitive advantages for organizations. This foundational knowledge equips one to tackdle more complex data visualization challenges and contributes to growth as a data professional.

# Case study

*Arati_FreshMart* India's transformative journey exemplifies how integrating cultural intelligence with advanced retail analytics can redefine market success. This case study illustrates how leveraging business intelligence architecture turns cultural insights into strategies that propel growth:

- **Executive summary**: *Arati_FreshMart*, a fast-growing chain of 50 organic food stores across India, faced cut-throat competition from local markets and e-commerce platforms. To gain a competitive advantage, the company overhauled its BI architecture. *Arati_FreshMart* transformed its operations by implementing a holistic ETL process, designing robust OLAP cubes, and utilizing Power BI for advanced data modelling. They crafted culturally aware dashboards, resulting in an 18% increase in sales and a 30% boost in customer engagement. This strategic move solidified their position in the Indian organic retail market.

- **Introduction**: India's retail sector is quite diverse. It reflects different consumer preferences, regional differences and deep cultural influences. Navigating this complex landscape is a big challenge. It is especially hard for *Arati_FreshMart*, a company trying to succeed in a competitive market. Local vendors enticed customers with personalized services steeped in tradition, while e-commerce giants attracted the masses through aggressive discounts and unparalleled convenience. Among this fierce competition, *Arati_FreshMart* grappled with fragmented data systems that obscured holistic insights, leaving it ill-equipped to fully understand and serve its diverse customer base.

  Since the market was changing rapidly, agility was essential. Swift decision-making was not just advantageous but necessary to meet consumers' evolving needs. Recognizing that data could be the key to unlocking its potential, *Arati_FreshMart* envisioned integrating cultural nuances into its **business intelligence (BI)** infrastructure. This strategic move aimed to transform challenges into opportunities, turning the rich complexities of India's retail market into a powerful asset for growth and customer engagement.

- **BI architecture implementation**: *Arati_FreshMart* adopted a centralized BI architecture to unify data sources by integrating various systems into a single platform. This architecture supported advanced analytics, enabling complex data analysis and real-time reporting, which enhanced decision-making by providing actionable insights at all levels of the organisation. Designed to scale with growth, it accommodated increasing data volumes and types while incorporating cultural context to reflect regional and cultural nuances in data analysis. This comprehensive architecture formed the foundation for the ETL process, OLAP cube design, data modelling and dashboard creation.

- **ETL process and data warehouse design:** To build a comprehensive dataset for analysis, *Arati_FreshMart* collected data from multiple sources, including point-of-sale systems capturing in-store transactions, online platforms recording e-commerce sales, supplier databases providing inventory and procurement details, loyalty programs offering insights into customer behavior and preferences and social media feedback reflecting customer sentiments and cultural trends. The rich dataset included both transactional and cultural information. First, the data was cleaned by fixing mistakes and removing duplicates. Then, categories and formats were standardized, and geographic codes, timestamps, cultural events, and language preferences were added to enrich the data. The transformed data was then loaded into a data warehouse with a dimensional model, optimizing query performance and facilitating informed decision-making across the firm. By integrating cultural data, *Arati_FreshMart* enhanced its understanding of consumer behaviour across regions.

- **OLAP and cube designs**: Purpose of OLAP and Cube Designs are to facilitate multi-dimensional data analysis incorporating cultural factors:

o **Design**

o **Dimensions**

o **Time**: Year, Quarter, Month, Day, Festival/Occasion

o **Location**: Region, State, City, Store

o **Product**: Department, Category, SKU

o **Customer**: Age Group, Occupation, Language Preference

This design enables comprehensive multi-dimensional data analysis by incorporating cultural factors.

Exhibit 1: OLAP Cube Structure:

| Dimension | Levels |
|---|---|
| Time | Year > Quarter > Month > Day > Festival |
| Location | Region > State > City > Store |
| Product | Department > Category > Sub-category > SKU |
| Customer | Age Group > Occupation > Language Preference |

*Table 6.13: OLAP Cube Structure:*

- **Analytical capabilities**: Analytics capabilities unlock the power of data. Slice and Dice enables analysis across multiple dimensions, providing a multifaceted perspective. Drill-down and Roll-Up navigate between detailed and summarized data and Pivot reorients data to uncover hidden patterns. Mastering these tools transforms raw data into actionable insights, uncovering trends, informing decisions and driving business growth.

- **Data modelling with Power BI**: In leveraging Power BI for data modeling, *Arati_FreshMart* built relationships by linking data tables encompassing sales, products, and customers with cultural attributes. Inconsistencies and duplicates were removed from the data to clean it. Then, categories and formats were standardized, and the data was enriched by adding geographic codes, timestamps, cultural events, and language preferences:

*Festival_Sales_Growth (%) = (Festival Period Sales–Previous Period Sales/Previous Period Sales) ×100*

This measure allowed *Arati_FreshMart* to quantify sales growth during festival periods accurately. Another key metric was the Cultural Product Preference Index, calculated as:

*Preference_Index= (Sales of Cultural Products during Festival/Total Festival Sales) ×100*

This index helped identify the proportion of sales attributed to cultural products during festivals. Hierarchies were established within the Time and Location dimensions to reflect cultural events and regional structures, enabling detailed analysis across various levels. This comprehensive approach enabled culturally informed decision-making and fostered targeted marketing and inventory strategies, aligning business operations with regional and cultural nuances.

- **Dashboard design and data visualization**: *Arati_FreshMart* developed dashboards tailored to different stakeholders, embedding cultural insights into their data visualizations. The Executive Dashboard showcased **key performance indicators (KPIs)** with visualizations of financial metrics enhanced by cultural overlays, such as sales figures during festivals, and included trend lines highlighting the impact of these events on overall performance. The Regional Manager Dashboard focused on local sales trends, inventory levels, and customer preferences, incorporating cultural event planning to help managers tailor strategies to their specific regions. The Marketing Dashboard analyzed campaign effectiveness during festivals and monitored regional social media sentiment, providing insights into customer engagement and allowing for timely adjustments in marketing initiatives. Visual tools like maps, line graphs, and bar charts illustrated the metrics across all dashboards, facilitating clear communication and informed decision-making.

- **Results and impact**: The implementation of *Arati_FreshMart's* culturally integrated BI system led to significant quantitative and qualitative improvements. Sales increased by 18% to reach ₹250 crore, with festival sales accounting for 40% of the annual revenue, highlighting the effectiveness of culturally tailored strategies during key periods. Customer engagement intensified as loyalty program memberships rose by 30%, and stockouts were reduced by 25% due to improved forecasting aligned with cultural events. Enhanced customer experiences from tailored offerings greatly improved satisfaction levels, while cultural competency training boosted employee morale and enabled staff to provide more personalized service. Additionally, Arati_FreshMart's active participation in local events strengthened community relations, fostering goodwill and reinforcing the brand's commitment to celebrating diverse cultures. This holistic approach not only solidified Arati_FreshMart's market position but also built a strong foundation for sustained success, demonstrating the significant impact of integrating cultural insights into business practices.

- **Implementation challenges and solutions**: During its BI transformation, *Arati_FreshMart* encountered several implementation challenges. Cultural diversity management was a significant hurdle, as navigating regional differences required a deep understanding of local customs and consumer behaviors. To overcome this, *Arati_FreshMart* employed local experts and created a cultural calendar, enabling the company to tailor strategies to each region effectively. Multilingual data handling posed another challenge due to data integration across various languages. The company addressed this by standardizing data formats and implementing multilingual support systems, ensuring seamless data integration and analysis. Supplier coordination was also critical, particularly in ensuring the timely supply of regional products. By partnering with local suppliers and improving forecasting methods, *Arati_FreshMart* enhanced its supply chain efficiency and responsiveness to regional demands. Lastly, technological variance across different areas presented difficulties, especially in regions with limited infrastructure. *Arati_FreshMart* optimized its BI tools for low-bandwidth environments and developed mobile solutions to accommodate varying technological capabilities, ensuring consistent performance across all locations.

- **Conclusion**: *Arati_FreshMart's* integration of cultural context into its BI systems led to unified data enriched with cultural insights, significantly enhancing their understanding of diverse consumer behaviors across India. By innovatively tailoring strategies beyond standard practices, they tapped into regional nuances, gaining a competitive advantage that increased market share and strengthened customer loyalty. Moreover, aligning business operations with cultural values allowed *Arati_FreshMart* to deepen community bonds and foster stronger customer relationships. This transformation underscores the critical importance of cultural intelligence and technological innovation in driving success in diverse markets. *Arati_FreshMart* 's experience demonstrates that embracing cultural diversity, supported by advanced BI tools, is essential for businesses aiming to thrive in a multifaceted retail landscape.

- **Looking ahead**: Looking ahead, the company plans to use predictive analytics with machine learning to anticipate trends. They are expanding collaborations with local suppliers to strengthen regional partnerships. By promoting eco-friendly practices and cultural preservation, they are supporting sustainability and heritage.

- **Strategic questions**:
  1. How can cultural diversity be leveraged globally?
  2. What ethical considerations arise with cultural data?
  3. How can technology deepen cultural understanding?

- **Key learning**: Integrating cultural elements boosts customer engagement, while leveraging technology offers nuanced market insights. Community involvement fosters loyalty and ethical practices build long-term trust. Together, these strategies are vital for businesses aiming for sustainable success in today's competitive market.

- **Final Insights:** *Arati_FreshMart's* journey showcases the power of combining cultural awareness with advanced BI tools to achieve significant business growth. By embracing India's cultural diversity and leveraging technology to understand and meet customer needs, *Arati_FreshMart* not only improved its market position but also strengthened its community connections. This case study demonstrates the critical role of cultural intelligence, ethical practices, and innovation in succeeding in diverse markets.

# Conclusion

BI architecture serves as the backbone of data-driven organizations by ensuring data flows to inform strategy and operations. ETL process and data warehouse design highlighted the importance of cleansing and harmonizing data into a unified warehouse, which is crucial for generating deep insights. The OLAP and cube designs section narrates multidimensional analysis, which identifies trends which is crucial for businesses aiming to stay agile in a shifting market. Data modeling with Power BI explored how modern tools enable users to construct sophisticated data models without strong knowledge in programming to unlock insights that drive strategic initiatives. Finally, delving into dashboard design and data visualization emphasized that visualizations are crucial for communicating insights effectively with well-designed dashboards at a glance and to assist informed decision-making.

This chapter projects a holistic picture of BI as a synergistic system where each component plays a vital role in transforming data into strategic assets. The key learning of the chapter focuses on BI as a continual process of leveraging data to gain a competitive advantage. In the next chapter, we are going to learn about Advanced Data Mining and Business Intelligence Techniques.

# Multiple choice questions

1. **What is the primary purpose of the pivot operation in OLAP?**
   a. To filter data based on specific criteria.
   b. To rotate the data axes in view to provide an alternative presentation.
   c. To remove duplicates from the dataset.
   d. To aggregate data according to a defined function.

2. **What is the role of a data warehouse in an organization?**
   a. To hold transactional information.
   b. To provide an integrated view of historical data for analysis.
   c. To serve as a backup for operational systems.
   d. To manage user access and security.

3. **In OLAP, the concept of drill down refers to:**
   a. The process of summarizing data during analysis.
   b. The ability to navigate to more detailed levels of data.
   c. The operational efficiency of processing queries.
   d. The exporting of summarized reports for external analysis.

4. **Which of the following operations is not part of the ETL process?**

    a. Data cleansing

    b. Data loading

    c. Data visualization

    d. Data transformation

5. **Which visual is best for showing trends over time?**

    a. Bar Chart

    b. Line Chart

    c. Pie Chart

    d. Tree Map

6. **Which language is used for data manipulation in Power BI?**

    a. SQL

    b. Python

    c. DAX

    d. M Language

7. **Which editor is used for data transformation in Power BI?**

    a. Visualization Pane

    b. Power Query Editor

    c. Report Editor

    d. Data Modelling Pane

8. **What is the primary use of Q&A in Power BI?**

    a. To apply themes to reports.

    b. To enable natural language queries.

    c. To create relationships between tables.

    d. To export data.

9. **When visualizing data with a line chart in Power BI which scenario is most appropriate for using the Continuous type on the X-axis?**

    a. When the X-axis represents categorical data like product names.

    b. When you have non-numeric data types.

    c. When you need to display all data points individually.

    d. When the X-axis represents a numerical field or date/time data.

10. **Which DAX function is best used to calculate the cumulative total (running total) over time in a report?**

   a. TOTALYTD

   b. SUMX

   c. CALCULATE

   d. DATESYTD

# Answers

1. b

2. b

3. b

4. c

5. b

6. c

7. b

8. b

9. d

10. a

# Practice exercises

1. Explain each step of the ETL process in the context of building a data warehouse. Provide detailed explanations of the ELT phases, emphasizing their roles in data warehousing.

   Using the Online Retail II dataset from the UCI Machine Learning Repository, design a dimensional model for a retail sales data warehouse. Identify the fact and dimension tables and explain your choices. Design a dimensional model by selecting appropriate fact and dimension tables based on the dataset and justify your selections.

   Dataset description: The Online Retail II dataset, available at **https://archive. ics.uci.edu/ml/datasets/Online+Retail+II,** contains transactional data for a UK-based online retailer from 2009 to 2011. It includes invoices, product details, quantities, prices, customer IDs, and countries.

2. Describe how you would perform the ETL process to consolidate data from different sources such as sales, inventory, and customer data into a single data warehouse using the Online Retail II dataset. Outline the steps involved in the ETL process to integrate multiple data sources into a unified data warehouse.

   List the tools and technologies you would use to implement the ETL process for this dataset, and justify your choices. Identify suitable ETL tools and technologies, explaining why they are appropriate for this task.

   **Dataset description:** The Online Retail II dataset can be accessed at **https://archive.ics.uci.edu/ml/datasets/Online+Retail+II** . It provides real-world e-commerce data suitable for practicing ETL processes and integrating multiple data sources into a data warehouse.

3. Using the Financial Sample dataset provided by Microsoft, outline the steps involved in creating a data model in Power BI. Include importing data and establishing relationships between tables such as Sales, Regions, and Products. Describe the process of building a data model in Power BI, focusing on data importation and relationship management.

   Explain how **Data Analysis Expressions (DAX)** functions enhance data modeling in Power BI, and provide an example of a calculated measure that calculates total revenue per country using this dataset. Demonstrate the benefits of using DAX functions and illustrate with a specific example of a calculated measure.

   **Dataset description**: The Financial Sample dataset is an Excel file provided by Microsoft, available at **https://go.microsoft.com/fwlink/?linkid=521962**. It contains sales and profit data across different countries and products, making it ideal for practicing data modeling and DAX calculations in Power BI.

4. With the Financial Sample dataset, discuss five best practices for designing an effective financial performance dashboard in Power BI. List and explain best practices to consider when creating a financial dashboard to ensure clarity and usability.

   Describe how the choice of visualization types can impact the interpretation of financial data in this dataset, and provide examples of appropriate visualizations for displaying revenue trends and profit margins across different regions. Discuss the influence of visualization choices on data comprehension and suggest suitable chart types for specific financial metrics.

   **Dataset description**: The Financial Sample dataset includes financial performance metrics such as gross sales, discounts, and profit by country and product. You can download it from https://go.microsoft.com/fwlink/?linkid=521962, providing a rich basis for dashboard design and data visualization exercises.

# References

1. Bose, R., & Sugumaran, V. (2009). *Challenges for deploying web services-based e-business systems in SMEs. International Journal of E-Business Research, 5(1), 1–18.*

2. Ministry of Law and Justice. (2019). *The Consumer Protection Act, 2019. Government of India.*

3. NITI Aayog. (2018). *National Strategy for Artificial Intelligence. Government of India.*

4. Press Information Bureau. (2020). *Digital payments surge with UPI. Government of India.*

5. Sharma, N., & Goyal, D. P. (2014). *Business intelligence and its implementation in retail. International Journal of Retailing & Rural Business Perspectives, 3(1), 734–738.*

6. Singh, S. (2020). *Cultural diversity in India: A qualitative study. Journal of Business and Management, 22(3), 45–52.*

# Join our book's Discord space

Join the book's Discord Workspace for Latest updates, Offers, Tech happenings around the world, New Release and Sessions with the Authors:

**https://discord.bpbonline.com**

# CHAPTER 7

# Advanced Data Mining and Business Intelligence Techniques

## Introduction

Traditional data mining techniques have laid the foundation, but the rapid expansion of data in volume, variety, and velocity demands more advanced approaches. The convergence of emerging technologies is redefining how we process, analyze, and leverage data across functional areas of business. This chapter delves into the forefront of advanced data mining and explores new methodologies and technologies are pushing the boundaries of what is possible. It tackles the evolving challenges of data mining professionals in making sense of unstructured data and handling massive datasets that surpass the capabilities of conventional methods. Through the implementation of these advanced techniques, it is possible to navigate the complexities of modern data ecosystems. At the same time, it is possible to acquire the knowledge, interpret data, and understand the underlying patterns and reasons for supporting informed decision-making. At the intersection of data and intelligent systems, this chapter serves as a gateway to the future of data analytics.

## Structure

This chapter covers the following topics:

- Text mining as advanced data mining technique
- Big data analytics in business
- Edge analytics

- Cognitive analytics
- Real time analytics and data streaming
- New era of creativity through generative AI
- Agentic AI as autonomous intelligence's future
- Future of continuous innovation and ethical integration
- Case study

# Objectives

This chapter introduces key concepts of modern advanced data mining. Readers will learn how to extract valuable insights from large collections of text data and understand techniques to analyze and find patterns in massive datasets with big data analytics. Readers will learn how edge analytics processes data directly at its source for quick decision-making. The exploration of cognitive analytics with the application of AI in data analysis explains what is happening in the data and why it is happening. This chapter will also describe how to interpret data as it is generated and allow for quick responses using real-time analytics and data streaming. Readers will know how machines can create new content and push creative boundaries with generative AI and also understand agentic AI where autonomous agents perceive their environment, make decisions and act with minimal human intervention. After going through the chapter, readers will have a clear understanding of these technologies and how they are shaping the future of advanced data mining.

# Text mining as advanced data mining technique

The primary objective of text mining is to convert unstructured text data into actionable insights. During the twenty-first century, organizations are drowned with massive text data from sources like customer reviews, **Internet of Things** (**IoT**) sensors, and social media feeds. So, it is essential to find out trends, patterns, and relationships within this text to make vital decisions.

## Preprocessing text data

Preprocessing transforms raw text into a clean and analyzable format to ensure that noise does not cloud our insights. For a holistic data mining analysis, effective processing of text data is essential. This process comprises various techniques to ensure data quality and consistency. Tokenization breaks down text into words or tokens to facilitate analysis of each word separately. To avoid variability due to differences of case sensitivity, lowercasing is accomplished to convert all characters to lowercase for standardization purposes. Stop words like *and* or *the* are eliminated, which do not add any analytical values. Punctuation marks are removed to simplify text. Similarly, stemming reduces the words to their base form by removing prefixes and suffixes. Lemmatization checks the context and converts the word to their dictionary form. In case the numeric data is irrelevant, these are removed. Whitespaces are also trimmed to eliminate extra spaces to ensure uniformity in text processing. On the whole, these preprocessing steps transformed text data into a clean and standard format.

# Bag of words modelling

Bag of words model is one of the basic techniques used to convert textual data into a numeric form. Let us work with the following two simple statements to understand the technique stagewise:

- **Review 1**: Advanced data mining is interesting.

- **Review 2**: Business intelligence is fun.

  Converting text into numerical representation enables machine learning algorithms to process it. This transformation allows algorithms to process and analyze text using mathematical methods. By grasping how we convert text into numerical form, we unlock the foundations of how machines work with language:

- **Stage 1:**

- **Count Vector Model**: The Count Vector Model is the most basic form of the BoW model that represents each document by counting the number of times each word appears.

  1. **Step 1**

     **Preprocessing the text:**

     Before counting, we need to preprocess the text to ensure consistency and remove noise.

     **Convert to lowercase:**

     **Review 1**: Advanced data mining is interesting

     **Review 2**: Business intelligence is fun

     **Tokenize the sentences:**

     **Review 1 tokens**: ["advanced", "data", "mining", "is", "interesting"]

     **Review 2 tokens**: ["business", "intelligence", "is", "fun"]

     **Remove Stop words** (common words that add little meaning, like "is")

     Review 1 Tokens after Stop word Removal: ["advanced", "data", "mining", "interesting"]

Review 2 tokens after Stop word Removal: ["business", "intelligence", "fun"]

2. **Step 2:**

   **Building the vocabulary:**

   Create a list of unique words from both reviews.

   **Vocabulary:**

   ["advanced", "business", "data", "fun", "intelligence", "interesting", "mining"]

3. **Step 3:**

   **Creating the count** vectors:

   Now, count how many times each word appears in each review.

   a. **Review 1:**

   | Term | Count |
   |------|-------|
   | advanced | 1 |
   | business | 0 |
   | data | 1 |
   | fun | 0 |
   | intelligence | 0 |
   | interesting | 1 |
   | mining | 1 |

   *Table 7.1: Word count-Review 1*

   b. **Review 2:**

   | Term | Count |
   |------|-------|
   | advanced | 0 |
   | business | 1 |
   | data | 0 |
   | fun | 1 |
   | intelligence | 1 |
   | interesting | 0 |
   | mining | 0 |

   *Table 7.2: Word count-Review 2*

   **Assembling the count vectors:**

   We can represent each review as a vector corresponding to the vocabulary terms.

Review 1 count vector: [1, 0, 1, 0, 0, 1, 1]

Review 2 count vector: [0, 1, 0, 1, 1, 0, 0]

Interpreting the count vectors

Each position in the vector corresponds to a term in the vocabulary. The counts represent the frequency of each term in the respective review.

- **Stage 2:**

**Term frequency (TF) vector model:**

The Term Frequency model refines the Count Vector by normalizing term counts by the total number of terms in the document. This accounts for document length differences. The formula is as follows:

$$TF\ (t, d) = (Number\ of\ times\ term\ t\ appears\ in\ document\ d)/$$

$$(Total\ number\ of\ terms\ in\ document\ d)$$

Review 1: Term frequencies

Total terms: 4

| Term | Count | TF calculation | TF value |
|---|---|---|---|
| Advanced | 1 | 1/4 | 0.25 |
| Business | 0 | 0/4 | 0 |
| Data | 1 | 1/4 | 0.25 |
| Fun | 0 | 0/4 | 0 |
| intelligence | 0 | 0/4 | 0 |
| interesting | 1 | 1/4 | 0.25 |
| mining | 1 | 1/4 | 0.25 |

*Table 7.3: Term frequencies-Review 1*

Review 2: Term frequencies

Total terms: 3

| Term | Count | TF calculation | TF value |
|---|---|---|---|
| advanced | 0 | 0/3 | 0 |
| business | 1 | 1/3 | 0.3333 |
| data | 0 | 0/3 | 0 |
| fun | 1 | 1/3 | 0.3333 |
| intelligence | 1 | 1/3 | 0.3333 |
| interesting | 0 | 0/3 | 0 |
| mining | 0 | 0/3 | 0 |

*Table 7.4: Term frequencies-Review 2*

**Collecting the TF vectors:**

Review 1 TF vector: [0.25, 0, 0.25, 0, 0, 0.25, 0.25]

Review 2 TF vector: [0, 0.3333, 0, 0.3333, 0.3333, 0, 0]

**Interpreting the TF vectors:**

TF values show term importance relative to document length. Longer documents do not overshadow shorter ones due to normalization.

- **Stage 3:**

**TF-IDF vector model:**

The TF-IDF model combines Term Frequency and Inverse Document Frequency to weigh terms. It highlights terms that are significant in a document but not common across all documents. The formula follows

**Term frequency (TF)**

*TF (t, d) = (Number of times term t in document d/Total terms in document d)*

**Inverse Document Frequency (IDF):**

$$IDF(t)=log(N/df(t))$$

Where,

N = Total number of documents.

df(t) = Number of documents containing term t.

**TF-IDF score:**

$$TF\text{-}IDF(t,d)=TF(t,d)\times IDF(t)$$

**Calculations:**

1. **Step 1:**

   Calculate IDF values

   Total documents (N): 2

   **Document frequencies (df(t)):**

   IDF calculations

   For each term:

   IDF(t)=log (2/1)≈0.6931

2. **Step 2:**

   Computation of TF-IDF scores

   **Review 1 TF-IDF scores:**

| Term | TF | IDF | TF-IDF Calculation | TF-IDF Score |
|------|-----|------|-------------------|--------------|
| advanced | 0.25 | 0.6931 | 0.25 × 0.6931 | 0.1733 |
| business | 0 | 0.6931 | 0 × 0.69310 | 0 |
| data | 0.25 | 0.6931 | 0.25 × 0.6931 | 0.1733 |
| fun | 0 | 0.6931 | 0 × 0.69310 | 0 |
| intelligence | 0 | 0.6931 | 0 × 0.69310 | 0 |
| interesting | 0.25 | 0.6931 | 0.25 × 0.6931 | 0.1733 |
| mining | 0.25 | 0.6931 | 0.25 × 0.6931 | 0.1733 |

*Table 7.5: Review 1 TF-IDF scores*

**Review 2 TF-IDF scores:**

| Term | TF | IDF | TF-IDF Calculation | TF-IDF Score |
|------|-----|------|-------------------|--------------|
| advanced | 0 | 0.6931 | 0 × 0.69310 | 0 |
| business | 0.3333 | 0.6931 | 0.3333 × 0.6931 | 0.2310 |
| Data | 0 | 0.6931 | 0 × 0.6931 | 0 |
| Fun | 0.3333 | 0.6931 | 0.3333 × 0.6931 | 0.2310 |
| intelligence | 0.3333 | 0.6931 | 0.3333 × 0.6931 | 0.2310 |
| interesting | 0 | 0.6931 | 0 × 0.69310 | 0 |
| mining | 0 | 0.6931 | 0 × 0.69310 | 0 |

*Table 7.6: Review 2 TF-IDF scores*

**Collecting the TF-IDF vectors:**

Review 1 TF-IDF vector: [0.1733, 0, 0.1733, 0, 0, 0.1733, 0.1733]

Review 2 TF-IDF vector: [0, 0.2310, 0, 0.2310, 0.2310, 0, 0]

**Interpreting the TF-IDF vectors:**

Review 1 emphasizes: "advanced", "data", "mining", "interesting"

Review 2 highlights: "business", "intelligence", "fun"

Higher TF-IDF scores indicate terms that are significant in distinguishing the content of each review.

**Visualizing the results:**

Let us compile all our findings into a comprehensive table:

| Term | Review containing term (df(t)) | IDF | Review 1 Count | Review 1 TF | Review 1 TF-IDF | Review 2 Count | Review 2 TF | Review 2 TF-IDF |
|---|---|---|---|---|---|---|---|---|
| advanced | 1 | 0.6931 | 1 | 0.25 | 0.1733 | 0 | 0 | 0 |
| business | 1 | 0.6931 | 0 | 0 | 0 | 1 | 0.3333 | 0.2310 |
| data | 1 | 0.6931 | 1 | 0.25 | 0.1733 | 0 | 0 | 0 |
| fun | 1 | 0.6931 | 0 | 0 | 0 | 1 | 0.3333 | 0.2310 |
| intelligence | 1 | 0.6931 | 0 | 0 | 0 | 1 | 0.3333 | 0.2310 |
| interesting | 1 | 0.6931 | 1 | 0.25 | 0.1733 | 0 | 0 | 0 |
| mining | 1 | 0.6931 | 1 | 0.25 | 0.1733 | 0 | 0 | 0 |

*Table 7.7: Combined term analysis table*

# Importance of the three models

- **Count Vector model**: This model is Simple and intuitive. It is useful for basic text analysis where term presence and frequency are important.

- **TF Vector model**: This model normalizes term counts. The model also accounts for document length differences.

- **TF-IDF Vector model**: This model highlights important terms unique to a document. It reduces the weight of common terms across documents.

TF-IDF is an essential tool used in many everyday applications. In search engines, TF-IDF ranks web pages. So, the most relevant results appear at the top when searched. For document classification, TF-IDF vectors help machine learning models categorize text into topics, genres, or sentiments. In information retrieval, TF-IDF enables systems to find documents similar to a given piece of text that is useful for things like legal research or recommending articles one might like. By measuring how important words are in context, TF-IDF helps to understand and navigate large amounts of text data.

# Visualizing with word clouds

A word cloud is a visual representation of text data. Here, the size of each word indicates its frequency or importance within the dataset. This technique helps in quickly deciphering the most prominent terms in large textual data such as speeches, articles, or social media posts. Word clouds are mostly useful in text analysis as they provide an intuitive way to grasp the main themes and trends. The arrangement of words in a word cloud is usually random, but the more frequently a word appears in the data, the larger and more centrally located it will be in the visualization. Word clouds are popular in data journalism, marketing, and educational settings as they offer a visually appealing and straightforward method to convey complex information.

Let us see how to create a word cloud using R:

```
#The package tm  provides functions for text manipulation and
preprocessing.

install.packages("tm")

#The package wordcloud allows  to create word clouds for visualizing word
frequency data.

install.packages("wordcloud")

#The package RColorBrewer offers a selection of color palettes to enhance
visualizations.

install.packages("RColorBrewer")

# Load necessary libraries

library(tm)

library(wordcloud)

library(RColorBrewer)

# Create your text data

text <- "
```

Organizations must implement stringent security measures to comply with regulations like the GDPR and safeguard data streams through secure networks. Dense wordcloud analysis, powered by state-of-the-art machine learning, delivers invaluable insights into privacy compliance while consistently revealing innovative patterns and driving continuous learning. To further enhance data protection, organizations implement additional stringent security measures that integrate advanced machine learning analysis with dense wordcloud techniques, reinforcing privacy standards and ensuring regulatory compliance. This dynamic approach, merging cutting-edge machine learning with robust innovation, enables organizations to generate deep insights, expose recurring patterns, and proactively comply with the General Data Protection Regulation, ultimately safeguarding data streams through resilient networks. Organizations must implement stringent security measures to comply with regulations like the GDPR and safeguard data streams through secure networks. Dense wordcloud analysis, powered by state-of-the-art machine learning, delivers invaluable insights into privacy compliance while consistently revealing innovative patterns and driving continuous learning. To further enhance data protection, organizations implement additional stringent security measures that integrate advanced machine learning analysis with dense wordcloud techniques, reinforcing privacy standards and ensuring regulatory compliance. This dynamic approach, merging cutting-edge machine learning with robust innovation, enables organizations to generate deep insights, expose recurring patterns, and proactively comply with the GDPR, ultimately safeguarding data streams through resilient networks:

```
# Create a text corpus
corpus <- Corpus(VectorSource(text))
# Clean and preprocess the text data
corpus <- tm_map(corpus, content_transformer(tolower)) # Convert text to
lowercase
corpus <- tm_map(corpus, removePunctuation)          # Remove punctuation
corpus <- tm_map(corpus, removeNumbers)              # Remove numbers
corpus <- tm_map(corpus, removeWords, stopwords("english")) # Remove common
stopwords
# Create a term-document matrix
tdm <- TermDocumentMatrix(corpus)
# Convert the term-document matrix into a matrix
tdm_matrix <- as.matrix(tdm)
# Calculate word frequencies
word_freq <- rowSums(tdm_matrix)
word_freq <- sort(word_freq, decreasing = TRUE)
# Create a data frame with words and their frequencies
df <- data.frame(word = names(word_freq), freq = word_freq)
# Generate the word cloud
set.seed(123)  # For reproducibility
wordcloud(words = df$word, freq = df$freq, max.words = 100,
          random.order = FALSE, colors = brewer.pal(8, "Dark2"))
```

Running this code generates a word cloud that visually displays the most frequent words in text data specified previously. The size of each word reflects its frequency, which allows to quickly identify the most prominent terms in the text:

*Figure 7.1*: Word cloud

# Sentiment analysis

Sentiment analysis is a technique used to determine the emotional tone behind a body of text. It classifies text as positive, negative, or neutral to permit organizations to gain insights into public opinion and sentiment trends. For example, in product reviews, sentiment analysis can help assess customer satisfaction by identifying whether the feedback is generally favorable or critical. In social media monitoring, it helps track brand reputation by analyzing posts and comments to understand how people feel about a company or product. In financial markets, sentiment analysis can be used to predict market movements by assessing the sentiment expressed in news articles and social media posts about stocks and companies.

# Topic modelling

Topic modelling is a method used to uncover hidden themes or topics within a large collection of texts. This is particularly useful for organizing and summarizing massive amounts of textual data. Techniques such as **Latent Dirichlet Allocation (LDA)** and Non-negative Matrix Factorization (**NMF**) are commonly applied for this purpose. LDA is a probabilistic model that assumes each document is a combination of topics and each topic is a combination of words. NMF factorizes the term-document matrix to decipher patterns and themes. These techniques are valuable in various applications, such as identifying the main subjects discussed in a collection of articles or discovering trends in customer feedback.

# Text classification and clustering

Text classification and clustering are useful techniques for organizing and making sense of large amounts of text. Text classification is like sorting books into predefined categories. For example, each text is assigned to a specific category based on its content, such as labeling emails as spam or not spam. This approach automates tasks like spam detection, keeping undesirable messages out of your inbox without manual effort. On the flip side, text clustering resembles grouping books based on similarities without preset categories. It automatically groups similar texts together, which is extremely useful for document organization when predefined labels are not there. Clustering can be used to automatically categorize documents in a content management system to make it easier to search and retrieve relevant information. By using these techniques, one can enhance efficiency, improve searchability, and effectively handle large volumes of data to turn overwhelming text collections into well-organized and accessible information.

# Question-answering systems and chatbots

Question-answering systems and chatbots or conversational agents are designed to provide automated responses to the queries of customers. These systems are widely used in customer support to handle common inquiries and provide assistance. For example, chatbots on e-commerce websites can answer questions about product availability, shipping, and returns. In educational environments, interactive learning tools use question answering systems to respond to student inquiries and provide explanations and resources to aid learning. These technologies enhance user experience to offer immediate and accurate responses to a wide range of questions.

# Challenges and considerations

Text analytics faces many challenges due to the complexities of human language, which include ambiguity, variability, sarcasm, multilingual processing, and ethical concerns. Words with multiple meanings (homographs), like lead (to guide or a metal), and synonyms, complicate exact interpretation. However, techniques like word sense disambiguation and resources like WordNet help algorithms understand context. Detecting sarcasm and irony is difficult because literal meanings may mask true sentiments. Analyzing broader contexts and employing advanced models like deep learning can uncover these nuances. Multilingual and cross-language processing introduce issues like handling low-resource languages and code-switching that can be addressed through transfer learning and designing multilingual models. Ethical and privacy concerns arise when biased data leads to unfair outcomes or when handling personal information, necessitating regular model evaluation for bias, dataset adjustments, and data anonymization to protect privacy. By tackling these challenges, we improve the accuracy, fairness, and effectiveness of text analytics in the field of data mining.

# Scalability and efficiency

Text analytics often involves processing large datasets, which requires optimized algorithms to ensure scalability and efficiency. For instance, analyzing terabytes of text data in real-time poses significant computational challenges. Techniques such as parallel processing and distributed computing can help manage these demands to enable instantaneous analysis and decision-making in various applications starting from real-time social media monitoring to financial market predictions.

# Future trends

Integrating multimodal data involves combining text with images, audio, and video. This approach improves user experiences by offering richer context and better analysis. For example, using both text and images can enhance content recommendations on social media, and adding audio data can make speech recognition systems more effective. Pre-trained language models like GPT- prove how computers understand and generate language. These models are trained on massive amounts of text and can perform many language tasks accurately to enable more natural interactions with machines with chatbots and virtual assistants. As language models become more complex, it is vital to understand how they make decisions. **Explainable AI (XAI)** helps to interpret model outputs and reasoning, build trust and make it easier for people to understand and validate results. Ethical AI and governance involve creating standards and guidelines for responsible AI development and use so that these technologies benefit everyone equally and operate in a trustworthy manner. For instance, using both text and images can enhance content recommendations on social media and adding audio data can make speech recognition systems more effective.

# Big data analytics in business

Due to digital transformation, there is rapid growth of technological innovation and diffusion that massive data generations in social media, sensors, and transactional records. So, the traditional data mining ecosystem fails to derive insights from these big data. Big data is a collection of large and complex datasets that are difficult to fetch and process using traditional databases and architecture. Social media data, stock exchange data, retail data, sensor data, conversational data, and video data, etc. are of the order of exabytes, zettabytes, and even yottabytes. So, big data analytics is a process to extract insights from these bigdata to uncover hidden patterns, market trends, and customer preferences. Big data can be categorized as structured, unstructured, and semi-structured. Structured data are usually relational database data with a fixed number of columns and tabular in nature. Unstructured data do not have any fixed structure or an unknown structure. These data can be videos, images, Google Search data, etc. Similarly, semi-structured data contains both the form of data. The examples are CSV, XML, Email, and JSON files. In a similar fashion to traditional data, big data can also be of four types. Descriptive, diagnostics, predictive, and prescriptive analytics can also be addressed here with different databases and architecture.

## Characteristics of big data

Usually, big data is characterized by the following five Vs:

- **Volume**: Huge data is generated every second which of the order of tera byte and above. These data are generated due to internet search, streaming services, and user interactions on the web.

- **Velocity**: Data is generated at an unbelievable speed. For example, social media platforms are generating data due to posting and interaction at an incredible speed in a second. So, these data must be processed.

- **Variety**: Data are of multiple types like structured, semi-structured and unstructured. These data are generated from multiple sources.

- **Veracity**: As data is sourced from multiple sources, ensuring the trustworthiness and quality of data can be challenging.

- **Value**: The value of data is most crucial in the context of bigdata. The primary objective of big data analytics is to derive insights from these data for competitive advantages.

Let us look at the types of tools used in big data:

- **Hosting of processing in big data environment**: Processing is hosted in bigdata environment in distributed servers and cloud platforms. Amazon EC2, Elastic Beanstalk, Google App Engine, etc. support scalable and flexible infrastructure which are crucial for processing bigdata. Amazon EC2 permits customized configurations to meet specific needs. Google App Engine simplifies deployment with managed platform services to streamline the development process. Elastic Beanstalk automates resource provisioning and scaling with negligible effort to adapt to changing workloads. By integrating these dynamic cloud services, it is possible to host applications and tackle data-intensive tasks carefully. Exploration of these platforms boost efficiency and opens up new horizons for innovation in the world of big data.

- **Data storage in big data environment**: Storage of massive amounts of information demands robust and scalable solutions like Amazon S3 and **Hadoop Distributed File System** (**HDFS**). Amazon S3 is a cloud storage service providing a simple web interface to store and retrieve any amount of data at any time to confirm high availability and durability. It uses an object storage architecture that easily handles vast amounts of data, making it ideal for big data applications. HDFS designed specifically for big data on clusters of commodity hardware, divides data into blocks and distributes them across multiple nodes to ensure redundancy and fault tolerance. This system is built to handle large-scale datasets with high throughput, perfect for analytics and processing. Both Amazon S3 and HDFS support the big data environment and offer the reliable and scalable storage needed to manage the ever-growing data deluge, ensuring data is always accessible and secure.

- **Programming model**: When working with big data, it is vital to use MapReduce and Spark, which can spread tasks across many machines to get the job done efficiently. In particular, MapReduce breaks down complex tasks into two main parts. Map processes chunks of data at the same time and reduces gathers and combines the results. This method makes handling massive amounts of data much more manageable. Spark takes things a step further with its super-fast and in-memory processing. Unlike MapReduce, which stores data on disk between steps, Spark keeps everything in memory to speed things up significantly. Spark is not just for batch processing. It also handles real-time data and machine learning tasks all in one framework. Spark and Hadoop are both big data processing frameworks, but they have distinct differences. Spark is significantly faster due to its in-memory processing, whereas Hadoop MapReduce writes intermediate results to disk. Spark's user-friendly **application programming interface** (**API**) facilitates multiple languages and offers versatility in handling batch processing, real-time processing, ML, and graph computations within a single framework. In contrast, Hadoop primarily handles batch processing. Spark surpasses in speed and efficiency and making it ideal for iterative tasks like machine learning. Spark uses **Resilient Distributed Datasets (RDDs)**, and Hadoop relies on HDFS for data replication. On the whole, Spark's speed, ease of use and broad capabilities make it a powerful tool. At the same time, Hadoop remains robust for batch processing and storage.

- **Data storage and indexing in big data environment**: NoSQL databases are built to handle large amounts of unstructured or semi-structured data and make them flexible and scalable for modern applications. Unlike traditional SQL databases, NoSQL databases are schema-free and allow data to be stored in various formats and easily adapted with fewer constraints. For example, MongoDB stores data in a JSON-like format to enable quick access and updates with powerful indexing options. CouchDB uses JSON documents and offers customizable indexing for efficient data retrieval. Cassandra is a wide column store that organizes data into column families, where each row can have a dynamic set of columns and utilizes primary and secondary indexes to enable rapid data access. These databases are designed for horizontal scalability to distribute data across multiple servers to handle high traffic and large datasets efficiently. Their in-memory processing and distributed architecture confirm high performance and fault tolerance as data is replicated across nodes for redundancy. NoSQL's flexibility, performance, and scalability make it ideal for managing dynamic datasets in the ever-evolving world of technology to drive innovation and growth.

- **Operations performed on data in big data environment**: In a big data environment, various operations are performed on data to extract meaningful insights to take data-driven decisions. Processing of analytics, which comprises tasks like data mining, statistical analysis, machine learning, and predictive modelling, helps uncover patterns, trends, and correlations within massive datasets. This facilitates organizations to make accurate forecasts and optimize business strategies. At the same time, semantic processing focuses on interpreting the meaning of data through techniques like natural language processing. This permits computers to understand and analyzes human language, categorize and tag data, and generate insights from unstructured sources. Both these operations transform raw data into valuable knowledge and empower organizations to make informed decisions, improve efficiency, and stay competitive in a data-driven world. Analytic and semantic processing are crucial for leveraging the full potential of big data, unlocking new opportunities for innovation and growth.

- **Real-time data processing in big data ecosystems**: In the dynamic world of big data, real-time data processing makes a paradigm shift. Tools like Apache Flink, Apache Storm, and Apache Kafka Streams excel at processing and analyzing data on-the-fly as stream processing frameworks. Apache Flink is famous for its high-throughput, low-latency stream processing capabilities that is ideal for complex event-driven applications. Apache Storm offers robust, real-time computation systems for processing unbounded streams of data to ensure reliable performance and scalability. Apache Kafka Streams provides a lightweight yet powerful solution for building real-time applications and microservices with ease. These capabilities are crucial for applications such as fraud detection, where immediate action is needed to prevent loss, and dynamic pricing, which adjusts prices based on real-time demand and market conditions. By leveraging these stream processing frameworks, businesses can respond to events as they happen to make data-driven decisions faster and more effectively than ever before.

# Challenges to big data analytics

Handling big data comes with a set of complex challenges. Big data refers to extremely large datasets that are too vast for traditional data processing tools to handle efficiently. Dealing with big data introduces challenges in storage, processing, and analysis due to its immense size and complexity. First, managing massive amounts of data from different sources can be daunting. Ensuring this data is accurate and fixing any issues is crucial for reliable results. The process of integrating and preparing data is also complex and requires advanced tools. Companies need to find a balance between cost and efficiency when scaling their big data systems. Extracting useful business insights depends on choosing the right big data technologies. Finding and keeping skilled professionals in the field is becoming more challenging. Managing costs while maintaining strong governance over the big data environment is essential to avoid financial risks. Lastly, making sure the data is relevant and fits specific use cases is key to making informed decisions. In the next decade, the challenges of big data will continue to evolve. With the rise of generative AI and agentic AI, data management and quality assurance will become more automated. Integration processes will become simpler with better data integration platforms. Innovations in cloud-based solutions and edge computing will help scale data systems more cost-effectively. Real-time analytics and predictive modelling will play a bigger role in generating business insights. The talent gap may decrease as education and industry efforts ramp up to train more professionals. Effective governance and ethical guidelines will become more important as data privacy and security concerns grow. Ensuring data is relevant and understandable will remain a priority, supported by improved data visualization and storytelling tools. Finally, big data challenges will persist. However, constant technological advancements and strategic approaches will help in finding more effective solutions.

# Emerging trends in big data analytics

Big data analytics is experiencing a transformative wave of innovation. Emerging trends are enhancing existing processes and redefining what is possible. From processing data at the edge to making AI more interpretable, these advancements are set to revolutionize how to derive insights from vast datasets.

| Emerging trends | Description |
|---|---|
| Edge analytics and fog computing | Processing of data at the edge of the network i.e. closer to the data source to reduce latency and bandwidth usage critical for IoT applications. |
| Quantum computing potential | Quantum algorithms are responsible to transform data analytics by solving problems that are currently beyond the scope of classical computers. Their potential to swiftly process and analyze massive amounts of data can lead to groundbreaking advancements in various fields. |
| Blockchain integration | In big data environments, blockchain integration enables secure and transparent data sharing to ensure data derivation and integrity. |
| **Automated machine learning (AutoML)** | AutoML tools automate the end-to-end process of applying machine learning to real-world problems and make advanced analytics more accessible for all. |
| XAI in big data | XAI develops models that are powerful and interpretable. It facilitates all stakeholders to understand how decisions are made. |

*Table 7.8: Emerging trends of big data analytics*

# Future ahead

The future of big data analytics is set to be transformative, driven by pioneering advancements and innovative applications. In the current context, generative AI and agentic AI will revolutionize how we process and utilize data, which will lead to the creation of more intelligent and autonomous systems. These systems will not only improve efficiency but also introduce new levels of sophistication in decision-making and problem-solving. Graph mining and network analysis will become crucial tools for exploring complex relationships and patterns within vast datasets, which will offer deeper and more comprehensive insights. By leveraging these techniques, professionals can uncover hidden trends that were previously unapproachable. Lakehouses combine data lake flexibility with warehouse structure will streamline data storage and access to effectively bridge the gap between traditional databases and modern data analytics. These architectures will provide a unified and scalable platform for managing and analyzing diverse data types to enhance the overall efficiency and agility of data-driven operations.

Techniques such as fuzzy logic and rough sets will play a crucial role in enhancing decision-making processes by addressing uncertainties and imprecision in data. These methods will enable more robust and accurate analysis to lead to better-informed decisions across domains. Genetic algorithms will continue to optimize problem-solving by mimicking the principles of natural evolution to offer efficient solutions to complex optimization problems. Along with neural networks and deep learning, these algorithms will solve new possibilities in predictive analytics and ML to drive significant improvements in these fields. Time series applications will gain increasing importance across various industries, from finance to healthcare, to assist in more accurate forecasting and trend analysis. These applications will support better resource allocation, risk management, and strategic planning. On the whole, these innovations will boost big data analytics into an era of unprecedented capability and impact to transform how organizations leverage data to drive growth, innovation, and competitive advantage.

# Edge analytics

Edge analytics is a revolution for data mining and business intelligence professionals. Here, data are processed at the periphery of a network where the data is generated without transferring data to a centralized data center. So, the processing of data happens in close proximity to sources like IoT sensors and local servers.

# Importance and advantages of edge analytics

Edge analytics represents a paradigm shift in data processing to bring analysis to the forefront of data generation. It offers numerous advantages across various sectors as an indispensable tool for modern data management, such as:

- **Real-time data processing**: Edge analytics enables the immediate processing of data from IoT devices, sensors, and a local server to eliminate the delay caused by transmitting data to centralized data centers. This is crucial for applications requiring real-time insights and rapid decision-making, such as autonomous vehicles, smart grids, and industrial automation.

- **Lower latency**: Edge analytics minimizes latency through local data procession that improves the performance and responsiveness of applications. This is particularly crucial for mission-critical systems where even every millisecond counts.

- **Optimized bandwidth usage**: Sending large volumes of raw data to a central data center can be both resource-intensive and costly. Edge analytics addresses this issue by processing data locally and transmitting only the most relevant insights or summaries to optimize bandwidth usage.

- **Enhanced security and privacy**: Local data processing at the edge reduces the volume of sensitive information transmitted over networks to enhance security and privacy. This localized approach makes it more difficult for potential cyber threats to tamper with critical data.

- **Scalability and flexibility**: Edge analytics provides scalable data processing across a distributed network of edge devices. This flexibility eases the deployment and management of analytics applications in diverse and dynamic environments such as remote locations and extensive industrial sites.

- **Cost efficiency**: By shifting data processing tasks from centralized data centers to edge devices, organizations can achieve substantial cost savings. This efficient use of computing resources reduces infrastructure costs and optimizes operational expenses.

Edge analytics is revolutionizing data management by meeting the growing demand for real-time insights, reduced latency, and enhanced security. Its applications span a wide range of industries, from healthcare to manufacturing, underlining its critical role in the modern technological landscape.

# Challenges of edge analytics

Edge analytics faces several significant challenges that must be addressed for effective implementation. Hardware limitations are a primary concern as edge devices often have limited computational power compared to centralized data centers, which makes complex data analysis difficult to perform locally. The initial investment required is substantial since implementing edge analytics infrastructure requires significant spending on edge computing devices and related technologies. Scalability is another significant challenge, as managing and expanding a large number of edge devices across diverse environments can be both challenging and resource-intensive. Additionally, confirming data consistency is complex in distributed systems to maintaining consistent and accurate data processing across multiple edge devices requires robust solutions to handle synchronization and integrity issues. Addressing these challenges is crucial to fully realizing the benefits of edge analytics in modern computing environments.

# Applications

Edge analytics is weaving intelligence into every part of our world. From the busy streets of smart cities to critical systems in healthcare and energy, this technology not only improves how things work today but also opens doors to future innovations. Let us look at some applications:

| Industry | Applications | Benefits |
|----------|--------------|----------|
| Smart cities | Edge analytics supports public safety, traffic management and energy efficiency by adapting traffic lights in real time to optimize vehicle and pedestrian flow based on immediate data. | This results in smoother travels and safer streets, enhancing the overall urban experience for everyone. |
| Healthcare | It monitors vital signs with wearable devices and detects anomalies immediately using medical equipment. | This allows for timely interventions that can save lives and improve patient outcomes without delay. |

| Industry | Applications | Benefits |
|---|---|---|
| Manufacturing | Edge analytics analyses sensor data from machinery to predict equipment failures before they happen and schedules maintenance proactively. | This reduces downtime and cuts costs, much like an experienced mechanic who knows exactly when a part needs fixing. |
| Retail | It transforms the shopping experience by empowering personalized promotions and adjusting inventory management in real time. | This enhances customer engagement and optimizes stock levels, making the shopping experience more engaging and efficient. |
| Energy and utilities | Edge analytics monitors and manages energy consumption, detects faults instantly and optimizes energy distribution across the grid. | This ensures that integrating renewable energy sources is efficient and reliable to support a sustainable energy future. |

*Table 7.9: Applications of edge analytics in different industries*

## Future of edge analytics

The future of edge analytics is promising with advancements in AI, ML and edge computing. As edge devices become more powerful and capable, the scope of edge analytics will expand, enabling more sophisticated data processing and decision-making. So, to say, edge analytics is revolutionizing data mining and business intelligence by processing data directly at its source. This approach brings computation closer to where data is generated and lead to faster insights and reduced latency. By integrating AI and ML algorithms into edge devices, it is possible to enable advanced data analysis and predictive capabilities right on these devices. This means one can perform complex computations and make real-time decisions without relying on centralized servers. The result is a more efficient system that responds swiftly to data as it is created. The rollout of 5G connectivity enhances this by providing faster and more reliable data transmission to boost the performance of edge analytics. Edge-to-cloud integration allows seamless collaboration between edge and cloud environments and combines the strengths of both approaches into hybrid analytics models. Emerging edge computing platforms and frameworks can simplify the deployment and management of these solutions. As technology continues to evolve, edge analytics will play an increasingly vital role in driving innovation and efficiency across various industries by offering real-time insights, reducing latency, and enhancing data privacy.

# Cognitive analytics

Cognitive analytics leverages AI, ML, natural language processing, and big data analytics to mimic human thought processes in deciphering and interpreting data. In the era of big data, it goes beyond the basic data mining analysis and facilitating systems to learn, understand, and interact with natural data. So, texts, videos, images and audio are processed to uncover hidden patterns, forecast future and generate actionable insights.

# Importance for data mining and BI professionals

In the current data-driven culture, organizations are flooded with unstructured data that are beyond the control of traditional data mining tools to process. Cognitive analytics addresses these challenges by extracting valuable insights from sources rich in unstructured data. By understanding complex trends, cognitive analytics improves the accuracy of the active models. As a result, it opens new scopes for product innovations, services, and also business models to harness for better decisions for competitive advantages in the market.

# Advantages of cognitive analytics

Cognitive analytics unlocks significant advantages by offering a holistic approach to data analysis that was unimaginable before. By integrating and examining diverse data types like sales records, customer feedback, and social media interactions, it weaves together a 360-degree view of business operations. When different data sources are combined, hidden patterns are found. For example, a company might notice that when social media engagement increases, sales also go up. This insight would be missed if each data source were analyzed separately. This powerful tool increases customer understanding by delving into sentiments and behaviors, which in turn elevate customer experiences and foster loyalty. Retailers can use sentiment analysis to monitor customer reactions to products in real time. If a new product receives negative feedback on social media, it can quickly adjust their offerings or marketing strategies. By responding swiftly to customer concerns, they can turn potential dissatisfaction into stronger customer relationships. Adaptive learning is a crucial aspect of cognitive analytics. The technology does not stay the same. Instead, it continuously learns from new data to refine models to remain relevant in ever-changing environments. For example, in the finance sector, models adapt to market fluctuations to provide up-to-date risk assessments and investment insights. It is like having a financial advisor who evolves with the market, always offering the most current and insightful advice.

When it comes to decision support, cognitive analytics assists in complex processes by providing insights that are both data-driven and context-aware. Supply chain managers might optimize logistics by simultaneously considering weather patterns, fuel costs, and demand forecasts. This multifaceted analysis enables more efficient operations and cost savings, much like a chess player anticipating several moves ahead to secure a win. Automation of complex tasks further increases efficiency and reduces human error. Banks employ cognitive analytics to automate fraud detection, analyzing transaction patterns to flag anomalies without manual intervention. This not only accelerates the detection process but also enhances accuracy, safeguarding assets and customer trust.

# Challenges of cognitive analytics

However, embracing cognitive analytics does not come without challenges. High-quality data and effective integration of disparate data sources are essential. Achieving this can be daunting due to inconsistent data formats or siloed information systems—it is like trying to assemble a puzzle with pieces that do not quite fit. Without seamless integration, the full potential of cognitive analytics remains untapped. Complex implementation is another hurdle. The sophisticated technologies involved demand specialized expertise in AI and data science. Organizations may need to invest heavily in training or hiring skilled professionals to effectively deploy these solutions. This requirement can be a significant barrier, especially for companies without substantial resources or those new to advanced analytics. Interpretability and trust are critical issues as well. Complex models, especially deep learning networks, can function like black boxes, making it difficult to understand how decisions are made. This opacity can hinder trust among stakeholders who require transparency. For instance, if a predictive model recommends discontinuing a product line, managers need to understand the reasoning to make informed decisions.

Ethical considerations cannot be overlooked. Cognitive analytics raises questions about data privacy, potential biases in AI models, and the ethical use of AI in decision-making. A hiring algorithm, for example, that inadvertently discriminates against certain groups could lead to unethical outcomes and legal repercussions. Ensuring that models are fair, transparent, and respectful of privacy is paramount. Resource requirements are substantial, demanding significant computational power and potentially sizable investments in infrastructure and talent acquisition. This can strain budgets and require careful planning to balance costs with anticipated benefits. Understanding these advantages and challenges is crucial for effectively leveraging cognitive analytics in data mining. By proactively addressing data quality issues—perhaps by standardizing data formats and breaking down information silos—organizations can lay a strong foundation. Investing in specialized expertise, whether through hiring or training, equips teams to navigate complex technologies. Prioritizing ethical practices ensures that the deployment of cognitive analytics aligns with legal standards and societal values, building trust with stakeholders.

Looking ahead, staying informed about advancements in explainable AI can help overcome interpretability challenges. Technologies that make AI decisions more transparent enable stakeholders to understand and trust the insights generated. Exploring cloud-based solutions might alleviate some resource demands by providing scalable computing power without the need for significant upfront infrastructure investments. As the field evolves, continuous learning and adaptation will be key to harnessing the full potential of cognitive analytics. Professionals and students alike must embrace a mindset of lifelong learning, keeping pace with technological advancements and emerging best practices. By doing so, they can transform data into actionable insights, driving innovation and maintaining a competitive edge in an increasingly data-driven world.

# Applications

Cognitive analytics is revolutionizing various industries with its ability to derive deep insights. Let us explore some practical applications:

| Industry | Application | Description |
|---|---|---|
| **Healthcare** | Medical diagnostics | Cognitive systems interpret patient data, medical images and research literature to assist in diagnosing diseases with higher accuracy. |
| | Personalized treatment plans | By understanding individual patient profiles, cognitive analytics helps formulate personalized treatment strategies tailored to individual needs. |
| **Financial Services** | Risk assessment and fraud detection | Perform analysis of transactional data in real-time to detect fraudulent activities and assess credit risks to enhance security and trust. |
| | Investment analysis | Processes vast amounts of financial news, reports, and market data to provide insightful investment recommendations and strategies. |
| **Retail and e-commerce** | Personalized marketing | Customize promotions and product recommendations based on individual customer preferences and behaviors to boost engagement and sales. |
| | Supply chain optimization | Predicts demand and optimizes inventory levels by analyzing market trends and consumer data to improve efficiency and reducing costs. |
| **Manufacturing** | Predictive maintenance | Monitors equipment through sensor data to predict failures before they occur, reducing downtime and maintenance costs. |
| | Quality control | Interprets production data to identify defects and enhance manufacturing processes to lead to higher product quality. |
| **Telecommunications** | Network optimization | Study the network traffic patterns to optimize performance, reduce outages and improve user experience. |
| | Customer service enhancement | Utilizes chatbots and virtual assistants to handle customer inquiries efficiently to provide prompt support and reducing workload on human agents. |
| **Energy and utilities** | Smart grid management | Analyses energy consumption patterns to optimize distribution and integrate renewable energy sources to promote efficiency and sustainability. |
| | Predictive analytics for resource management | Forecasts demand and assists in maintenance scheduling to ensure reliable service and efficient resource utilization. |

*Table 7.10: Applications of cognitive analytics*

Cognitive analytics is redefining the boundaries of what is possible in data mining and business intelligence. By harnessing the power of AI and machine learning, organizations can unlock deeper insights from vast and complex datasets. For professionals and students in this field, cognitive analytics presents an exciting frontier that promises to enhance decision-making, drive innovation, and shape the future of industries worldwide. As we stand on the cusp of this transformative era, embracing cognitive analytics is not just an option. It is a strategic imperative. The ability to think, learn, and adapt hallmarks of cognitive analytics will be the defining factors of success in the data-driven landscape of tomorrow.

# Real-time analytics and data streaming

Real-time analytics and data streaming are transforming the landscape of data mining and business intelligence by enabling organizations to process and analyze data as it is generated. This immediacy allows for timely insights and actions, which are critical in today's fast-paced, data-driven environments. Unlike traditional batch processing that handles data in large groups at scheduled intervals, real-time analytics processes data continuously, delivering up-to-the-moment information.

## Concept and importance

Real-time analytics refers to the ability to process and analyze data immediately after it is collected, providing instant insights and allowing for prompt decision-making. Data streaming involves the continuous flow of data from various sources, such as sensors, devices, social media, and transactional applications, which can be processed in real-time or near-real-time.

The importance of real-time analytics and data streaming lies in their capacity to enable organizations to respond swiftly to emerging trends, anomalies, and opportunities. In an era where data is generated at unprecedented volumes and velocities, the ability to harness this data in real-time offers a significant competitive advantage. It allows businesses to be more agile, improve customer experiences, reduce risks, and optimize operations.

## Advantages of real-time analytics and data streaming

Real-time analytics and data streaming are transforming how organizations operate by providing immediate insights into operations, customer behaviors, and market trends. This instant visibility empowers businesses to respond proactively. For example, retailers can dynamically adjust pricing or promotions based on live consumer behavior to enhance customer experiences through personalized interactions and timely offers. Streaming analytics-customized services to individual preferences on the fly lead to higher customer satisfaction. At the same time, real-time data plays a crucial role in risk mitigation by detecting anomalies and potential issues as they occur. This allows companies to prevent fraud, security breaches, and operational failures. Financial institutions utilize real-time analytics to detect and respond to suspicious transactions immediately and safeguard assets and trust. Operational efficiency is also heightened as organizations optimize supply chains, manage inventory, and allocate resources with real-time information. Manufacturers can adjust production schedules dynamically in response to demand fluctuations to ensure agility and reduce waste.

Eventually, the instant decision-making enabled by real-time analytics provides a competitive edge. Companies that can capitalize on real-time opportunities and adapt quickly to market changes position themselves ahead of competitors. For data mining professionals, embracing real-time analytics is not just about speed. It is about leveraging continuous data flows to extract actionable insights that drive strategic decisions. This technology streamlines operations and opens doors to innovation in algorithms and modelling techniques. It is exciting to see how real-time data processing is reshaping predictive analytics and ML applications. Exploring data mining methods optimized for streaming data or discussing real-time data integration challenges could unveil even more opportunities in this dynamic field.

# Challenges of real-time analytics and data streaming

Implementing real-time analytics and data streaming presents many challenges that data mining professionals must skillfully navigate. Managing the data volume and velocity requires robust infrastructure and scalable systems, as handling high-speed and large quantities of streaming data can significantly strain resources. The complexity of integrating real-time analytics with existing IT environments and different data sources adds another layer of difficulty to making unified data flow across various platforms a tough task. Ensuring data quality in real time is tough. With little time to validate and clean data, keeping it accurate becomes hard. Bad data can lead to wrong insights and poor decisions. Real-time processing is also resource-intensive, demanding substantial computational power that can escalate operational costs and necessitate investment in high-performance hardware and software. Additionally, there is often a skill gap as implementing and managing these advanced systems require specialized expertise that may be scarce, increasing the demand for professionals proficient in streaming technologies. These challenges highlight the need for strategic planning and innovation in handling real-time data to fully harness its potential.

# Applications

Real-time analytics and data streaming are applied across various industries to drive innovation and efficiency:

| Industry | Application area | Description |
|---|---|---|
| **Financial services** | Real-time fraud detection | Real-time fraud detection systems analyze transactional data instantly to identify and prevent suspicious activities to enhance security and trust. |
| | High-frequency trading | Stock exchanges utilize streaming data to facilitate high-frequency trading to allow rapid execution of trades based on current market conditions. |
| **E-commerce and retail** | Personalized recommendations | Real-time recommendation engines provide personalized product suggestions based on current browsing and purchasing behavior to boost engagement and sales. |
| | Dynamic inventory management | Retailers adjust inventory levels dynamically by analyzing live sales data to ensure optimal stock levels and reduce overstocking or shortages. |
| **Telecommunications** | Network performance monitoring | Network providers use real-time analytics to monitor network performance, manage traffic and enhance service quality to prevent outages and optimize bandwidth. |
| | Service quality enhancement | Real-time data helps in proactive maintenance and customer service improvements by addressing issues as they arise. |
| **Manufacturing** | Real-time production monitoring | Production lines employ real-time monitoring to detect equipment malfunctions and ensure quality control to reduce downtime and production errors. |
| | Predictive maintenance | Analyzes sensor data continuously to predict equipment failures before they occur to lower maintenance costs and extend machinery lifespan. |
| **Healthcare** | Patient monitoring systems | Real-time patient monitoring alerts medical professionals to critical changes in patient conditions to enable rapid intervention and improve outcomes. |
| | Wearable health devices | Wearable devices stream health data continuously to allow for ongoing health assessments and early detection of potential medical issues. |

| Industry | Application area | Description |
|---|---|---|
| **Energy and utilities** | Smart grid management | Smart grids interpret consumption data in real-time for demand forecasting and efficient energy distribution to integrate renewable sources effectively. |
| | Demand forecasting | Provides real-time analytics for accurate demand prediction to assist in resource management and reducing energy waste. |
| **Transportation and logistics** | Real-time tracking | Enables tracking of shipments and fleet management in real time to augment delivery efficiency and providing transparency to customers. |
| | Fleet optimization | Uses live data to optimize routes, improve fuel efficiency and reduce delivery times which saves cost and provides better service quality. |

*Table 7.11: Application of real-time analytics and data streaming*

# Future of real-time analytics and data streaming

Integrating real time analytics with edge computing is transforming data mining and unlocking innovations we once thought impossible in past. By processing data right at its source from factory sensor, wearable health device, or a smart appliance, edge computing drastically reduces latency and boosts performance. This immediacy is crucial for IoT applications that demand instant responses. For example, industrial machinery equipped with sensors can detect anomalies and take corrective actions immediately to prevent failures without the delays of transmitting data to distant servers. As these technologies advance, one can envision personalized healthcare interventions delivered instantly or smart cities that adapt in real time to residents' requirements. The fusion of real time analytics with edge computing is enhancing existing technologies and paving the way for a future where data driven decisions happen instantaneously to reshape industries and daily life alike.

AI and ML are further augmenting real-time analytics by enabling systems to predict outcomes and learn from new patterns in data. These technologies allow for adaptive algorithms that can adjust to new information on the fly. In the realm of cybersecurity, AI-driven real-time analytics can identify and neutralize threats by recognizing unusual patterns of network activity before they cause harm. Similarly, e-commerce platforms use machine learning to analyze customer behavior in real time to offer personalized recommendations that improve the shopping experience and increase sales. The explosion of IoT devices has led to a massive volume of streaming data to make real-time analytics even more essential. In smart cities, vast networks of sensors collect data on everything from traffic flow to energy usage. Real-time analysis of this data allows city officials to manage resources more efficiently. For example, traffic data can be analyzed instantly to adjust signal timings to reduce congestion and commute times. This immediate responsiveness enhances urban livability and can lead to significant economic benefits through improved productivity. The widespread adoption of 5G technology is another game-changing development supporting faster data transmission and more advanced real-time applications. With its high speed and low latency, 5G enables technologies like autonomous vehicles to communicate instantaneously with each other and with infrastructure. This real-time communication is vital for navigating complex environments safely. In healthcare, 5G enables remote surgeries by allowing doctors to perform procedures on patients miles away without lag, extending access to specialized medical care and saving lives when time is critical. Cloud-based streaming services are democratizing access to advanced analytics by offering scalable and pay-as-you-go models. This means that businesses of all sizes, starting from startups to multinationals, can leverage powerful real-time analytics without heavy upfront investments in infrastructure. For example, a small retail company can use cloud-based services to analyze customer data in real time to adjust marketing strategies on the fly to boost engagement and sales. However, this rapid progress brings significant responsibilities. As more data is processed in real time, there is an increased focus on data privacy and security. Protecting sensitive information requires the development of robust real-time data governance frameworks. Organizations must implement stringent security measures and comply with regulations like the **General Data Protection Regulation** (**GDPR**) to safeguard data as it streams through networks. The GDPR enforces transparent practices in collecting and processing personal data, ensuring that users give informed consent and retain control over their information. It also requires organizations to document their data-handling procedures and act swiftly in the event of breaches, thereby reinforcing accountability and maintaining trust. Failure to do so can result in legal repercussions and damage to reputation. Real-time analytics and data streaming have become essential components of modern data strategies to allow organizations to gain immediate insights, respond swiftly to changing conditions, improve customer experiences, and maintain a competitive edge. In the financial industry, firms use real-time data to make instantaneous trading decisions to capitalize on market movements as they happen. In supply chain management, companies track inventory levels and shipment statuses in real time to optimize logistics and reduce costs.

Due to these technological innovations, data mining professionals can innovate, optimize, and lead significant changes across industries. Staying current with these technologies enables professionals to design systems handle vast amounts of data efficiently and extract actionable insights that drive strategic decisions. Whether it is developing algorithms that enhance personalized medicine, creating models that predict equipment failures before they happen, or designing platforms that offer real-time recommendations to users, the opportunities are vast.

The future of real-time analytics and data streaming is exciting and transformative. As these technologies continue to evolve, they will play an increasingly critical role in shaping the way organizations operate and compete. For data mining professionals, understanding and leveraging these tools is key to unlocking new possibilities and driving innovation in a data-driven world.

# New era of creativity through generative AI

Generative AI represents a revolutionary leap in artificial intelligence, where the spotlight shifts from merely analyzing data to creating fresh, original content. Imagine advanced algorithms and deep learning techniques coming together to weave text, paint images, compose music, and even build entire virtual worlds—this is the magic of generative AI.

# Core concepts of generative AI

Generative AI understands and mimics the intricate patterns and structures within data. The following are some of the major techniques driving this innovation:

- **Generative adversarial networks (GANs)**: Let us imagine two neural networks collaborating in a creative partnership. One acts as the generator to produce new content from random inputs. The other serves as the discriminator to evaluate this content against real data and guides the generator to enhance its outputs. This dynamic duo was introduced by *Ian Goodfellow* during 2014 which revolutionized content generation.

- **Variational autoencoders (VAEs)**: VAEs learn the basic patterns hidden in data and use this knowledge to create new and realistic outputs. This makes them quite valuable tools in data mining and machine learning. By generating data that mirrors the original, VAEs help expand datasets and improve models. This leads to better data analysis and more accurate predictions. Their ability to understand and replicate data patterns results in more efficient and effective machine learning applications.

- **Transformers**: These powerful models, similar to the famous **Generative Pre-trained Transformer** (**GPT**) series, excel at generating human-like text. They achieve this by understanding context and recognizing relationships within data. By processing vast amounts of language data, they learn patterns and nuances that enable their outputs to appear remarkably natural and coherent. This ability allows them to produce text that closely resembles human writing across a variety of topics. Their competence spans natural language processing tasks like text completion, translation and summarization.

- **Generative AI applications**: Generative AI is transforming industries, breathing life into novel applications detailed in the following table:

| Functional area | Applications |
|---|---|
| Creative arts | Generative AI is revolutionizing the creative arts by producing fabulous artworks, captivating music and innovative fashion designs. Artists and designers leverage this technology to blend human creativity with machine precision resulting in unique and innovative pieces that push creative boundaries. |
| Content creation | In media and entertainment, generative AI assists in crafting scripts, themes and dialogues to boost the creative process. It generates realistic animations, special effects and virtual environments for movies and video games which significantly reduce production time and costs. |
| Healthcare | Generative AI facilitates improvements in drug discovery by simulating molecular structures and predicting their properties to accelerate the development of new medications. It also generates synthetic medical images to support training and research without compromising patient confidentiality. |
| Marketing and advertising | Businesses utilize generative AI to create personalized marketing copy and advertisements to engage customers more effectively. By analyzing consumer preferences, it customizes content to individual tastes and behaviors to enhance customer engagement and conversion rates. |
| Data augmentation | In machine learning, generative AI generates synthetic data to enrich real-world datasets. This is helpful when data is scarce or expensive to improve model performance by providing diverse and representative samples for training. |

*Table 7.12: Applications of generative AI*

# Ethical considerations and challenges of generative AI

Generative AI is transforming various fields by automating and enhancing creative and analytical processes. From revolutionizing the creative arts and content creation to accelerating advancements in healthcare, marketing, and machine learning, its impact is profound. However, alongside these advancements come ethical considerations that must be diligently addressed. Issues of authenticity, bias, intellectual property, and privacy present challenges that require ongoing attention and the development of robust solutions. By understanding both the potential and the pitfalls of generative AI, professionals can better navigate its applications and contribute to its responsible advancement. The balance between innovation and ethical responsibility is crucial to fully realize the benefits of generative AI while minimizing risks to society:

| Ethical consideration | Description |
|---|---|
| Authenticity and trust | The realistic content produced by generative AI can blur the lines between genuine and synthetic materials. This raises concerns about misinformation, deepfakes and the erosion of trust in digital media. It is essential to develop methods to authenticate content and maintain public confidence. |
| Bias and fairness | AI models may reflect biases present in their training data which leads to unfair or discriminatory outcomes. Ensuring varied and representative datasets is crucial to mitigate bias. Continuous monitoring and updating of models help promote fairness in AI-generated content. |
| Intellectual property | The flow in AI-generated content brings complex questions regarding ownership and intellectual property rights. Legal frameworks need to evolve to address issues such as authorship, licensing and the rights of creators versus the developers of AI systems. |
| Privacy and security | Generative AI might unintentionally expose sensitive information especially if trained on proprietary data or personal data. Responsible content management is essential to respect privacy and adhere to data protection regulations to safeguard individuals' rights. |

*Table 7.13: Ethical considerations and challenges of generative AI*

Generative AI is a powerful fusion of human creativity and advanced ML. As we continue to explore its potential and tackle its challenges, generative AI is set to play a pivotal role in shaping the technological and societal landscape of the future.

# Agentic AI as autonomous intelligence's future

Agentic AI is creating an environment where artificial intelligence follows pre-set rules, makes autonomous decisions, learns from its environment, and performs complex tasks without constant human intervention. This technique is built on many foundational principles that enable it to function independently and intelligently. They make decisions, initiate actions, and solve problems independently using their understanding of the environment and objectives. These AI systems utilize sophisticated ML algorithms to learn from experience and adapt to evolving conditions. As they continuously analyze past actions and outcomes, their performance improves, making them highly flexible and responsive. Guided by specific goals or objectives, agentic AI prioritizes actions that maximize goal achievement. Techniques such as reinforcement learning enable these systems to evaluate and optimize their strategies effectively. Agentic AI interacts seamlessly with other AI systems, human users, and its environment to foster collaborative problem-solving. This ability allows multiple agents to work together to address complex tasks efficiently.

# Applications of agentic AI

The autonomous and adaptive nature of agentic AI opens up a world of possibilities across various fields, like:

| Functional areas | Applications |
|---|---|
| Autonomous vehicles | Agentic AI powers self-driving cars and drones to enable them to navigate complex environments, make real-time decisions and safely transport passengers and goods. These systems continuously learn from their surroundings and boost their navigation and operational capabilities. |
| Healthcare | In the medical field, agentic AI assists with diagnosis, treatment planning and patient monitoring. AI-driven robots can perform surgeries with high precision while intelligent systems personalize treatment plans based on individual patient data and outcomes. |
| Finance and trading | In financial markets, agentic AI executes high-frequency trading strategies, manages investment portfolios and detects fraudulent activities. These systems analyse vast amounts of data in real time to make split-second decisions to optimize financial outcomes. |
| Supply chain and logistics | Agentic AI optimizes supply chain operations by predicting demand, managing inventory and coordinating the movement of goods. Autonomous robots and vehicles handle responsibilities such as warehouse management and delivery to improve efficiency and reducing costs. |
| Smart cities | In urban planning and management, agentic AI enhances infrastructure, optimizes energy consumption and improves public services. Intelligent traffic management systems reduce congestion and emissions by dynamically adjusting traffic signals and routes. |
| Customer service | AI-powered chatbots and virtual assistants provide personalized customer support, autonomously handle inquiries and resolve issues. These systems learn from interactions to improve responses and enhance the customer experience over time. |

*Table 7.14: Applications of agentic AI*

# Future of continuous innovation and ethical integration

Research in agentic AI is accelerating its capabilities and expanding its reach. Engineers and researchers are refining learning algorithms to enable even faster adaptation and a broader repertoire of tasks. Equally significant is the improvement of human-AI collaboration. By designing intuitive interfaces and robust communication channels, the strengths of human expertise and machine efficiency converge to achieve superior outcomes. Ethical and responsible development remains a cornerstone of progress. Establishing clear frameworks and guidelines ensures that the deployment of these advanced autonomous systems benefits society while mitigating risks. This ongoing effort is central to forging a future where technology stands as a true partner in human advancement.

# Case study

Let us look at an interesting case study:

- *Fusion_Intelli* drives data driven innovation in Asia:
    - **Background**: In a region marked by rapid digital transformation and diverse cultural consumer behaviors, Fusion_Intelli, a dynamic technology enterprise headquartered in Singapore, faced immense challenges and opportunities. With booming ecommerce, emerging smart cities and intricate supply chain networks spanning Asia, traditional analytics tools struggled to keep pace with the torrents of data from social media, mobile transactions, and IoT enabled infrastructures. Determined to lead in this fast-evolving landscape, Fusion_Intelli launched an ambitious project to redefine its business intelligence framework using advanced data mining techniques.
    - **The integrated analytics approach**: Fusion_Intelli's strategy was to build a unified analytics system that transcended conventional limits. Leveraging cutting-edge techniques, the company developed a platform capable of analyzing data from multiple streams and delivering real-time insights to facilitate agile decision making. Key components of the system included

        To capture the rich nuances of consumer sentiment across Asia's multilingual digital landscape, Fusion_Intelli deployed text mining techniques. Processing vast amounts of unstructured data in languages such as Mandarin, Hindi, Japanese and Bahasa Indonesia enabled the company to uncover trends that directly influenced localized product innovation and customer service improvements.

        The company integrated extensive datasets from retail transactions in bustling markets to detailed operational logs from large scale manufacturing hubs. Big data analytics allowed Fusion_Intelli to map market patterns unique to Asian economies, optimize inventory levels, forecast evolving demand trends and adjust pricing strategies with agility in competitive environments.
    - Fusion Intelli adopted edge analytics to process data locally across densely populated urban centers and sprawling industrial areas. By analyzing information directly at the source, whether at a smart manufacturing facility in South Korea or at a connected retail outlet in India, the company made immediate decisions, reduced latency and responded swiftly to challenges such as sudden shifts in consumer behavior.

To address the complexity of regional consumer nuances, Fusion_Intelli employed cognitive analytics. Advanced models capable of mimicking human reasoning detected subtle market signals and predicted emerging trends in multilayered environments, allowing the company to adjust strategies proactively before clear patterns emerged.

Recognizing that speed is a competitive advantage in Asia's fast paced markets, Fusion_Intelli implemented real-time analytics platforms to process continuous data streams. With the ability to monitor live customer interactions and key operational metrics, the company rapidly reacted to significant events, such as demand surges during local festivals or unexpected supply chain disruptions, ensuring sustained agility across the region.

Embracing generative AI as a creative partner, Fusion_Intelli harnessed these tools to develop innovative marketing campaigns, design forward-thinking product prototypes, and generate localized content that resonated with diverse Asian audiences. This creative leap enhanced brand recognition while enabling rapid iteration and dynamic product development.

At the culmination of its integrated system, Fusion Intelli piloted an agentic AI platform designed for autonomous decision making. Continuously learning from real-time data, this intelligent system optimized logistics, managed regional inventory, and fine-tuned resource allocations with minimal human intervention. The result was an agile and adaptive framework capable of meeting the complexities of Asia's dynamic markets.

o **Implementation and outcomes**: Within a year, Fusion Intelli's robust, integrated approach began yielding significant benefits. On the operational front, the combined power of edge and real time analytics reduced response times and enhanced system resilience during peak periods. These initiatives resulted in a substantial increase in operational throughput across expansive networks. By leveraging advanced text mining and cognitive analytics, Fusion Intelli gained deep insights into the diverse preferences of consumers throughout Asian supply chains. This data-driven understanding empowered the organization to deliver highly personalized interactions, significantly boosting customer satisfaction and engagement across various regional markets.

# Key insights and lessons learned

Integrated intelligence combining advanced techniques from text mining to agentic AI yields a layered analytical system that produces insights far beyond the sum of its parts, proving essential for multifaceted markets. Local impact through decentralized processing data on site via edge analytics facilitates immediate action, a critical advantage in densely populated urban centers and regions with varied infrastructure capabilities.

Cultural nuances and real-time adaptation cognitive and real time analytics empower organizations to interpret subtle regional consumer behaviors, enabling them to craft targeted and effective engagement strategies. Balancing innovation with autonomous efficiency while generative AI fosters creativity, agentic AI drives operational autonomy. Together, these approaches demonstrate how technology can bolster creative innovation while streamlining efficiency.

# Summary

Fusion Intelli's case exemplifies how advanced data mining and business intelligence techniques can be seamlessly integrated into a unified strategy. By leveraging text mining, big data analytics, edge and cognitive analytics, real time streaming, generative AI and agentic AI, the company addresses immediate market challenges and anticipates future trends which is a vital capability in Asia's diverse and rapidly evolving landscape. This comprehensive transformation sets a benchmark for businesses seeking to harness data driven innovation in the digital era. In today's rapidly evolving digital landscape, forward-thinking companies are harnessing the power of advanced analytics to redefine success.

# Conclusion

This chapter narrated key ideas of advanced data mining. Readers are familiar with pulling useful information from large text data and identifying patterns in massive datasets using big data analytics. They have learned that edge analytics processes data right where it is created to permit quick decisions. The chapter also explained how cognitive analytics uses AI to see what is happening in the data and why. Readers understand real-time analytics and data streaming, which facilitate data as it is produced for fast responses. Readers understand the concept of generative AI and its creation of new content. The concept of agentic AI as autonomous agents was discussed. After going through the chapter, the readers will have a good grasp of these technologies and their impact on the future of advanced data mining.

# Multiple choice questions

1. **In text analytics, which of the following methods converts a collection of documents into a matrix of word frequencies?**

    a. One-hot encoding

    b. Bag-of-words model

    c. Term Frequency-Inverse Document Frequency

    d. Latent semantic indexing

2. **Which distributed computing framework uses the MapReduce programming model for processing large data sets?**

    a. Apache Hadoop

    b. Apache Kafka

    c. PyTorch

    d. TensorFlow

3. **Edge analytics mainly processes data as follows:**

    a. In the cloud after transmitting data.

    b. On centralized data servers.

    c. Locally, near the source of data generation.

    d. Using third-party data centers.

4. **Which of the following platforms is planned for distributed stream processing and real-time analytics?**

    a. Apache Spark Streaming

    b. NoSQL

    c. MySQL

    d. Hadoop Distributed File System

5. **Generative adversarial networks consist of which of the following?**

    a. Two competing neural networks known as the generator and the discriminator.

    b. A single network trained on labeled data.

    c. Multiple networks working independently.

    d. Networks that only perform data classification.

6. **Agentic AI systems are characterized by which of the following?**

    a. Performing pre-programmed tasks without adaptability.

    b. Autonomous decision-making and actions within an environment.

    c. Reliance solely on human input for every action.

    d. The inability to interact with their environment.

7. **Cognitive analytics enhances decision-making by?**

    a. Ignoring unstructured data sources

    b. Utilizing only historical data without context

    c. Incorporating context and learning from new data

      d.  Relying solely on human intuition

8. **Spark is preferred over Hadoop MapReduce for certain applications because Spark ___.**

      a.  Is exclusively for data storage.

      b.  Processes data only in batch mode.

      c.  Offers in-memory computing for faster processing.

      d.  Lacks support for real-time data processing.

9. **Which if the following is a benefit of edge analytics over traditional cloud analytics?**

      a.  Higher costs due to advanced hardware requirements

      b.  Increased data privacy by processing data on-site

      c.  Longer latency in data processing

      d.  Dependence on constant internet connectivity

10. **Which technique in text mining reduces inflected words to their root form?**

      a.  Lemmatization

      b.  Tokenization

      c.  Part-of-speech tagging

      d.  Parsing

# Answers

1. b
2. a
3. c
4. a
5. a
6. b
7. c
8. c
9. b
10. a

# Practice exercises

1. How does text mining enable a business to extract actionable insights from unstructured data? Discuss real-world examples relevant to Asian markets and evaluate the challenges and opportunities that arise when deploying text-mining techniques for customer sentiment analysis and product innovation.

2. Compare and contrast big data analytics, edge analytics, and real time data streaming. How do these approaches complement one another to enhance decision-making in dynamic business environments like those found in Asia? Illustrate your response with examples that highlight the unique roles and applications of each technique.

3. Examine how cognitive analytics, generative AI, and agentic AI are transforming the landscape of autonomous intelligence in contemporary businesses. What differentiates these technologies in terms of functionality and strategic impact, and what are the potential benefits and risks of integrating these advanced techniques into an organization's digital transformation roadmap?

# Join our book's Discord space

Join the book's Discord Workspace for Latest updates, Offers, Tech happenings around the world, New Release and Sessions with the Authors:

**https://discord.bpbonline.com**

# CHAPTER 8

# Data Mining and Business Intelligence Ethical Framework

## Introduction

In the current data-driven world, businesses leverage data mining and business intelligence to drive innovation, optimize operations, and maintain a competitive edge. As organizations collect and analyze massive datasets, the ethical implications of these activities have become increasingly significant. Establishing robust ethical guidelines and frameworks is essential to ensure responsible data usage and to protect individual rights and privacy. The presence of algorithmic bias poses a considerable threat, leading to adverse impacts across industries by reinforcing inequalities and perpetuating unfair practices. Understanding the ethical dimensions of data mining is critical across all business disciplines to influence decision-making processes and shape corporate reputations. So, transforming ethical responsibilities into tangible actions is imperative as a legal obligation and as a fundamental aspect of sustainable and socially responsible business operations.

## Structure

This chapter covers the following topics:

- Ethical guidelines and framework
- Adverse impact of algorithmic bias in industries
- Merging ethical insights, data mining and BI
- Turning ethical responsibilities into action

# Objectives

This chapter aims to provide a holistic exploration of the ethical frameworks that govern data mining and business intelligence. Readers will delve into established ethical guidelines, examining how they apply to practical business scenarios and the consequences of non-compliance. The chapter will investigate the adverse impacts of algorithmic bias to highlight real-world examples where inherent biases have led to detrimental outcomes. The ethical dilemmas faced across various business disciplines will be addressed. By examining these issues, the importance of integrating ethical considerations into every aspect of data practice is underscored. Ultimately, the main goal is to provide business professionals with the knowledge and tools they need. This will help them turn ethical principles into practical strategies. By doing this, data-driven initiatives can be carried out responsibly, transparently, and fairly.

# Ethical guidelines and frameworks

In the era of the big data revolution, each click, swipe, and online interaction adds to our digital footprints, making personal data valuable and vulnerable. Personal data is not just about what we are willing to share. It is also about how our information is collected, stored, and used without our full awareness. Understanding these laws is not just about remembering acronyms. It is about recognising how they empower us and protect our privacy. It is a curious question who holds the power over our personal data. The global concern is to move towards stronger data protection, leading to laws that safeguard privacy and hold organizations accountable. The regulations expect transparency, control, and respect in the digital space. Now, let us discuss a few of the most influential data protection laws reshaping our digital world.

# Data protection laws and their ethical imperatives

In the current context, personal data is quite valuable for organizations. Hence, countries worldwide have enforced legislation to protect individual privacy and personal information laws such as **General Data Protection Regulation** (**GDPR**), **California's Consumer Privacy Act** (**CCPA**), Digital Personal Data Protection Act of India and Brazil's **General Data Protection Law** (**LGPD**) towards establishment of strict standards for data protection. Technological innovations are evolving quite rapidly. So, these laws face challenges in fully protecting privacy. As a result, there is a need for a cultural shift towards ethical data practices.

## General Data Protection Regulation

The GDPR is established by the European Union as a regulation to protect personal data and privacy. It enforces strict rules on how organizations collect, use, and store personal information. This regulation's objective is to provide individuals with greater control over their data and ensure responsible handling of data by organizations. GDPR principles are leveraged by regulatory authorities to address ethical complexities in data mining algorithms, Artificial intelligence systems, and large language models. However, GDPR as a protector of personal data does not always guarantee complete privacy. The challenge lies in applying existing regulations and also in fostering a culture where ethical data practices are integral to data mining algorithm development and deployment. Organizations may find loopholes to satisfy their hunger for data to indicate that compliance alone is not sufficient. It is really crucial to imbibe an environment where both treating data and collecting data ethically are important. The GDPR requires companies to obtain clear and informed consent before using personal data. However, some organizations comply superficially by crafting overly complex or vague consent forms. For example, a shopping app might hide data-sharing agreements deep within lengthy terms and conditions, leading users to unknowingly consent. This loophole allows companies to technically meet GDPR requirements while compromising transparency and user control over their data.

# California Consumer Privacy Act

The CCPA boosts privacy rights and consumer protection for residents of California. Currently, there is increasing concern over personal data exploitation. CCPA grants individuals the right to know what personal information is collected by an organization about them, to request deletion of their data, and to opt out of the sale of their personal information. CCPA aims to empower customers by establishing foundational concepts like transparency, purpose limitation, data minimization and accountability. However, concerns persist about its effectiveness within the ethical framework of data mining and business intelligence practices. In an era where technological progressions often overtake legislation, trusting solely on laws like the CCPA may not be sufficient. Organizations must fundamentally review how they perceive and handle personal information to prioritize the protection of individual identities as a core aspect of their data strategies.

# Digital Personal Data Protection Act of India

The Digital Personal Data Protection Act is significant legislation enacted by the government of India to protect personal data in the rapidly growing evolving digital era. It establishes a framework that empowers individuals while fostering innovation and economic growth. This act grants individuals rights to access, correct, and erase their personal data held by firms to ensure transparent and informed consent. Strong security measures are delegated to protect data from breaches, and user-friendly grievance redressal systems enhances trust and accountability in how organizations handle personal information. By embracing a *digital by design* approach, this act promotes seamless digital interactions, ease of living and doing business in the digital age. However, its effectiveness depends on organizations embodying ethical data practices beyond compliance. Protecting personal information is an evolving journey that requires collective responsibility and a genuine commitment to ethical principles. India's **Digital Personal Data Protection (DPDP)** Act emphasizes the importance of individual control over personal data. It mandates explicit consent before data use, ensuring users are fully informed about how their information is processed. For example, an e-commerce platform must obtain clear approval before tracking user activities, empowering individuals to manage their digital footprints effectively and strengthen their privacy rights. Additionally, the Act enforces strict accountability, requiring organizations to implement robust safeguards that protect data from misuse or breaches. This fosters a culture of transparency and trust in an increasingly digitized society

## Brazil's General Data Protection Law

LGPD of Brazil signifies a fundamental shift in the nation's approach to personal data and privacy. Just like GDPR, it establishes strict standards for how firms gather, process, and protect personal information. Fundamental task of LGPD is to grant greater autonomy to individual on their data and compel organizations to operate with transparency and accountability. The impact of the LGPD extends beyond legal mandates. It is about cultivating a culture where ethical data practices are inherent to every facet of data mining model development and deployment. Organizations must surpass mere compliance to proactively close gaps that could undermine privacy rights and embrace a genuine commitment to ethical integrity. It is clear that legislation alone cannot fully shield personal information.

# Adverse impact of algorithmic bias in industry

 In the current world of big data, algorithms are vital for making business decisions in all functional areas of business. However, they can inadvertently inherit and amplify biases that already exist in the data they are trained on. So, existing prejudices are unknowing supported by the decision-making tools. By identifying these biases, one can work towards creating impartial algorithms that lead to better outcomes.

## Historical data bias

Historical data bias occurs when algorithms learn from past data that already has biases. So, these algorithms inherit those biases and can produce unfair or prejudiced outcomes. This can be particularly problematic in areas like criminal justice, finance, employment, education and healthcare where biased outcomes can have serious consequences. To counteract this, it is essential to carefully evaluate and adjust the data that these algorithms are trained on.

For example: Amazon's recruiting tool.

Amazon's experimental AI recruiting tool was developed during 2014 to streamline their hiring process by scoring job applicants' resumes. This is an example of historical bias. The algorithm was trained on resumes from last ten years. It was a period when the technology industry was mostly dominated by males. So, the tool favoured male candidates and did not shortlist resumes of women. Hence, we see an issue of not recruiting diverse talents due to gender disparities in technology employment. The selection process creates gender imbalance in hiring practices of the company.

# Facial recognition bias in Indian law enforcement

India's **Digital Personal Data Protection** (**DPDP**) Act emphasizes the importance of individual control over personal data. It mandates explicit consent before data use, ensuring users are fully informed about how their information is processed. For example, an e-commerce platform must obtain clear approval before tracking user activities, empowering individuals to manage their digital footprints effectively and strengthen their privacy rights. Additionally, the Act enforces strict accountability, requiring organizations to implement robust safeguards to protect personal data from misuse or breaches. This fosters a culture of transparency and trust in an increasingly digitized society.

Facial recognition bias has raised significant concerns in the context of India's diverse population. Law enforcement agencies have quickly adopted facial recognition techniques, but biases persist within these systems. For instance, a trial by the Delhi police reported a 2% misidentification rate, primarily affecting individuals from marginalized communities with darker skin tones and distinct facial features. A 2020 study highlighted that facial recognition systems show higher error rates for darker-skinned individuals, stemming from inadequate representation in training data and algorithmic design flaws. These inaccuracies lead to wrongful detentions, violating citizens' rights and eroding public trust in law enforcement. To address this, regulations must ensure transparency and fairness, while systems must be improved to represent India's diversity inclusively. This would allow all citizens to benefit from technology without bias while reinforcing public trust.

# Sampling bias

Sampling bias arises when the sample used in a study is not representative of the population from which it was drawn with skewed and unreliable output. To avoid sampling bias, it is vital to ensure that the sample is diverse and truly represents the whole group being studied.

Let us look at some examples of sampling bias:

- **Political polling**: Political polling is often detected with sampling bias. For example, if a survey is administered to predict election outcomes, it would include urban area responses and ignore rural people. The result may not accurately reflect the voting preferences of the entire population. So, polls may overestimate the support for candidates who are more popular in urban areas.

- **Surveys on customer feedbacks**: Companies frequently use customer feedback surveys to measure satisfaction and identify areas for improvement. However, if these surveys are primarily filled out by highly satisfied customers or those with extreme dissatisfaction, the data may not represent the sentiments of the average customer. As a result, the company may make decisions based on a biased understanding of customer needs and preferences.

- **Measurement bias**: Measurement bias occurs when the data collection process introduces systematic errors and produces inaccurate or misleading results. To reduce measurement bias, it is important to use accurate and well-maintained tools and methods for data collection.

  Example:

  o **Blood pressure monitoring**: Consider a study monitoring blood pressure levels in a population. If the sphygmomanometers are not properly calibrated, they might consistently show higher or lower readings than the actual values. So, the miscalibration can conclude the prevalence of hypertension within the population.

  o **Employee appraisal**: In employee appraisal, measurement bias can occur if managers have personal biases that affect their evaluation. For example, if a manager consistently rates employees from a particular department or background more favourably, the appraisal data collected will be biased. This will lead to unfair promotions and rewards.

- **Algorithmic processing bias**: Algorithmic processing bias occurs when the algorithms used in data analysis or decision-making processes introduce systematic errors or unfair treatment of certain groups. To minimize algorithmic processing bias, it is essential to constantly review and update the algorithms to ensure they are fair and unbiased.

  **Example**:

  o **Credit approval system**: Let us consider a credit approval system that uses an algorithm to evaluate applicant's credit-worthiness. If the data mining algorithm is trained on historical data that includes biased lending practices, it may unfairly deny loans to certain demographic groups. Say, for example, if the training data shows a trend of rejecting loan applications from individuals in low-income neighbourhoods, the algorithm may preserve this bias and continue to discriminate against these applicants.

# Mitigation of algorithmic bias

In our data-centric era, fairness thrives through a proactive and multidimensional strategy. Combining technical corrections with inclusive practices lays a robust foundation for unbiased algorithms. By anticipating and addressing potential pitfalls early, organizations can foster transparency and trust throughout their data systems:

- **Dataset balancing**: Adjusting the training dataset to ensure equal representation of genders can help mitigate bias. By including resumes from both males and females in equal numbers, algorithms can learn from a diverse dataset. This balancing approach prevents the algorithm from favouring one gender over the other.

- **Exclusion of sensitive features**: Removing information that could reveal sensitive attributes such as gender, race, or ethnicity is crucial before applying the dataset to the algorithm. Ensuring data anonymity is also essential. For example, eliminating gender identifiers and gender-specific names of applicants before feeding data into a recruitment algorithm allows it to focus solely on the qualifications and experience of applicants. Excluding this information leads to a fairer recruitment process.

- **Detection and correction of biases**: Regularly auditing algorithms is necessary to detect and correct biases. Systematic reviews help ensure that the algorithm's decisions treat all candidates equally, regardless of their gender. If any bias is detected, adjustments can be made to eliminate it from the dataset. Implementing these steps leads to a fairer recruitment process that evaluates all job applicants equally, promoting diversity and inclusion in the workplace. A diverse team can boost creativity and improve a firm's performance.

- **Inclusive development teams**: Having a development team from diverse backgrounds helps create bias-free data mining models, which might not be possible with homogeneous teams. Team members from different backgrounds can identify prejudices present in the dataset. Such a team can challenge the status quo and the rationale behind the decisions of data mining algorithms. They bring a balanced mix of experiences, leading to innovative solutions. Additionally, these teams can understand customer needs and issues with empathy.

- **Transparency and explainability**: Making algorithms transparent enables us to clearly understand the rationale behind their decisions. Transparency empowers individuals to challenge and correct unfair practices. When organizations are honest about how their algorithms work, they build trust and accountability among customers and society. As technology becomes an integral part of human civilization, building credibility is essential. Implementing transparency can transform our relationship with technology to be more human-centric. For example, transparent algorithms can help patients understand treatment decisions in a hospital, fostering trust between medical professionals and patients. In universities, it can support the use of fair assessment tools that both professors and students understand.

- **Data-driven policing**: Data-driven policing algorithms aim to predict where crimes are likely to occur based on historical crime data. If the dataset used to train the algorithm is biased, the system may disproportionately target certain neighbourhoods. For instance, if the training data reflects a history of over-policing in minority communities, the algorithm may reinforce these biases, leading to increased surveillance and harassment of these populations

On the whole, transparency in algorithms is both a technical endeavor and a societal imperative. Organizations devoted to fairness as core principles are confident to address algorithmic biases. With the addition of people from diverse backgrounds who are affected by communities in creating technology ensures it serves all fairly. Teaching teams about ethics and how to reduce bias empowers them to use AI responsibly. So, we must be ready to demand and embrace openness that can redefine our relationship with technology.

# Merging ethical insights, data mining and BI

In the digital transformation era, data mining and business intelligence are transformative tools that revolutionize how businesses operate. So, understanding complex applications and dilemmas in these practices is crucial. Let us discuss the importance of data mining and business intelligence across various functional areas of business enriched with real-world examples.

# Transforming data into decisive consumer insights

Data mining is instrumental in understanding the buying behaviour of consumers, and decipher trends that were previously hidden. Say, for example, a retail company finds that customers who buy baby products also often purchase coffee. This finding helps create targeted promotions, boost customer satisfaction, and drive sales. However, it also raises the ethical dilemma of privacy invasion. How much personal data should businesses collect and analyse? Striking a balance between personalized marketing and respecting consumer privacy requires thoughtful consideration.

| Application | Benefits | Dilemmas |
|---|---|---|
| Data analysis | Personalized marketing strategies | Privacy invasion |
| Targeted promotions | Enhanced customer engagement | Ethical concerns |

*Table 8.1: Marketing applications: benefits and dilemmas*

# Strengthening finance with risk management and fraud prevention

In finance, the risks are high, and the margin for error should be minimal. So, data mining and business intelligence tools are invaluable in managing risks and detecting fraud. By analysing financial transactions in real-time, financial institutions can detect unusual patterns indicative of fraudulent activities. When a customer's account shows a sudden increase in transactions, it can start an investigation and help the bank avoid big losses.

However, automated systems ca sometimes gives big false alarms or miss tricky fraud schemes that make them less reliable.

| Application | Benefits | Dilemmas |
|---|---|---|
| Fraud detection | Real-time fraud prevention | Risk of false positives |
| Risk management | Better investment decisions | Over-reliance on automated systems |

*Table 8.2: Balancing financial tools: advantages and risks*

# Maximizing operational excellence for efficiency and productivity

Operational efficiency is the foundation of any successful business. Data mining and Business Intelligence play a vital role in optimising supply chain, inventory control and production processes. By predicting demand and identifying inefficiencies, businesses can reduce costs and enhance productivity. For example, an online store might use data analysis to forecast which products will be in high demand during the holiday season to ensure popular items are well-stocked. However, adding BI systems to their current setup can be complicated and expensive. At the same time, there is always the risk of data breaches and cybersecurity issues. By using predictive analytics to manage inventory, the store can prevent stockouts and excess stock, which improves customer satisfaction and boosts sales.

| Application | Benefits | Dilemmas |
|---|---|---|
| Supply chain | Optimized inventory control | Integration complexity |
| Production processes | Enhanced productivity | Cybersecurity threats |

*Table 8.3: Optimizing operations: advantages and challenges*

# Enhancing hiring and workplace satisfaction

In human resource practices, data mining and business intelligence are transforming the way organizations recruit and manage talent. By interpreting resumes, performance reviews, and employee feedback, HR professionals can identify the best candidates, assess job satisfaction, and predict turnover rates. For example, a company might use BI tools to analyse employee feedback surveys and find that flexible working hours greatly enhance job satisfaction. However, using data in HR raises ethical issues such as the risk of algorithmic bias and the invasion of employee privacy. These tools also help identify that flexible working hours not only improve job satisfaction but also reduce turnover rates.

| Application | Benefits | Dilemmas |
|---|---|---|
| Recruitment | Identification of top candidates | Potential algorithmic bias |
| Employee satisfaction | Predicting turnover rates | Privacy concern |

*Table 8.4: Employee insights: advantages and ethical concerns*

# Strategies for decision making and competitive advantage

At the strategic level, data mining and BI provide the insights required for informed decision-making and maintaining competitive advantages. By interpreting market trends, competitive performances, and internal metrics, businesses can formulate strategies that are data-driven and aligned with market demands. Relying too much on data can limit creativity and innovation, leading to overly data-focused decisions that lack human insight. For example, a tech company uses BI tools to analyse market trends and competitor performance. This helps them launch new products that meet market demands before their competitors do.

| Application | Benefits | Dilemmas |
|---|---|---|
| Market analysis | Informed decision-making | Over-reliance on data |
| Competitive edge | Strategic advantage | Stifling creativity |

*Table 8.5*: *Strategic applications: benefits and dilemmas*

On the whole, data mining and business intelligence are game-changers for businesses. They offer invaluable insights that boost efficiency, customer satisfaction, and strategic success. However, these powerful tools come with significant challenges, including ethical concerns and operational issues. As organizations increasingly rely on data, it is crucial to balance the benefits of technology with ethical standards. Only by doing so can we navigate the complex landscape of data mining and business intelligence to ensure a future that is innovative, responsible, and ethical. Balancing technological advancements with ethical values is a challenge that every business must face as we move forward.

Let us go through a case study to grasp the concepts and issues in a holistic way.

**Case let–Revolutionizing retail**: The power of data mining and business intelligence:

- **Context**: *Fashion_Ruby*, as a mid-sized retail company, is seeking to boost customer engagement and streamline its operations by utilizing data mining and business intelligence. By leveraging advanced analytics, *Fashion_Ruby* aims to gain deeper insights into customer behaviours and preferences. This approach will enable the company to tailor shopping experiences, predict emerging trends, and maintain a competitive advantage in the market. On the operational front, implementing business intelligence tools can optimize their supply chain management, reduce operational costs, and improve decision-making processes. This case let highlights the transformative potential of data-driven strategies in the retail industry and demonstrates how technology can drive growth and innovation.

- **Application of data mining and business intelligence:**
  - **Inventory management**: *Fashion_Ruby* leveraged advanced data mining solutions to carefully analyse historical sales data, seasonal trends, and intricate customer preferences. This comprehensive approach enabled them to forecast demand with heightened accuracy and strategically optimize their inventory levels. By aligning their stock precisely with customer needs, they significantly reduced both stockouts and excess inventory to lead to improved customer satisfaction and operational efficiency. Understanding the variation of customer demand was pivotal. They discovered that certain fashion accessories, such as traditional jewellery and festive attire experienced a surge in popularity during specific seasons and cultural festivals. By identifying these patterns, *Fashion_Ruby* could proactively adjust its inventory ahead of time.

    **Example**: During the lead-up to Diwali, *Fashion_Ruby* noted a consistent spike in demand for ethnic wear and complementary accessories like embroidered scarves and handcrafted earrings. In previous years, they faced challenges with stockouts on these high-demand items, which resulted in missed sales opportunities and customer dissatisfaction. Armed with this insight, they increased their inventory of festive items by 40% well in advance of the holiday season. They collaborated with suppliers to ensure timely deliveries and negotiated better terms due to bulk purchasing. Customers searching for the perfect outfits for Diwali celebrations were delighted to find a wide selection of new arrivals available both in-store and online.

    This strategic move led to a 25% increase in sales revenue during the festive period compared to the previous year. Stockouts on popular items decreased by 50%, and excess inventory was minimized to reduce warehousing costs. Moreover, customer satisfaction scores improved significantly as shoppers appreciated the availability of desired products during peak shopping times.

    By utilizing data-driven strategies in inventory management, *Fashion_Ruby* boosted sales and strengthened customer loyalty. This example highlights how business intelligence and data mining can transform retail operations into agile and customer-centric models that effectively anticipate and meet market demands.

  - **Personalized marketing**: *Fashion_Ruby* leveraged business intelligence tools to conduct an in-depth analysis of customer purchase histories and behaviours. This exploration revealed a fascinating pattern where customers purchasing formal wear also showed significant interest in accessories like ties and cufflinks. Recognizing this trend, *Fashion_Ruby* developed personalized marketing campaigns that targeted these customers with tailored promotions for relevant accessories. This planned approach enriched the customer experience by offering items that genuinely matched their preferences. As a result, the company observed a notable increase in conversion rates, and customers felt more engaged and valued. This boosted immediate sales and nurtured stronger customer loyalty. By aligning their marketing efforts closely with customer interests, *Fashion_Ruby* successfully enhanced both revenue and customer relationships.

**Example**: Through their sophisticated business intelligence tools, *Fashion_Ruby* identified a segment of customers who frequently purchased formal wear but seldom added accessories to their carts. Take, for example, a customer named Somu who regularly bought suits and dress shirts for work. By analysing his purchasing behaviour, they discovered that while he invested in high-quality attire, he rarely indulged in complementary items like ties, cufflinks or belts. Recognizing this opportunity, *Fashion_Ruby* crafted a personalized promotion for Somu to offer a 15% discount on accessories that perfectly matched his previous purchases. The promotion highlighted a range of silk ties, elegant cufflinks and premium leather belts that complemented his style. Tempted by the tailored recommendation, Somu decided to purchase several accessories during his next visit. This not only enhanced his wardrobe but also elevated his shopping experience by making it more personalized and convenient. As a result, his average spending per visit increased from 16,500 rupees to 22,700 rupees. This tactical use of data mining boosted immediate sales and also strengthened customer loyalty. Customers like Somu felt understood and valued, encouraging repeat business and positive word-of-mouth referrals.

o  **Fraud detection**: *Fashion_Ruby* recognized the critical importance of securing financial transactions to protect both the company and its customers. To address potential threats, they integrated sophisticated fraud detection algorithms into their transaction processing system. These algorithms continuously monitored transactions in real time to analyse patterns and decipher any unusual activities that deviated from normal customer behaviour. By employing advanced machine learning and data analytics, the system adapted to emerging fraud tactics to become more effective over time. This proactive approach prevented fraudulent activities, safeguarded the company's revenue, and upheld customer trust.

**Example**: The fraud detection system identified an unexpected surge in transactions originating from a single customer account. Unlike typical purchases, these transactions involved high-value items and were made in rapid succession at unusual hours. Recognizing these anomalies, the system promptly flagged the account for investigation. The risk management team reviewed the flagged activity and discovered that the account had been compromised by unauthorized users attempting fraudulent purchases. Immediate action was taken to suspend the account, cancel the illegitimate orders and notify the legitimate customer about the suspicious activity.

This timely intervention prevented potential financial losses of over 500,000 rupees and protected the company's assets and reputation. The customer appreciated the quick response to reinforce their confidence in *Fashion_Ruby'* commitment to security. By continuously monitoring transactions and leveraging intelligent fraud detection algorithms, *Fashion_Ruby* maintained a robust defence against fraudulent activities. This strategy minimized financial risks and enhanced customer loyalty by providing a secure shopping environment.

Through the strategic application of data mining and business intelligence, *Fashion_Ruby* was able to transform its operations, boost customer engagement and achieve significant business growth. This case let demonstrates the tangible benefits of leveraging these technologies while also highlighting the importance of addressing ethical and operational challenges.

# Turning ethical responsibilities into action

This section builds on the foundation from the last three sections titled, *Ethical guidelines and framework*, *Adverse impact of algorithmic bias in industry* and *Importance of data mining and business intelligence practices and dilemmas across business disciplines*. Here, focus on the practical steps to turn ethical responsibilities into actions. The primary goal is to close the gap between ethical theory and real-world practice to ensure that data practices are fair, transparent, and trustworthy.

## Establishing a strong ethical foundation

Let us imagine an organization as a ship sailing through the unknown waters of the complex world of data governance. On this journey, ethical guidelines serve as a compass, providing clear direction and keeping on course as we manage data responsibly. Just like a ship's crew relies on precise navigation tools, the team depends on clear, documented, and communicated ethical standards. These guidelines are like the North Star, a constant inspiration ensuring that everyone from new employees to top executives understands and follows the organization's ethical commitments.

For example, a global financial services company recognized the relevance of data ethics in their operations. To address this, they developed an ethical framework outlining acceptable and unacceptable uses of customer data. This framework became a key part of the company's culture and was included in employee training programs to ensure compliance at all levels. Employees received clear guidance on responsible data handling to reduce risks of data misuse and strengthen customer trust.

By integrating robust data ethics into daily operations, organizations empower their teams to navigate complex challenges while reinforcing a culture that prioritizes integrity and responsible decision-making. Zero Trust architecture complements these efforts by treating every user and every access attempt as unverified until verified, like a constant ID check.

This proactive model ensures that no one is inherently trusted, strengthening security by continuously verifying access credentials and minimizing the risks of unauthorized data access:

- **Insight**: Establishing a strong ethical foundation is like building the keel of a ship. It is the primary structure that ensures stability and provides direction. This foundation anchors data practices in integrity to help navigate challenges with confidence. A solid ethical base prevents straying from core values and maintains the trust of customers, partners, and regulators.

- **Advanced insight**: Forming an Ethics Committee can provide a well-rounded approach to ethical decision-making. This committee, comprising members from various departments such as legal, compliance, information technology, and human resources, brings diverse perspectives together. By meeting regularly and engaging in collaborative discussions, they review and update ethical guidelines to ensure they remain relevant and effective amid evolving technologies, regulations, and societal expectations. Promoting cross-departmental collaboration helps rapidly address ethical dilemmas and strengthen a culture of accountability and transparency.

# Ensuring data privacy and security

Imagine an organization as a fortress with high walls, deep moats and vigilant guards. This is how your data privacy and security measures should be designed. Safeguarding data from unauthorized access, breaches, and misuse is essential. To keep a fortress secure, one should implement strong encryption and strict access controls and conduct regular security audits. By doing so, one can safeguard sensitive information, maintain trust with stakeholders, and reduce risks.

**For example**: An e-commerce company uses advanced encryption techniques and performs regular security audits to protect customer data. They ensure that only authorized personnel have access to sensitive information, which helps prevent data breaches and builds customer trust:

- **Insight**: Ensuring data privacy and security is like fortifying your castle. It strengthens relationships with stakeholders and protects valuable assets from external threats.

- **Advanced insight**: Regularly training employees on data security best practices and simulating phishing attacks can help create a culture that is aware of security risks. Additionally, adopting a zero-trust architecture where all users, inside or outside the organization, are continuously verified can significantly enhance data security.

# Promoting transparency and accountability

Transparency is like sunlight that brightens an organization's data practices and makes them visible to all stakeholders. Let us imagine operating in a glasshouse where every action is open and clear. By regularly publishing transparency reports, engaging openly with stakeholders, and establishing clear mechanisms for accountability, one can promote trust and credibility. This openness addresses ethical dilemmas by emphasizing the need for honesty to build strong relationships.

**For example**: A healthcare provider publishes an annual transparency report detailing their data practices. This report explains how they collect and share patient data and is made available to patients and stakeholders. By doing this, they build trust within their community and demonstrate a commitment to ethical data management:

- **Insight**: Transparency and accountability are the foundations of trust. By shedding light on data practices, one can establish credibility and encourage a culture of openness. Stakeholders are more likely to engage positively with an organization that is honest about its operations.

- **Advanced insight**: Implementation of a digital platform where stakeholders can track how their data is used in real time can elevate transparency to a new level. This platform can include features that allow stakeholders to control their data preferences and offer opt-out options for data sharing. Empowering individuals in this way strengthens relationships and shows a deep respect for their rights and privacy.

- **Hypothetical example**: Imagine a healthcare portal where patients can see exactly how their data is being used in real time. With a simple dashboard, they can review data-sharing activities and opt out of specific uses instantly. Such a platform gives users a sense of control and reinforces trust by demonstrating the organization's commitment to respecting privacy.

# Mitigating bias and ensuring fairness

Bias in data and algorithms can cause unfair results, like playing on an uneven field where not everyone has an equal chance. To ensure fairness, organizations should use diverse datasets, regularly check algorithms, and employ tools to detect bias. It is akin to having a referee in a fair game to ensure everyone follows the rules. Addressing bias is crucial for justice and equality in data handling.

**For example**: A technology company routinely reviews its hiring algorithms to ensure they do not favour any gender, ethnicity, or background. By promoting fair hiring practices, they ensure every candidate has an equal chance based on their skills and qualifications, creating a diverse and inclusive workplace:

- **Insight**: Reducing bias is like creating a level playing field, supporting equality and fairness. Companies that focus on fairness not only meet ethical guidelines but also benefit from diverse perspectives and skills that a varied workforce brings.

- **Advanced insight**: Using advanced bias mitigation techniques can further enhance fairness. Methods like reweighting data for balanced representation, using adversarial debiasing during algorithm training, and incorporating fairness constraints can reduce biases. Explainable AI helps in understanding decision-making processes, making it easier to identify and address potential biases. By proactively addressing bias, organizations show a strong commitment to ethical practices and contribute to a fairer society.

# Fostering an ethical culture

Creating an ethical culture within an organization is similar to nurturing a garden. It requires continuous care, attention, and dedicated leadership. Leaders need to cultivate an environment where ethical considerations are integral to every decision. To foster this culture, organizations should hold regular workshops on ethical data practices and encourage open discussions about ethical dilemmas. Demonstrating a commitment to integrity in all actions reinforces the importance of ethical behavior to make it a shared value among all team members. When ethical practices are woven into the fabric of the organization, they naturally guide employees' choices and actions, promoting a responsible culture and strengthening trust among employees, customers, and stakeholders.

**Example**:

A data analytics firm regularly conducts seminars on ethical data practices, encouraging employees to openly discuss and address ethical challenges. By providing a safe space for dialogue, the organization fosters an atmosphere where employees feel comfortable raising concerns and collaborating on solutions. This approach enhances the company's ethical standards and cultivates a culture of integrity:

- **Insight**: Building an ethical culture requires ongoing care and commitment. When leaders invest time and resources in nurturing this environment, ethical practices flourish, leading to better decision-making and strengthening trust among employees, customers, and stakeholders.

- **Advanced insight**: Implementing an Ethics Ambassador program can further embed ethical standards within the organization. Volunteer employees serve as ambassadors who promote and uphold ethical practices within their teams. They act as points of contact for ethical concerns and spread awareness about best practices. Empowering employees to take ownership of ethical initiatives ensures that everyone contributes to maintaining high standards. Actively cultivating this culture enhances the organization's reputation and builds a solid foundation of trust and integrity to lead to long-term success. Focusing on ethics at all levels helps people make good decisions, benefiting both the organization and the community.

By proactively nurturing ethical practices and empowering teams with dedicated initiatives, organizations transform everyday decisions into strategic actions that boost integrity and sustainable success.

**Case let**: Ethical data practices at *Jayanti_HeathInsights:*

- **Context**: *Jayanti_HeathInsights* is a top healthcare analytics company that focuses on enhancing patient outcomes through the power of data-driven insights. Understanding the high sensitivity and confidentiality of healthcare data, *Jayanti_HeathInsights* places a strong emphasis on maintaining the highest ethical standards in its operations. For them, trust is a foundational element, and they are committed to taking substantial actions to ensure their data practices adhere to ethical guidelines. This means implementing strict data protection measures, ensuring data accuracy, and being transparent about how they handle data.

- **Scenario**: *Jayanti_HeathInsights* embarked on a project aimed at analyzing patient data to improve treatment outcomes. The main challenge they faced was balancing the extraction of valuable insights with the necessity of ethical data practices. This project required them to investigate deeply into patient data, which involves sensitive information that needs to be handled with utmost care. The company was determined to find actionable insights without compromising patient privacy or ethical standards. They faced the challenge of using advanced data analytics techniques to identify patterns and trends while ensuring their methodologies were ethical and safeguarding patient privacy by anonymizing data and employing robust security measures.

- **Actions taken–Establishing ethical guidelines**: *Jayanti_HeathInsights* created detailed ethical guidelines for collecting, using, and sharing patient data. These guidelines are part of the company's daily operations and are included in training programs. Workshops, seminars, and online courses ensure everyone understands and follows these principles.

  **Example**: Patient data can only be used with explicit consent. Before use, data must be anonymized to protect privacy. Employees learn the importance of consent and how to anonymize data properly.

  Ethical guidelines set clear rules and standards for handling patient data. By making these guidelines part of daily operations and providing regular training, *Jayanti_HeathInsights* ensures that all employees are aware of and adhere to these standards. This approach helps prevent misuse of data and reinforces the company's commitment to ethical practices.

- **Ensuring data privacy and security**: *Jayanti_HeathInsights* uses advanced encryption to protect patient data. Strict access controls ensure only authorized personnel can access sensitive data. Regular security audits and vulnerability assessments help identify and fix potential weaknesses.

**Example**: The company secures patient information with top-notch encryption algorithms. Multi-factor authentication adds an extra security layer. Analysts must pass rigorous verification to access data, ensuring only qualified personnel handle it.

Protecting data privacy and security is crucial in healthcare. By implementing advanced encryption and access controls, *Jayanti_HeathInsights* ensures that patient data is safeguarded from unauthorized access. Regular audits and assessments help maintain the integrity of the data and identify any potential security threats.

- **Promoting transparency and accountability**: *Jayanti_HeathInsights* keeps patients and stakeholders informed about data practices through an annual transparency report written in clear language. This report details data collection, usage, and sharing practices, helping to build trust.

  **Example**: The report includes information on data usage policies, partnerships, and privacy protection measures. Patients can see how their data contributes to medical advancements and can ask questions or voice concerns.

  Transparency and accountability are essential for building trust with patients and stakeholders. By providing clear and accessible information about data practices, *Jayanti_HeathInsights* demonstrates its commitment to ethical standards and allows for open communication. This approach helps foster a sense of trust and participation among patients.

- **Mitigating bias and ensuring fairness**: To prevent biases in data analysis, *Jayanti_HeathInsights* uses diverse datasets representing various populations. They regularly audit algorithms to detect and correct biases, working with medical professionals and data scientists to ensure fairness.

  **Example**: An initial algorithm under-recommended treatments for elderly patients due to biased training data. After auditing, they retrained the algorithm with a more representative dataset, ensuring fair treatment for all patients.

  Bias in data analysis can lead to unfair treatment recommendations. By using diverse datasets and regularly auditing algorithms, *Jayanti_HeathInsights* ensures that their analysis is fair and representative of all populations. This approach helps prevent discrimination and promotes equality in healthcare.

- **Fostering an ethical culture**: *Jayanti_HeathInsights* promotes ethical practices through workshops and open discussions. Leadership sets an example, and an Ethics Ambassador program encourages employees to uphold ethical standards.

  **Example**: In one workshop, employees discussed a case where using patient data could lead to breakthroughs but might infringe on privacy. They debated and proposed solutions that balanced innovation with privacy.

  Fostering an ethical culture within the organization is key to maintaining high ethical standards. By encouraging open discussions and leading by example,

*Jayanti_HeathInsights* creates an environment where ethical considerations are prioritized. The Ethics Ambassador program further promotes ethical behavior by having dedicated individuals who champion these values within their teams.

## Outcome

Jayanti_HeathInsights' proactive measures ensured their data practices were ethical and compliant with regulations:

- **Enhanced patient trust**: Patients felt confident their data was handled responsibly, leading to more participation in data-sharing.

- **Improved treatment outcomes**: Ethical data analysis led to better treatment strategies and patient care.

- **Industry leadership**: *Jayanti_HeathInsights* set a benchmark for ethical data management in healthcare.

- **Strengthened relationships**: Transparent practices fostered strong partnerships and trust with regulators and the medical community.

# Expanding on the steps for ethical responsibility

Growing on the steps for ethical responsibility opens up a deeper conversation about how we express our values in everyday actions. Ethical responsibility is not just a concept. It is a practice that requires constant reflection and commitment. By delving into each step, we can uncover richer insights and more meaningful ways to align our behavior with our moral compass. Consider how embracing transparency not only builds trust but also fosters genuine connections. When we are open about our intentions and actions, we create an environment where honesty flourishes. Taking accountability goes beyond acknowledging mistakes, it is about learning from them and using those lessons to drive positive change.

Furthermore, by actively engaging in ethical decision-making, we challenge ourselves to consider the broader impact of our choices. This means thinking critically about how our actions affect others and the world around us. It is about moving from self-interest to a mindset of collective well-being. In exploring these expanded steps, we might also look at inspiring examples from history and current events.

Leaders and communities who have supported ethical practices can offer valuable lessons on courage and integrity. Their stories remind us that ethical responsibility is a powerful force for change. Questions may arise: How can we cultivate ethical habits in our daily lives? What obstacles might we face, and how can we overcome them? Reflecting on these can lead to personal growth and a stronger commitment to living ethically. Let us also consider how technology and globalization are presenting new ethical challenges. In a rapidly evolving world, staying grounded in our values becomes even more crucial.

Exploring these contemporary issues can provide fresh perspectives and encourage proactive approaches to ethical responsibility:

- **Establishing a strong ethical foundation**: Guidelines must be dynamic and updated to reflect new challenges. *Jayanti_HeathInsights* has an Ethics Committee overseeing compliance and ethical decision-making.

  **Advanced insight**: Regular updates and employee involvement in developing guidelines ensure they remain relevant.

  Ethical guidelines need to evolve with changing technologies and societal norms. By regularly updating guidelines and involving employees in the process, *Jayanti_ HeathInsights* ensures that their ethical framework remains current and effective. The Ethics Committee plays a vital role in overseeing compliance and addressing any ethical concerns that arise.

- **Ensuring data privacy and security**: Regular training and simulations create a security-aware culture. A zero-trust architecture continuously verifies all users.

  **Advanced insight**: This approach significantly enhances data security. Ongoing training and simulations help employees stay vigilant about data security. Adopting a zero-trust architecture, where all users are continuously verified, provides an additional layer of protection against potential threats. This approach ensures that data privacy and security are consistently maintained.

- **Promoting transparency and accountability**: Engage stakeholders through regular meetings and public forums. This dialogue builds trust and openness.

  **Advanced insight**: Transparency is not just about reports but about meaningful engagement with stakeholders. Regular meetings and public forums provide opportunities for stakeholders to ask questions, voice concerns, and provide feedback. This open dialogue helps build trust and ensures that *Jayanti_ HeathInsights* remains accountable to its patients and partners. Transparency goes beyond just publishing reports; it involves actively engaging with the community.

- **Mitigating bias and ensuring fairness**: Implement techniques like reweighting and explainable AI to enhance fairness and understand biases in algorithms.

  **Advanced insight**: These methods ensure equitable treatment recommendations. Advanced techniques like reweighting and explainable AI help identify and address biases in algorithms. By understanding the underlying factors contributing to bias, *Jayanti_HeathInsights* can take corrective actions to ensure fair and equitable treatment recommendations. This proactive approach helps maintain integrity in data analysis.

- **Fostering an ethical culture**: Regular training and discussions on ethical dilemmas deepen understanding and commitment to ethical standards.

  **Advanced insight**: A strong ethical culture is crucial for effective data practices. Regular training sessions and open discussions on ethical dilemmas help employees internalize ethical principles and apply them in their daily work. By fostering a culture of ethics, *Jayanti_HeathInsights* ensures that ethical considerations are integrated into all aspects of its operations. This commitment to ethics is essential for maintaining high standards in data practices.

# Conclusion

This chapter explored the complex landscape governing data mining and business intelligence practices. It starts with essential guidelines and frameworks to establish a foundation for understanding the ethical responsibilities of organizations. The importance of finding and fixing algorithmic bias was highlighted with real-world examples showing its negative impact on industries. The critical role of ethical practices in data mining and business intelligence across various functional areas of business was evaluated to address dilemmas professionals may encounter. By acknowledging these challenges, the necessity of integrating ethical considerations into every stage of data-driven initiatives was highlighted. Finally, actionable strategies to transform ethical principles into practice were discussed. By empowering business professionals with the knowledge and tools to execute these principles responsibly, data-driven endeavors can be carried out with transparency and fairness. This holistic approach boosts trust and accountability and fosters a more equitable business environment.

# Multiple choice questions

1.  **Which principle is not a foundational concept established by the CCPA?**

    a.  Transparency

    b.  Purpose limitation

    c.  Data minimization

    d.  Data sales

2.  **Why is there a need for a cultural shift towards ethical data practices, as per the provided content?**

    a.  Technological innovations are evolving rapidly

    b.  Data protection laws are outdated

    c.  Data sales are increasing

    d.  None of the above

3.  **What challenge is associated with GDPR in terms of personal data protection?**

    a.  Guaranteed complete privacy

    b.  Organizations finding loopholes to satisfy their hunger for data

    c.  Elimination of data protection laws

    d.  None of the above

4. **What is the main focus of the Digital Personal Data Protection Act in India?**

   a. Protecting personal data while fostering innovation and economic growth

   b. Promoting data sales

   c. Eliminating data protection laws

   d. None of the above

5. **What is a fundamental task of Brazil's General Data Protection Law?**

   a. To hinder digital innovation

   b. To grant greater autonomy to individuals on their data

   c. To promote data sales

   d. None of the above

6. **What does digital by design indicate in the context of the Digital Personal Data Protection Act?**

   a. Encouraging digital innovation without regulations

   b. Promoting seamless digital interactions and business

   c. Selling digital data for profit

   d. None of the above

7. **What is a key ethical imperative mentioned in the context of the General Data Protection Regulation?**

   a. Selling personal data for profit

   b. Ensuring responsible handling of data by organizations

   c. Promoting online marketing

   d. Reducing data storage costs

8. **Which act emphasizes transparency, purpose limitation, data minimization and accountability for residents of California?**

   a. GDPR

   b. CCPA

   c. LGPD

   d. Digital Personal Data Protection Act

9. **What does LGPD of Brazil emphasize in its approach to personal data and privacy?**

   a. Data sales

   b. Technological innovation

    c. Greater autonomy to individuals on their data

    d. Data monopoly

10. **What is the primary goal of the General Data Protection Regulation?**

    a. To increase data sales

    b. To provide individuals with greater control over their data

    c. To promote online marketing

    d. To reduce data storage costs

# Answers

1. d
2. a
3. b
4. a
5. b
6. b
7. b
8. b
9. c
10. b

# Practice exercises

1. Design a consent form for a mobile application that collects user data. Ensure that the form is clear, concise, and transparent. Include sections on what data is being collected, how it will be used, and how users can opt out. Explain why you chose the specific wording and structure for your form.

2. You have been given a dataset used to predict creditworthiness. Develop a method to identify potential biases in the algorithm trained on this dataset. Describe the steps you would take to detect biases and propose strategies to mitigate them. [Hint: You may use any public dataset like the German Credit Dataset from the UCI Machine Learning Repository]

3. Create a mock transparency report for an imaginary company that uses data mining for targeted advertising. The report should outline what data is collected, how it is used, and the measures taken to protect user privacy. Include a section on how the company addresses ethical concerns.

4. Conduct an ethical impact assessment of a data mining project aimed at analyzing social media behavior to predict trends. Identify potential positive and negative impacts on individuals and society. Propose ways to enhance the positive impacts and mitigate the negative ones.

# Role-playing scenario questions

1. Board meeting on data privacy:

   a. **Roles**: CEO, data scientist, legal advisor, privacy advocate.

   b. **Scenario**: The company plans to launch a new feature that involves extensive data collection. The CEO supports the feature for its business potential, but the privacy advocate raises concerns about user privacy. The data scientist explains the technical details, and the legal advisor assesses legal compliance. Conduct a board meeting to discuss the ethical implications and reach a consensus.

2. Customer complaint resolution:

   a. **Roles**: Customer, customer service representative, data protection officer.

   b. **Scenario**: A customer discovers that their data was used for targeted marketing without their explicit consent. They file a complaint with the company. Role-play the interaction between the customer, the customer service representative, and the data protection officer as they work to resolve the issue and prevent future occurrences.

3. Ethical review panel:

   a. **Roles**: Data ethics officer, marketing manager, data analyst, external ethics consultant.

   b. **Scenario**: The company wants to use data mining to personalize advertising campaigns. The ethical review panel must evaluate the ethical considerations of this project. Each role presents their perspective and the panel collectively decides whether to proceed, modify, or halt the project based on ethical grounds.

## Join our book's Discord space

Join the book's Discord Workspace for Latest updates, Offers, Tech happenings around the world, New Release and Sessions with the Authors:

**https://discord.bpbonline.com**

# Index

www.ingramcontent.com/pod-product-compliance
Lightning Source LLC
Chambersburg PA
CBHW061808210326
41599CB00034B/6924